Defending the
Little Desert

Defending the Little Desert

The Rise of Ecological Consciousness in Australia

LIBBY ROBIN

MELBOURNE UNIVERSITY PRESS

MELBOURNE UNIVERSITY PRESS
PO Box 278 Carlton South, Victoria 3053, Australia

First published 1998

Typeset by Syarikat Seng Teik Sdn. Bhd., Malaysia in 10/13 pt Sabon
Printed in Malaysia by SRM Production Services Sdn. Bhd.

National Library of Australia Cataloguing-in-Publication entry

Robin, Libby, 1956– .
Defending the Little Desert: the rise of ecological consciousness in Australia.
Bibliography.
Includes index.
ISBN 0 522 84831 1
1. Environmental protection—Australia—Citizen participation.
2. Environmental responsibility—Victoria—Little Desert
National Park. 3. Ecosystem management—Victoria—Little
Desert National Park. 4. Environmentalism—Australia.
5. Conservation of natural resources—Victoria—Little.
6. Little Desert National Park (Vic.). I. Title.
333.783099458

Publication of this book was assisted by a special publications grant from the University of Melbourne Publications Subcommittee.

Contents

Introduction: The Little Desert   1

1 The Dispute   11
2 Crosbie Morrison's National Parks Campaign   25
3 The Local and the Global   41
4 The Ecologists   55
5 A Wimmera Perspective   76
6 The Bureaucrats   90
7 Public Participation and New Bureaucracies   113
8 Conservation and Environmentalism   134

Notes   155
Bibliography   180
Index   197

Illustrations

Location of the Little Desert   xii

'I never knew the Little Desert was in Dandenong' (*Age*)   20

Wimmera River near Dimboola (Libby Robin)   *facing* 84

Ebenenezer Aboriginal Mission (Libby Robin)   85

Typical open heath, Little Desert (Peter Attiwill)   85

Sir William McDonald with parliamentary
colleagues, 31 October 1969 (*Age*)   *between* 100–101

The border between Victoria (left) and South Australia,
1969 (Peter Attiwill)

View from the highest of the 'Sisters' hills (Libby Robin)

Philip Crosbie Morrison (from *Along the Track
with Crosbie Morrison*)

Keith Hateley (*Wimmera Mail Times*)

Mrs Valerie Honey and family, 1960s
(courtesy V. Honey)

Victorian National Parks Association conservation
campaigners (James Calder)

An inseparable trinity (NRCL Archives)   *facing* 116

Agricultural Botany students, Little Desert, 1969
(Peter Attiwill)   116

The 'McDonald Highway' (Peter Attiwill)   117

Acknowledgements

My first thanks must go to Professor Rod Home and Dr Malcolm Calder who co-supervised the PhD thesis on which this book is based, and who continued to offer encouragement and support for the book long after. Their complementary talents provided a bridge across the science–humanities divide, and their insightful comments were much appreciated.

My research has taken me to diverse community, conservation and scientific organisations, archives and libraries, and I have been grateful for the helpful assistance of the staff of the following: Australian Academy of Science, Australian Science Archives Project, the Department of Natural Resources and Environment (especially its Archives and its Historic Places Section), Environment Victoria, the Field Naturalists Club of Victoria, the Goolum Goolum Aboriginal Co-operative, the Mirimbiak Nations Aboriginal Corporation, the National Herbarium, National Library of Australia, the Natural Resources Conservation League, the Parliamentary Library of Victoria, the State Library of Victoria, Trust for Nature Victoria, the University of Melbourne Archives, the Urimbirra Co-operative and the Victorian National Parks Association.

Thank you also to my colleagues at the Humanities Research Centre, Australian National University, and to my former colleagues, the staff and students of History and Philosophy of Science and Botany at the University of Melbourne, Politics at La Trobe University and at the Sir Robert Menzies Centre for Australian Studies, University of London.

Research for *Defending the Little Desert* has been supported by the ANZ Charitable Trust, the University of Melbourne and the Australian Research Council.

All of the informants listed in the bibliography gave generously of their time and helped shape my thinking on the project. To them and to their families, thank you. I also appreciate the wise comments of Geoffrey Bolton, Judith Brett, Helen Cohn, Linden Gillbank, Richard Gillespie, Sara Maroske, Brian Wilder and an anonymous reader for Melbourne University Press.

Finally I want to thank Tom Griffiths, whose love and ideas sustained the whole enterprise, and our children Kate and Billy Griffiths who have given enthusiastic support to this project all their lives.

Libby Robin
Canberra
February 1998

For my family
Elizabeth, Tom, Kate and Billy

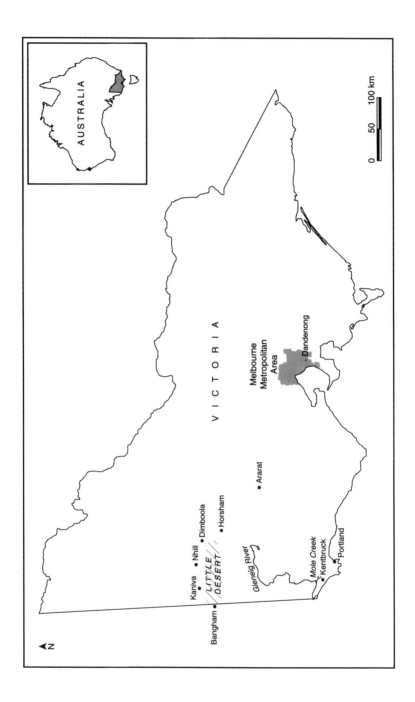

Introduction:
The Little Desert

At a time when we are told that primary producers are facing many problems in satisfactorily disposing of their present level of production, it seems incredible that Sir William McDonald is intent on opening up yet more Crown Land . . . [The Little Desert is] known to be only marginal country—requiring . . . large capital expenditure and . . . highly expert farm management. No complete fauna study of the Little Desert has ever been made and it is more than likely that much knowledge is yet to be gained from the area.

Gwynnyth Taylor, President of the Victorian
National Parks Association, in a letter to the *Age*,
28 April 1969

In the Melbourne suburb of Greensborough, Valerie Honey read this letter and saw red. Sir William McDonald, the Victorian Minister for Lands, was proposing to put farms on the Little Desert, an isolated area of undeveloped country near her birthplace in Western Victoria. Honey had nostalgic memories of visiting the area near her uncle's farm, where she sometimes spent school holidays:

> I didn't know it was the Little Desert . . . we used to call it 'the scrub' and we went out there and I was crammed in the old truck cabin with some other farmers and my uncle . . . It was sunset and the sun was

1

going with rays across this little salt lake, just one of the several salt lakes out there. There were birds and parrots and the salt lake had turned red . . . It was the most magnificent sight![1]

Gwynnyth Taylor's letter roused Honey to action. 'That's it,' she vowed. 'I'm going to contact her and see what I can do!'[2]

Honey was an assiduous newspaper reader, but had never been a conservation activist before. 'I wasn't in the National Parks Association or anything like that . . . My whole life was . . . I'd got married and I had four kids to look after and that was it.'[3] The Little Desert became an 'obsession'. Honey became a familiar figure, sitting at a table at art shows in the nearby suburb of Eltham, talking to people about a petition to stop the Little Desert Settlement Scheme. She demanded to see her local Member of Parliament, and through him organised a deputation with Gwynnyth Taylor to present her petition with 4000 signatures to the Acting Premier in July 1969.

Honey loved the wild country of Victoria's north-west. She and her family holidayed at Wyperfeld National Park in the same region, a little further north.

I knew there was something going on because we'd [talked with the ranger] at Wyperfeld and from then on I seemed to be seeing . . . letters in the *Age* . . . And these letters kept coming . . . and then the one that fired me up finally was one from Gwynnyth Taylor.[4]

Taylor and Honey met through this letter and became firm friends; they were still exchanging Christmas cards more than twenty years after the Little Desert Settlement Scheme was abandoned.

Many unusual alliances were forged through the Little Desert campaign. The dispute has lived on as a 'watershed' in conservation history. The passage of time has not assuaged its protagonists' anger that a Minister of Lands could press ahead with a scheme to farm some of the poorest land in Victoria, ignoring both the public outcry and the considered advice of economists and land-management experts. Geoff Mosley, a leading figure in the Australian conservation movement, described the dispute as having 'ultimately spawned more conservation reforms than any other land-use conflict in Australia'.[5]

The Little Desert dispute is not simply an episode in the history of Victorian politics. It is a cultural icon, a key event, marking what J. M. Powell has described as a 'complex transformation in Australian society'.[6] The Little Desert protagonists saw it as a watershed at the time, and now look back on it with nostalgia. The Little Desert was 'saved', retained as bushland, not 'vandalised' by unsuitable agricultural development. The result was a win for conservation.

The Little Desert campaign took place in Victoria in 1969, but it speaks to today's Victorians, who have witnessed another revolution in government, including the dismantling of public participatory mechanisms that were central to the resolution of the Little Desert dispute. It also speaks to a wider Australian and international audience. Conservation and environmental politics operate in various spheres: government, science and the wider community. A close focus on the case study of the Little Desert campaign illuminates the interactions and tensions between these spheres.

Ecology in Australia is a powerful example of a 'public science' that has become central to government, bureaucracy and community. The Little Desert dispute offers an opportunity to analyse the role of scientific ecology in the political arena. Historically, the discipline emerged with strong support from government initiatives in the agricultural and pastoral sector. By the 1950s it was becoming central to 'conservation science'.[7] In the past few decades it has also become the voice of 'biodiversity', a new international priority with strong local ramifications under the economic–scientific banner of 'ecologically sustainable development'. The ecologists who defended the Little Desert against agricultural and pastoral development were some of the early advocates of biodiversity politics. The public dimensions of their science forged new relationships with land management departments and the wider community.

Many of the histories of conservation and environmental movements, in Australia and internationally, have been written by activists and focus on the post-'green' period since the 1970s. These studies often emphasise the autonomy, originality and radicalism of 'popular' movements at the expense of the 'establishment' contribution made by earlier conservation bureaucrats and scientists. The defence of the Little Desert, however, involved alliances that cut across this neat dichotomy. I was not a participant in this dispute, but I have interviewed many of its key figures. The opposition to the scheme was multifaceted, so my task has been to balance the views from the Wimmera and the city, the economic and conservation arguments, and the voices of community activists and people working within the bureaucracies that regarded themselves as 'protectors of the public interest'.

The oral testimony of the participants makes it clear that government, science and community are interdependent. Each of the actors has built on or rebelled against traditions, at the time and in their reminiscences. But the traditions to which they react are not just their own—the bureaucrats are influenced by science, the scientists by community concerns and the community by bureaucratic systems. The categories are not distinct, but mutually referencing. This interdependence has enormous implications for understanding how environmental concerns emerge.

The central focus of this book is 'the rise of ecological consciousness', by which I mean a growing awareness of the political dimensions of concerns about the natural world and the place of people in nature. Ecological consciousness is necessarily a multifaceted concept. It includes 'ecological' in both its scientific and philosophical guises, and 'consciousness' in the individual, collective and political senses. 'Ecological consciousness' is itself a time-dependent notion, meaning different things in different historical contexts. Sensitivity to the context of the past, however, does not free the author or reader from hindsight. The book seeks to strike a balance between multiple contexts: the 1960s context of the actors, the memories of the actors who are still living and whose stories have enriched this study, and the later context of the reader.

The Little Desert dispute reveals ways of thinking about the natural world that have antecedents in diverse utilitarian, scientific, aesthetic and romantic traditions. It offers a rich lode of ideas to mine. It is a key to analysing a point of convergence of traditions, and provides a local perspective on the rise of ecological consciousness, which is an international phenomenon. At the same time, although the 'environmental revolution' is international, each community's participation is distinctive. In this case, the international patterns were important in creating the climate in which the fate of the Little Desert was disputed, but the individuals who acted in the dispute had their particular philosophical inheritances and, indeed, still have their own opinions today on what has followed.

The shift from 'conservation' to 'environmentalism' is striking, yet has been little studied.[8] Because the Little Desert dispute coincided with this shift, it offers a unique historical window on changing ideas, a way to 'slice' through earlier and later stories. Environmentalism changed the world-views of some and alienated others, but none denied that 'something had happened'.

Environmental concerns are built around conceptions of place: the land, the air, the sea, the built environment, the planet as a whole. They may be about a location with a personal or nostalgic association—or about a principle, a democratic right. The Save Our Bushlands Action Committee, which was the focus of the community campaign for the Little Desert, represented both a sense of place and a defence of public rights, working together. Its manifesto was *An Outline for a Bushlands Magna Carta*, which documented the rights of people to undeveloped bushland—whether they visited it or not. It did not go so far as to advocate legal rights for nature itself, as Roderick Nash and others have since done,[9] but it pressed the public's right to bushland, and its right to participate in decisions about the future uses of the land. It was a surprisingly strong stance for activists to take on the Little Desert, a place that was neither conventionally picturesque nor especially accessible to the city people who spearheaded its defence.

The Place and Its People

The Little Desert lies within the country of the Wotjabaluk people, whose traditional territory centres on the Wimmera River, extending east to the Richardson River, west to just beyond the present South Australian border, south to about Edenhope and north to Pine Plains in the Mallee.[10] Although the Little Desert is sandy and arid, it is not bare, but on the contrary supports a dense vegetation. Surviving Aboriginal artefacts found there suggest that before European invasion its harsh, prickly heathlands were sparsely inhabited hunting grounds. The cultural focus was on the big Wimmera River and, to a lesser extent, the waterholes and soaks in the Little Desert. The nineteenth-century Aboriginal community centred itself on the Ebenezer Moravian mission station established in 1859 at Antwerp, near Dimboola, close to the Wimmera River.[11] Aboriginal people were positively involved in the mission from the start.[12] At the end of its first year, two young English-speaking Wotjabaluk teenagers, Pepper (later baptised Nathaniel Pepper) and Charley (later Phillip Pepper), took up residence, and in early 1860 they went out into the bush and encouraged fifty others to come and live at Ebenezer. The community's decision to move to the mission may also have been influenced by the fact that its site, known to the Wotjabaluk as Punyo Bunnutt (Bunyo-Budnutt), was regarded as a traditional gathering place. It had also been the site of a massacre in 1846.[13]

In 1886 the *Aboriginal Protection Law Act* was amended, dramatically reducing the Protection Board's coverage and forcing people of mixed descent off the missions. The Ebenezer mission's financial support was curtailed, and the mission was officially closed in 1904. Aboriginal people were sent out of the district, to Lake Tyers and elsewhere, but as 'Uncle' Jack Kennedy proudly recalls: 'most of 'em come back again'.[14] Sixty-eight people, including his family, eked out a living on the Crown land of the mission reserve during the depression of the 1920s and 1930s. 'Everyone said then that it was the Aboriginal reserve and no one went anywhere near it or interfered.' The Little Desert was their back yard:

> We went out to the Little Desert when we wanted a feed of kangaroos or emus—or porcupine—or *yulawil*—as we call it. Always come out there for a feed.

Individuals went away, but they came back. The community continued. The length of family memory and the strength of intergenerational links is striking. When I interviewed 82-year-old Jack Kennedy in 1997, he spoke of his childhood friendship with Bobby Kinnear, who in 1883 became the first Aboriginal person to win the prestigious Stawell Gift foot-race. Jack recalled being allowed to drive Bobby's horse and cart as a small child. After distinguished war service abroad, Jack Kennedy moved around for more than thirty years, working on the railways, but he came back to Dimboola to retire.

The younger generations also return, more so than their non-Aboriginal counterparts. 'After so many years I decided that—oh well, this is where I *should* be, so I've come back,' says Peter Kennedy, now in his thirties. 'I was born and bred in Dimboola,' says his cousin 'Cape', about the same age '. . . and I'll die there'.[15] The idea of returning to where you belong in order to die is very strong among Wotjabaluk people. Jack speaks movingly of the deaths of his brother and cousin, both of whom walked out to Antwerp to die near the Wimmera River.[16] Despite their many dislocations, the Wotjabaluk have a strong connection to their country, including the Little Desert, that traditional hunting ground, which is highly valued by the Wotjabaluk communities in Dimboola, Horsham and further afield.

European settlers also focused their first energies on the Wimmera River and waterholes near by. Explorers found the country very inhospitable. The first to cross a small section of the south-eastern Little Desert was G. W. C. Stapylton, travelling with Major Mitchell's 'Australia Felix' expedition in July 1836. The sand and winter mud made the going heavy, and Stapylton could not get close enough to the Wimmera River to follow it. His account is full of 'country dreadfully deep and the Cattle nearly brought to a stand still' and concerns about the necks of the bullocks, which were injured by all the whipping.[17]

A different prospect confronted Edward John Eyre in 1838. Arriving in high summer, Eyre successfully followed the waterholes of the Wimmera River up to Lake Hindmarsh and beyond, but failed to reach the Murray River because of the lack of water.[18] Early squatters settled on waterholes and sank wells into soaks, knowing that this effectively tied up large acreages in a land without fences.[19]

The other difficulty for the European surveyors of the 'new country' was the lack of vantage points. The land was not flat, being criss-crossed with sandstone ridges, but there were few points where one could see as far as the next reliable source of water.

Mitchell viewed the country from Mount Arapiles (which he called Mount Broughton) to the south-east. He sent Stapylton out in search of water:

> I . . . came to A new feature of Country and of forest Land and commencement of white sand Banks[ia] Heath and Demiosa [*Dumosa*] Scrub—pursued my course for six miles further ascending elevation after elevation upon the Heath in the hopes of gaining sight of the Lowest Land and our river comeing round to the South-West—but alas nothing prospectively but an endless undulating moor to the north and N-W I never had a more dismal ride.[20]

Later travellers concurred about the difficulty of crossing the Little Desert. In midsummer 1852 Alexander Tolmer passed through the region on an expedition to 'establish an escort to bring back gold-dust to Adelaide from the Victoria diggings' at Mt Alexander. He encountered 'slow travelling, heavy sand; this I regret to say continued for fifteen miles'.[21] Edward Snell, another adventurer crossing from South Australia about two weeks after Tolmer, described it as 'Bay of Biscay' country, a reference to the rough passage, and also to the ocean-like appearance of this undulating land clad in blue-green heath.[22] Until the 1880s the area was simply known to Europeans as the 'scrub country'.[23]

The bane of travellers in the Little Desert was the region's distinctive ridges, which run north-north-west/south-south-east. These were such a feature of the area that they were dubbed Lowan ridges, after the shire in which they occurred.[24] They long remained a scientific mystery. In 1836 Stapylton advanced one explanation for their form:

> How happens it that all the Lakes are circular indeed every hollow on the surface of the earth is round wether wet or dry Small Hills also so exactly similar as though they had been cast in A mould can such be the origanal formation of the earth and does the same formation exist under the sea it is reasonable to suppose that the salt water on these Lakes has been left there by the receding of the Ocean because we now stand extremely low we have descended gradually 300 feet during the last three days Journeys.[25]

In 1918 Charles Fenner suggested that the ridges and valleys were traces of old river courses,[26] but this explanation could not be reconciled with the discontinuities in the 'river courses', especially in the western Little Desert near Kaniva. It was then hypothesised that the distinctive 'Lowan' sand between the sandstone ridges was the result of a weathering process.[27] Another theory, put forward in 1946, after the massive dust storms of the 1930s droughts, was that the sands were blown from South Australia.[28] In 1962 Gerard Blackburn returned to Stapylton's original idea, and suggested that the elevations were 'stranded beach ridges' or dunes. He supported this with later work showing that only the notion of the westerly recession of the inland sea could account for all the features distinctive to the area: the Lowan sands, the calcareous clay that separates the ridges elsewhere, and the 'lunettes', ridges that are concave to the west around the crescent-shaped lakes to which Stapylton referred.[29]

The pattern of different soils, ridges, salt lakes and freshwater soaks, combined with low rainfall, has resulted in enormous biodiversity in the flora and fauna of the Little Desert. Paradoxically, poor, infertile soils and arid conditions (or a low-resource base) result in greater ecological specialisation, and therefore diversity, than the high-resource base of richer soils.[30] The Little Desert, like other heathland areas of Australia, is rich in species, though not agriculturally productive. It also supports some substantial stands of yellow gum in the west, where the rainfall is higher, and there are fine river red gums along the Wimmera River and around significant waterholes. Early European field naturalists found the area rewarding. St Eloy D'Alton mentioned more than 200 plant species of the area when he addressed the Field Naturalists' Club of Victoria in 1913. Others continued to visit the Little Desert to botanise, and by the 1960s the count had grown to more than 600 species.[31]

Of the 280 native faunal species recorded in the Little Desert, the most distinctive is the mallee-fowl or lowan (*Leipoa ocellata*). One of the earliest reservations in the Little Desert was the Kiata Lowan Sanctuary, established in 1955 to provide a conservation refuge for this mound-building bird. Its habitat is mature stands of mallee-broombush—not strictly 'Little Desert' country, but rather the country that fringes the sandy tongue of the Little Desert. By the mid-1950s there was an urgent need for mallee-fowl conservation because development was threatening all the mallee-broombush country, which was significantly more valuable for agricultural, pastoral and other purposes than the adjacent heathland.[32]

The story of conservation in the Little Desert begins with a series of small reservations—one near Dimboola in 1946 and the Kiata Lowan Sanctuary, which was later extended—and the strong local defence of 'special features' such as Broughtons Waterhole in the western Little Desert and the 'Crater', a distinctive geological feature of the central Little Desert. The vast tracts of the eastern Little Desert, with their many distinctive salt lakes, were not under pressure from encroaching development, and their reservation as national park in 1969 was politically simpler than the battle for the smaller pockets in the west.

Gradually, as 'improvements' encroached on every side, the Little Desert acquired its wholeness, its sense of being an island of nature surrounded by civilisation. Nowhere is this clearer than on the Little Desert's extreme western edge, the South Australian border. That border, the subject of an acrimonious dispute between surveyors from 1849 and 1865 as to where exactly Victoria ended and South Australia began, is now clearly marked by an abrupt fence-line.[33] On the Victorian side of the border there is 'wild country', while on the South Australian side the 'improvements' of wheat and sheep farming extend to the fence. The dramatic barbed-wire fence marks more than a State boundary; it creates a frontier between 'settled' and 'unsettled' lands. All around the Little Desert sands, to the north, the south and the east, are the rich black soils of the well-tilled Victorian Wimmera. The 'desert' forms an island of biodiversity in a sea of monoculture. It was the fight for this 'last frontier country' that inspired the surprising passion of the Little Desert dispute.

1

The Dispute

*In the final analysis, perhaps the person who
made the greatest contribution towards the
preservation of the Little Desert and Kentbruck
Heathland was Sir William McDonald himself.
He united the conservationists as never before.*

Fred Davies

The Little Desert Settlement Scheme of 1968 was among the last of
a long line of proposals for the 'settlement' of Australia's semi-arid
lands. Agricultural and pastoral development had been the backbone of settler Australia, and the source of its national mythology.
'How anybody in their senses could believe that the development of
land to carry more stock was wrong is beyond my comprehension',
thundered the Victorian Minister of Lands, Sir William McDonald,
more than twenty years after he first ventured the scheme to develop
the Little Desert:

> If the people who founded Australia had adopted that point of view,
> Australia would be a pretty miserable place today. Most of it is due
> to development. In one way or another the outback has been devel-
> oped by putting more water points on it. The inside country has
> been developed, originally by the use of phosphate, latterly by trace
> elements.[1]

Developing the outback was also profitable. The Australian
Mutual Provident (AMP) Society was one of many large financial
groups to underwrite and profit from land subdivisions for new

settlements, particularly in South Australia, just across the border from the Little Desert. The 'desert country' could be made to carry more stock through the use of 'sub and super' routines—planting deep-rooted subterranean clover and applying superphosphate—and the addition of copper, zinc, trace elements, molybdenum and cobalt to ensure the health of stock. Scientists discovered these techniques during the first half of the twentieth century, making it possible to decrease the size of holdings and to increase the population in country that had formerly been very sparsely inhabited. Such discoveries also created the opportunity for significant profits for the companies who took on the expense and risk of subdivision.

The Waite Agricultural Research Institute in South Australia played a key role in developing the pasture science that was being used to open up the country, so the natural places to choose were those in continuity with existing South Australian schemes.[2] The Little Desert had been earmarked for development several times before 1968. Various schemes were mooted in the 1950s, and at least one of these proposals was on a scale sufficient to be publicised in interstate newspapers. In mid-1951 the Council of the Field Naturalists' Club of Victoria (FNCV) urged that reserves be established to protect flora before an AMP development scheme for the area proceeded.[3] A botanical survey was prepared to support the FNCV's case.[4] Ros Garnet, secretary of the National Parks Committee of the FNCV, wrote to Clive Stoneham MLA asking about the effects of the development schemes on Wyperfeld National Park and the Little Desert, and was assured that 'such areas as Natimuk, Dimboola, Kiata and Wyperfield [sic] are well away from the range of operations in the proposed scheme'.[5] The major development that occurred in the area during the early 1950s was in the Big Desert, well north of the Bordertown–Kaniva–Nhill road, close to the South Australian border. It is possible that the FNCV's questions prevented the Little Desert from being included in the early 1950s experiment, although there was no mention of the area in a 1951 report by the State Development Committee on Victoria's national parks, which included suggestions for additional national parks.[6]

In the late 1950s there was some development in the area known as Lemon Springs, near Minimay, on the southern edge of the Little Desert.[7] This was regarded by some as a 'pilot scheme' for larger plans to develop the Little Desert. By the late 1960s, when the future of the bigger McDonald scheme lay in the balance, opponents of development made much of the lack of success of these blocks.

In 1963 the AMP Society put forward a definite proposal to subdivide the Little Desert for agricultural or pastoral development. It had developed a few blocks there in the 1950s, but this was to be a bigger venture. After lengthy negotiations with the local community and significant economic and agricultural market research, the company decided that the steadily declining wool and wheat prices made the scheme economically risky. The AMP tried to negotiate an agreement to have the necessary road development subsidised by the government, but in the face of government indecision and the continuing decline in commodity prices, the scheme was abandoned in March 1967.[8]

Within months of the AMP's withdrawal, Sir William McDonald was appointed Victorian Minister of Lands. 'Jack' McDonald had been knighted for his long service to the Victorian Parliament as Speaker since 1955. Sir Henry Bolte, the Premier of Victoria, wanted him in Cabinet and gave him his choice of portfolios. Sir William chose the Lands portfolio because of the opportunity it offered for land development and for increasing the productivity of marginal land. He also became Minister for Conservation, a brief that he interpreted as mainly being concerned with soil conservation and other practices that improved agricultural productivity in the long term.

McDonald had an energetic personal interest in the border country between South Australia and the Victorian Wimmera. He was a farmer with properties on both sides of the Victorian–South Australian border, one of which abutted the Little Desert. He was aware that government indecision had been a factor in aborting the AMP plan for development, and was keen to give the government a decisive 'new look' through his Lands portfolio. McDonald was an experienced developer. He was proud of his role in the 1950s development of Heytesbury in south-western Victoria as an intensive dairy-farming area. He had also considerably intensified production on his own properties.[9]

In June 1967, soon after his appointment as Minister of Lands, McDonald addressed a public meeting in Kaniva on the issue of developing the nearby Little Desert.[10] McDonald knew the area well —both the place and its politics. He cited the example of the deep sands country at Bangham to the west, just on the other side of the South Australian border, where lucerne grew successfully, given agricultural lime and superphosphate.[11] There was even optimistic discussion of growing wheat in the Little Desert. The local people of Kaniva were initially enthusiastic about the proposal, hoping that an influx of new settlers might make it possible to maintain the local high school and other amenities that were threatened with closure because of the area's declining population.[12] Early in 1968 McDonald announced a government-backed subdivision proposal, the Little Desert Settlement Scheme.[13]

Closer settlement and decentralisation had been a focus of heated political debate in Victoria for more than a hundred years. From the 1850s there had been a public clamour to 'unlock the land' held by large pastoralists under Crown lease and break it up into smaller blocks. The popularity of these schemes grew out of British ideas of the virtue of the small 'yeoman farmer', who was often regarded nostalgically as the backbone of England before the Industrial Revolution swept the country.[14] In Victoria the language of agrarianism appealed to people of diverse political views. Conservative elements were keen to recreate an English yeomanry as a force for social stability, while radicals sought a rightful share of the land for all.[15]

It was in this climate that the Department of Crown Lands and Survey was established in 1855. The 1860s saw it develop into an important arm of government, with three major Land Acts being passed in less than a decade. These Acts were intended to make farms available to small agricultural settlers who would fill the country and utilise its potential. Although the closer settlement campaign was more successful in Victoria than in several of the other colonies, the pastoralists' sheer wealth made them difficult to dislodge.

In the early decades of the twentieth century, fear of perceived 'threats from the north' prompted a new round of schemes to fill

outback Australia.[16] Among the largest of these were the soldier
settler schemes of the 1920s, under which returned soldiers were
given assistance to purchase small blocks of marginal land. Many of
these projects failed dismally, especially during the depression and
droughts of the 1930s, when many settlers walked off their lands.[17]
Nevertheless, after World War II the rhetoric of 'decentralisation'
was again boosted by concern about national defence. High rural
commodity prices and new agricultural and transport technologies
gave further impetus to the push into the semi-arid zone.

McDonald enthusiastically endorsed decentralisation and the
agricultural endeavour. His philosophy echoed that of one colonial
Victorian who wrote: 'the man who furnishes his fellow beings
with the staff of life increases the *real wealth* and prosperity of
his country'.[18] Like his predecessors in the Lands Department,
McDonald saw land as there to be developed, not 'wasted'. He
also understood the political advantage of any scheme that could
appeal simultaneously to the supporters of patrician notions of the
'worthy yeomanry' and the egalitarian idea of opportunity for all.
McDonald's idealism overrode the cautionary tales from the failed
soldier settlement schemes; such was his confidence in the new
technologies that he believed this small-holding 'settlement scheme'
would prosper and give families a living where others had not.

The Little Desert was a final frontier and there were, at last, the
knowledge and fertilisers to improve the land for agricultural
purposes. McDonald took it for granted that the scheme was politically viable. He expected the Victorian people to support this new
settlement opportunity.[19] He was prepared to gamble that the
scheme would pay its way financially in the medium to long term.
His philosophy was simple: 'We can't afford *not* to develop this
land'.[20]

Distinguished economists and agricultural scientists, including
senior university academics and officials of the State Department of
Agriculture, did not share McDonald's optimism.[21] Their views
were publicised through the media, notably in a special series on the
ABC 'Country Hour' in mid-1968.[22] According to these experts,
the Little Desert Settlement Scheme was not economically viable.
The agricultural climate was bleak, with poor wool and wheat prices

and problems of overproduction. The cost of improving such poor land was prohibitive, and the rainfall was lower than in the comparable country in South Australia. Why should public money be invested in something that could never succeed?

At the point where economic advisers had garnered sufficient information to show that the time was not right for the Little Desert Settlement Scheme, a new vision for the Little Desert emerged. Conservation activists advocated a major national park to preserve habitat for the Little Desert's many species and simultaneously provide the region with a tourist attraction. A fight about national parks was the last thing that Sir William McDonald had expected. Like many others, he did not view the 'scrub' country of the Little Desert as scenic. He shared the view of the journalist who wrote: 'Who on earth would want to preserve this horrid piece of land?'[23] McDonald's idea of beauty was, in the words of one of his critics, to convert the area into 'grass—as far as the eye could see'.[24]

National parks had been a hot political issue in the 1950s. In 1956, a year after Bolte had come to power, his government had passed a National Parks Act after strong campaigning by the FNCV, the newly established Victorian National Parks Association (VNPA) and other groups. Over the preceding decade, eight successive Victorian governments had failed to agree on such a bill, so the Bolte team felt they had reasonable credentials in this area. Initially it was not clear whether the conservation protest about the Little Desert in 1969 was electorally representative, or was just a protest by a few 'birds-and-bugs fanatics'.

McDonald had vested considerable personal credibility in the Little Desert Settlement Scheme and a similar scheme to develop Kentbruck Heath near Portland in south-west Victoria (which was also opposed by national parks advocates). By mid-1969, however, he had been forced to acknowledge that the national parks lobby represented a significant proportion of the electorate. He had scaled down his original plan for forty-four wheat farms in the Little Desert to a mere twelve sheep farms. He also offered conservationists a national park. He announced that the 945-hectare Little Desert National Park, established in 1968, would be dramatically expanded to 35 300 hectares.[25] The new park included most of the eastern section of the Little Desert, which was the part with the very low rainfall, least suitable for settlement purposes. This decision was a purely political one; McDonald had not even thought to consult the Director of the National Parks Authority about it.[26] The conservationists were not appeased. The eastern Little Desert was not 'biologically representative' of the whole area, they argued. No settlement scheme should be contemplated in any part of the area until flora and fauna surveys had been undertaken so that more would be known about what would be lost.[27] National parks were not just 'worthless lands' available for recreational purposes; they must have some sort of ecological integrity.[28]

McDonald underestimated the force of the protest and misread its direction. The Little Desert represented 'a last frontier' for both sides. McDonald wanted to tidy it up, to civilise it. The conservationists wanted it as a monument to lost wilderness, an element of the past retained for the future.[29] A token national park in part of the area did not achieve this. It was the holistic ideal of the Little Desert that the conservationists sought to defend. In the battle between declining nature and sprawling civilisation, the urban defenders of natural bushland were far more vociferous than the local recreational users of the Little Desert, who might have been appeased by an allocation in the eastern section. McDonald's knowledge of local politics had blinded him to the force of the urban push.

New attitudes to frontiers had developed in Australia, as they had overseas. Frontiers, because of their increasing scarcity, required protection rather than conquest. In the USA, Roderick Nash's *Wilderness and the American Mind* was published in 1967.[30] There was a growing body of nature writing that counterpointed (good) nature against the evils of civilisation, and the popularity of this view was increasing as the certainty engendered by the technological revolutions of the 'Atomic Age' of the 1940s and 1950s faded.[31] At the end of the 1960s, after unprecedented boom times for consumer society, some people were seeking a balance to its excesses.

In times of extreme trouble such as the depression of the 1930s and the two world wars, many Australians had found solace in nature and in writings about nature. Those who felt that the new society cushioned people too much from the reality of life, or who perhaps could not believe that the good times would keep on happening, were attracted to an idealised 'nature' untouched by the evils of consumerism. Just as nature had provided a touchstone in earlier times when the affairs of the world had become stressful, so it seemed important again in the Brave New World of the booming 1960s. The conservationists, many of them old enough to remember the 1930s depression and the exigencies of war, sought to make the Bolte government aware that many voters were concerned about the moral poverty of the expanding materialist society.

McDonald's proposal spurred Melbourne-based conservationists to affiliate themselves into a new group, the Save Our Bushlands Action Committee. This represented the united forces of eight metropolitan conservation groups, the largest of which were the Field Naturalists' Club of Victoria (FNCV), the Natural Resources Conservation League (NRCL) and the Victorian National Parks Association (VNPA).[32] The Save Our Bushlands Action Committee's case was informed by an important document prepared by the Wimmera Regional Committee, a State government statutory body representing the region around the Little Desert, when it was considering the earlier AMP scheme. The regional committee had identified places for nature reserves in key parts of the Little Desert, and its recommendations had been included in a major government report on the Little Desert in 1968.[33] But the central locus of the desert protest was in the leafy eastern suburbs of metropolitan Melbourne, and it was here that the government was confronted by significant numbers of protesting voters.

The Save Our Bushlands Action Committee organised two major public meetings in Melbourne in August and October of 1969, each of which was attended by more than 1000 people. These meetings were supported by sympathetic press coverage of conservation issues and a barrage of letters to the editors of the *Age*, the *Sun* and the *Herald*, Melbourne's three big daily newspapers.[34]

In September 1969 the Save Our Bushlands Action Committee also sponsored a deputation to the Premier, Sir Henry Bolte, but to no avail.[35] Bolte believed and frequently said that ministers should be allowed autonomy to make their own decisions. 'Why keep dogs and bark yourself?' was his comment on the subject.[36] Bolte was sympathetic to the settlement scheme; he represented a rural constituency and was a farmer himself. He was comfortable with McDonald's decision to treat the Conservation portfolio as relating exclusively to the practical farming aspects of soil conservation and the improvement of agricultural resources. This had been the logic behind giving McDonald both Lands and Conservation.

In 1950 Bolte had been the State's first Minister for Conservation and had treated it as entirely a practical farming portfolio. In an article written for *Victoria's Resources* in 1960, Bolte, by then Premier as well as Minister for Conservation, chose for his subject the conservation of grass, 'a vital Natural Resource', urging that we should 'realise the value of grass . . . a bounty of Nature which we must cherish—or perish'.[37] Graham Pizzey, a journalist and naturalist who attended a 'Little Desert briefing' requested by Bolte late in 1969 has confirmed that this was still Bolte's notion of conservation at that time.[38]

By late 1969, despite the strong line taken by Bolte and McDonald, the Little Desert development scheme had few supporters and many opponents, especially in the metropolitan media. Letters to the editor about the proposed scheme were almost all against it. Sir William McDonald was the butt of cartoonists' satire and was increasingly caricatured by strident journalists as an 'enemy of conservation'.[39] The 'hero developer' image that he had hoped to cut was nowhere apparent. 'Hero developers' had fallen from grace. McDonald was left to construct an image of himself as a 'strong leader in the face of rag-bag opposition'. But, as the opposition's credibility continued to grow, he was increasingly seen as a bloody-minded minister unable to take advice.

The combined Labor and Country Party opposition forces held a majority in the Legislative Council, the Victorian Parliament's upper house, and seized the opportunity to discredit the government. A parliamentary inquiry into the Little Desert Settlement Scheme was established in October 1969, chaired by the Hon J. W. (Jack) Galbally, a Labor MLC, who had successfully used this type of inquiry to stop the building of a restaurant in Melbourne's Royal Botanic Gardens earlier in 1969.[40] The inquiry heard evidence

'I never knew the Little Desert was in Dandenong'

stretching over more than 250 pages of transcript. A significant number of the 'expert witnesses' were the same agricultural resource managers who had advised McDonald against the scheme when it was first mooted. Much of the data presented both at the inquiry and in the media was officially or unofficially supplied by bureaucrats frustrated because the government was not taking their well-considered advice. The staff of the Department of Agriculture were particularly active in opposing the scheme, within the limits of public service etiquette. Their political masters were well aware of this. McDonald did not speak to the Minister for Agriculture for some time because of the 'leaks' from his department.[41]

The parliamentary inquiry received generous media coverage on an almost daily basis. Even before the report of the inquiry was published in March 1970, evidence and popular opinion against the scheme had mounted. In December 1969, following a by-election in Dandenong that returned a disastrous result for the government, the Legislative Council voted to block funding to the scheme. Metropolitan Dandenong was a long way from the Little Desert, as one cartoonist pointed out, but resentment about the scheme had built to a point where it was now an issue of State-wide significance.[42] The supply vote led to a temporary halting of preparatory road-building and other activities in the Little Desert, and while it was in abeyance the protest gathered pace.

In particular, there was a growing concern about public consultation. As more and more evidence emerged from the parliamentary inquiry, it seemed that the only people who would be able to farm the new Little Desert blocks 'economically' would be those who needed to make a tax loss. This was not a question of depriving rural battlers of their dream block, of the yeoman ideal revisited. It was only an opportunity for 'Collins Street farmers'—business and professional people from the big city—to reduce their tax burden at the government's expense.

Sir Henry Bolte was old-fashioned in many ways, but he was politically astute enough to sniff the winds of change. It seemed that it was the new conservation vote that had decided the Dandenong by-election result against him. So he 'discovered' a more electorally appealing type of conservation just in time for the general election the following May. The post-election Minister for Lands, Bill Borthwick, recalled it thus:

> The Little Desert was a turning point . . . it caught Bolte—Bolte came to me for the 1970 policy speech and got me to write a segment on conservation—never been in a policy speech before. He knew it was time—Bolte was a great politician—he knew that things and attitudes had changed. I wrote the conservation issues . . . I took [the section] to [Dick] Hamer [who succeeded Bolte as Premier of Victoria in 1972] because I got it down to seven pages and I knew it should be seven paragraphs and Dick blue-pencilled it for me.

This departure from earlier policy did not go unremarked. Borthwick went on to recall wryly the reaction of journalists in an Ararat pub after the speech: 'We walked in on the press and they were saying "Who wrote Bolte's speech? He's saying things he doesn't understand."'[43]

Bolte promised that land management decisions would be taken in a new way that involved more public consultation via a 'Land Resources Council'. He also specifically promised that at least five per cent of the State would be reserved for national parks, wildlife reserves and forest parks.[44] The promise was an acknowledgement of the 'conservation vote', but it was not as generous as it sounds. At the time more than 30 per cent of the State was unalienated public land.

The speech was persuasive. The Liberal primary vote slipped only slightly, and Bolte's government was re-elected. Only two seats were lost, but one was Dundas, the 'safe' seat held continuously by Sir William McDonald for fifteen years.[45]

The loss of McDonald was no guarantee that the Little Desert Settlement Scheme would be abolished. Many conservationists at the time were anxious about what would happen after the election.[46] Sir William's demise, however, had to be attributed at least in part to the Little Desert controversy. Although twenty years later he would deny that the scheme had been his downfall, he faced an extraordinary number of independent opponents in that election, unlike any other, and the vote in Dundas was much more strongly anti-Liberal than in the rest of the State. The government had lost the scheme's most passionate proponent. The election results cooled the ardour of the other members of Cabinet, and even Bolte's support for the scheme waned. There was a general view that conservation interests needed to be taken seriously. This scheme was not a political winner.

The Little Desert dispute was not simply a case of conservation or preservation versus development. It was, rather, a rare moment when economists and conservationists found themselves arguing the same case. The public, which in the past had been supportive of development and decentralisation schemes, was sceptical about this one. Some felt that it was to cost the taxpayer too much, while others remembered individuals who had suffered because of the inadequacy of the land provided under the soldier settlement schemes.[47] A new group was emerging that was concerned about the cost to the land itself. But underlying all the opposition was a fundamental concern about 'due process'.

Letters to the editor in major metropolitan newspapers almost universally opposed the Little Desert Settlement Scheme, but as the year progressed the emphasis shifted towards questions of political process rather than economic arguments or even conservation values.[48] No single minister, it was argued, should have the power to act in the face of popular and expert opposition and create a land-use pattern that would be passed down to future generations. There was a strong call for more consultation and accountability. The

Little Desert dispute could not be said to be resolved until the matter of process had been tackled.

The whole system of public land management had to be reviewed. There was a new awareness that leaving options for future generations was more politically important than tidying up the frontier. The public demanded the right to be consulted about land-use decisions. Even before the 'green' ethic that crystallised in the 1970s, there was growing recognition that resources, especially land resources, were not unlimited. The images of the finite, blue and singular Earth that were beamed back from the Apollo 11 space mission of July 1969 shaped public consciousness, both consciously and unconsciously.

Conservationists realised that parliamentarians were listening to them as a unified pressure group. Theirs was the voice of 'finite resources'. They fought for the public's right to decide about appropriate uses for the 'last' lands, and they won. There was a tremendous sense of celebration. The phrases 'Little Desert' and 'Conservation Victory' were juxtaposed in the titles of radio programmes and photographic exhibitions.[49]

The successful result for the Little Desert lent confidence to the whole movement. On this wave of enthusiasm, the Conservation Council of Victoria (CCV) was established to act as an umbrella organisation for all conservation groups, to offer the government of the day representative advice on conservation matters.[50] The CCV took over from the informal and politically charged Save Our Bushlands Action Committee, and ensured that the government of the day had a liaison point for all conservation matters affecting the State.

Bolte handed the Lands portfolio to Bill Borthwick after the 1970 election. Borthwick described the Little Desert Settlement Scheme as 'a bad error of judgement on the part of my government', but he also saw that it had provided 'a peg on which conservationists could hang their hats'.[51] The lessons of the dispute became central to the way in which he reorganised the bureaucracy. The Little Desert became the 'peg' for a variety of 'hats'. Nature lovers, the emerging green movement and utilitarian conservationists alike claimed it as their victory. These groups had very different visions of land management—something that subsequent governments were to discover—but at the time of the Little Desert dispute it was possible for one iconic victory to satisfy all.

Borthwick recognised that it was politically important to develop a very different style of management for the Lands portfolio, and set about offering it through the mechanism of the Land Conservation Council. The change in name from Bolte's pre-election 'Land Resources Council' was indicative of Borthwick's new style. The council had to be credible to the concerned general public. Unless real public consultation could be seen to occur, the potential for a Little Desert type of protest was ever present. The new mechanism had to be 'above politics'. This authoritative, independent (although government-approved) body was charged with the responsibility for inquiring into all matters of public land management. Generally it is only a potentially divisive issue that will drive a government to risk a public inquiry for the sake of legitimising its own policy.[52] The Little Desert Settlement Scheme thus stands out as a very divisive issue, for its practical result was not just an inquiry, but rather a permanent mechanism for inquiry.

As a postscript to the dispute, in 1973 Borthwick demoted the Lands portfolio in order to promote a new, broader Conservation ministry. From 1973 Borthwick styled himself 'Minister for Conservation' rather than Minister of Lands. It was the beginning of the end for the Lands Department, which was abolished in 1983.[53] The Little Desert dispute made it clear that politically there was no longer a need for a department of frontier development. There were no new frontiers, only fragile, limited land resources, to be managed with a consciousness of conservation values.

Significantly, a further eighteen years were to pass before the Little Desert National Park was expanded to include the hard-won western end.[54] Yet during that time, the post-victory fervour gave conservationists faith that the new Land Conservation Council would 'do the right thing'. There was such optimism that conservationists even argued that the cooling-off period might benefit the conservation imperative. The resolution of the dispute could truly be said to reside not in the extension of the national park, but in the establishment of a mechanism for public consultation on land management.

2

Crosbie Morrison's National Parks Campaign

The birds and the beasts and wildflowers have no votes, and therefore they don't interest the politician.

Philip Crosbie Morrison[1]

Nature conservation entered the political agenda in the post-war era because of persistent hard work over a whole century by amateur nature lovers. It was they who convinced politicians and the wider population of the public's 'right' to bushland. Amateur nature lovers lobbied and chivvied, driven by passion rather than the economics that often determines political 'causes'. In Victoria there were two key groups, the Field Naturalists' Club of Victoria (FNCV), established in 1880, and the Victorian National Parks Association (VNPA), which grew out of it in 1952.

The VNPA was not the first national parks association for the State, but it was somewhat different from its predecessor. The first National Parks Association of Victoria, established in 1908, followed the British traditions of the National Trust.[2] It soon became concerned as much with the erection of historical monuments such as 'simple memorials to mark the routes travelled and the landing places of the early explorers'[3] as with the reservation of bushland. By the 1920s the National Parks Association had lost its separate identity and had been subsumed by the Town and Country Planning Association (TCPA) through the influence of Sir James Barrett (1862–1945), an eminent ophthalmologist with interests in both. In 1946 the TCPA renewed its interest in national parks, but as a quasi-professional planning organisation, not as a body primarily concerned with nature conservation.

The field naturalists of the FNCV, on the other hand, tended to concern themselves with particular places rather than with the processes of government. They loved the bushland haunts where they spent weekends 'birding' or 'botanising'. Special natural places belonged to the higher things of life; they were associated with relaxation, not with earning a living. Nature conservation was a moral, not an economic imperative. To make this moral imperative politically viable, though, it became more and more apparent that there was a need to engage with the labyrinthine structures of government.

In the 1940s the radio journalist and editor Philip Crosbie Morrison (1900–58), who was incontrovertibly the nature conservation movement's most notable public figure at the time, took up this challenge. During the early 1940s, as editor of the magazine *Wild Life*, Morrison promoted the contemplation of nature as providing a release from the horrors of war. He likened it to religion 'in the calm and contentment it brings to the mind and the soul . . . Religion is a matter for individual thought and conscience, but as a secular exercise, *Wild Life* commends to its readers the release from cares which contact with nature can bring.' In Morrison's book, to contemplate nature was not to escape one's duty to the nation. Demonstrating his sensitivity to wartime politics, Morrison tied patriotism to nature, and against Hitler: 'Hitler hates [the contemplation of nature]. That is why he has turned hiking parties and nature excursions into military youth movements, and has suppressed the universities where these things are studied'.[4] The association of nature with personal and moral values is crude and propagandistic, but offers an insight into how Morrison saw such values as becoming politically relevant.

Morrison's writing was predicated on a human value system developed through a personal ownership of nature, not by land title or collection but rather by familiarity and observation. In Morrison's writing there was always a human subject, a contemplator of nature, one who can be 'improved' by such contemplation. There was respect for nature but a constant otherness about nature itself. Morrison never implied the eighteenth-century subliminal romantic view, picked up by late twentieth-century extreme radical ecologists, where lover and beloved are one. Rather, the separation between the human and the natural placed a moral and political onus of 'stewardship' on the human contemplator.[5]

Morrison's philosophies of nature were strongly influenced by the work of the *Argus* journalist Donald Macdonald, whose nature columns, 'Nature Notes and Queries' and 'Notes for Boys', had created a niche for nature in Australian popular culture since the first decade of the twentieth century.[6] When Macdonald was seriously ill, not long before his death, Morrison, then a young journalist with the *Argus*, co-wrote several of the columns. Morrison took over both columns in the hiatus between Macdonald's death in 1932 and the appointment of his successor, ornithologist and senior journalist A. H. Chisholm (1890–1977), early in 1933.[7] Morrison again took over the column (by then called 'Notes for Boys and Girls') in mid-1937, when Chisholm became editor of the *Argus*. After just over a year Morrison left this job to take on the much bigger one of editing his own magazine, *Wild Life*, in which his question-and-answer correspondence column played an important role. Morrison's page, 'Along the Track', was inspired by readers' queries. This regular exchange between columnist and readers furthered Macdonald's notion of a 'nature club'. Morrison's 'Wild Life' radio programme, begun on the first Sunday in November 1938, was initially established to publicise his new magazine, but its astounding popularity meant that it quickly expanded beyond its original brief, running for sixteen years until 1954.[8] Within three months it had a 70 per cent share of the local audience at 6 p.m. on Sunday. It was later broadcast interstate and in New Zealand and South Africa.

In an era before telephones could be assumed to be part of every household, the 'Wild Life' show had almost a talkback dimension, using listeners' letters as cues for topics for discussion. For many of the avid listeners, these programmes became the starting point of a life-long commitment to nature and nature conservation.[9]

Morrison, who held a Master of Science degree in marine zoology, was more consciously scientific in style than his mentor Macdonald, but he embraced Macdonald's notion of writing for amateurs, answering questions and providing untrained naturalists with information about science. In Macdonald's time newspaper columns themselves provided a forum for scientific exchange between amateur and professional biologists, geologists and natural historians.[10] Macdonald encouraged his readers to observe for themselves directly, not simply to accept on authority. Occasionally he set particular tasks for his team of fieldworkers (his readers).

By the time Morrison was writing and broadcasting, however, growing scientific professionalisation and the move away from descriptive to analytical science had diminished the role of the scientific amateur. Morrison's columns were more consciously educative, encouraging a new generation into scientific careers as well as promoting nature study. They were also more political. There was important and urgent work for naturalists to undertake, irrespective of formal qualifications: nature conservation, demanding an active engagement in politics, was the major endeavour pursued co-operatively by Morrison and his readers.

'Stewards of nature' had an overtly political responsibility. Once the constraints of wartime rhetoric were past, Morrison identified specific sacrifices made by nature in the interests of patriotism, and a very different political tone emerged in his journalism. In 1946 he signalled the beginning of a campaign for what he called a 'local post-war New Deal for the wild things'.[11] The centrepiece of this 'New Deal' was a campaign to remedy the damage inflicted on Wilsons Promontory National Park by the military forces stationed there during the war:

> This remote area with its wide range and wild mountain country and extensive plains, and its short dividing fence, was the very place for certain military and air force purposes which at that time must at all costs be kept secret. The Commonwealth took it over for the period of the war. They made an aerodrome there. Some of the most secret of the war's 'hush hush' equipment was there. They trained commando troops there—they had to learn to travel light, to make booby traps and to avoid enemy booby traps; they had to become accustomed to living off the land, and what better land could there be to live off than a region which had been preserved as a fauna sanctuary for nearly half a century?[12]

Morrison urged that there be a 'stocktake' of wartime losses. His broadcast was framed in a way that provoked listeners elsewhere in Australia and New Zealand to start thinking about the effects of military operations in their own local areas. But for Victorian listeners Wilsons Promontory was not simply an example. It was 'The National Park', the most important and distinctive of the State's dedicated natural reserves.[13]

Wilsons Promontory

The naturalists J. B. Gregory, a lawyer, and A. H. S. Lucas, a senior science master, had been the first to commend Wilsons Promontory to their fellow enthusiasts, particularly the members of the FNCV, in the 1880s.[14] They described the area as 'inaccessible' and likened it to the Cornish peninsula, in that it was late to be discovered by tourists. They prophesied that 'a future yet awaits it as a summer haunt of lovers of nature, lovers of scenery'.[15]

The 'Prom' has some of the physical properties of an island. Its landscape contrasts sharply with the surrounding countryside, to which it is joined by a narrow isthmus. It is spectacular, scenic (in the traditional nineteenth-century sense) and diverse, with high mountain peaks, white sandy beaches and dunes, barren offshore islands and densely forested areas. It carries cultural associations based on the symbolism of an island: the Eden-like properties of a place apart, a place of adventure (a literary association from such works as *Treasure Island* and *Robinson Crusoe*) and its wholeness as an environment.[16]

Older members of the FNCV and others would have remembered or known of the long fight waged between 1884 and 1908 to preserve the 'Prom', a story that had become one of the great traditions of the club. Wilsons Promontory was reserved as a national park through a long and tortuous process that had many similarities to the Little Desert campaign. Although the people involved in the Wilsons Promontory campaign were several generations older than the Little Desert campaigners and the land they were fighting to preserve could not have been more different, the politics of the campaigns show significant parallels. The groups most active in seeking the reservation of Wilsons Promontory were the natural history societies and scientific societies of the day, especially the FNCV, the Australasian Ornithologists' Union,[17] the Royal Society of Victoria and the Victorian branch of the Royal Geographical Society of Australasia. The early National Parks Association of Victoria also emerged initially because of the Prom's new-found status as a national park.[18]

The publication of J. B. Gregory's descriptive account of his 1884 trip 'To Wilson's Promontory Overland', which appeared in four parts in the *Victorian Naturalist*, was quickly followed by political action. In July 1887 Gregory and his co-author, A. H. S. Lucas, heard of a Lands Department proposal to alienate 45 000 acres (18 000 hectares) near the Promontory to 'settle' immigrant crofters from the Isle of Skye in Scotland. Gregory asked the FNCV to take steps:

> to secure the vesting of Wilson's Promontory and the islands and waters adjoining in a board of Trustees, for the purposes of a national park, for the preservation of fauna and flora, for the conservation of the fisheries, and for public recreation.[19]

Lucas approached the Royal Society of Victoria with the same aim.[20] The Skye crofters plan was finally abandoned following a deputation from the FNCV, the Royal and Geographical Societies and the Academy of Arts.

Yet it was not until 1898 that the area was gazetted as a national park and 91 000 acres (37 000 hectares) of land were reserved.[21] A few years later the FNCV and the Royal Society were shocked to discover that this was only a temporary reservation. '[I]t was discovered that we had been living in a fool's paradise', commented Thomas Sergeant Hall, a former FNCV president. 'It is under the absolute control of the Ministry, and may be alienated at will.'[22] The discovery of the status of the reservation prompted the FNCV to wage a much more determined and well-informed campaign between 1904 and 1908, spearheaded by Alfred D. Hardy, an enthusiastic naturalist and also an officer of the Lands Department. Hardy was responsible for leading an extended excursion to Wilsons Promontory over the summer of 1905–06, 'so that the Club might be in a position to speak with authority on the present condition of its fauna and flora and future possibilities'.[23]

The decision to campaign using the voice of one or several clubs with expertise in science or natural history was a pattern repeated throughout the twentieth century. The clubs lent authority to conservation campaigns, and also gave anonymity to public servants such as Hardy, whose jobs constrained them from taking an overt political stance. It was more efficient to use existing infrastructure than to set up a series of single-issue campaign offices. The clubs also contained many members who would never have initiated a political effort, but were happy to go along with the office-bearers' efforts. So, when it came to lobbying, the club's representatives could say they were speaking on behalf of the whole membership, lending significant credibility to the campaign.

The permanent gazetting of Wilsons Promontory in 1908 represented the culmination of the efforts of naturalists, scientists and bureaucrats working together under the banner of the scientific and natural history societies. The choice of key personnel reflected the importance of science and natural history: Professor W. Baldwin Spencer, Professor of Biology at the University of Melbourne, was the first chairman of the committee of management for Wilsons Promontory National Park, while the first ranger, appointed in 1909, was Charles McLennan, a naturalist and contributor to the 'Nature Notes and Queries' column in the *Argus*.[24]

The campaign for Wilsons Promontory was the first of many major State-wide campaigns by natural history societies, and shaped the campaigns that followed. Never again was there confusion between temporary and permanent reservation. It was also a 'success story', something vital to the morale of conservationists in any era. The exigencies of World War II, however, swept away the power of permanent reservation. This was the background to Crosbie Morrison's disgust at the military's treatment of Wilsons Promontory during the war. His radio broadcast and subsequent editorials in *Wild Life* expressed a sense of sacrilege and indignation. They prompted renewed action through the FNCV to tackle the problem of representing nature in the era of post-war reconstruction.[25]

Wilsons Promontory was close to the hearts of Victorian nature conservationists. It was the closest thing Victorians had to a 'temple' of nature—despite the fact that the nature there was far from pristine, as Jane Lennon has convincingly argued.[26] The losses made during the war were compounded in 1951 by major bushfires. The Prom became the heart of the campaign for a structure to protect nature. The parlous state of the unmanaged wartime park was a shock to those who knew it from the pre-war years. When it was burnt out (possibly by an out-of-control grazing fire) in 1951, anger grew afresh. Personal and historical associations with Wilsons Promontory motivated people in the FNCV to become concerned about all Victoria's national parks and their management. Concern about the loss of a familiar and beloved place led on to a concern about process. What could be done to prevent such debacles in future?

The Two Conservations

Conservation bureaucracies in Victoria dated from early in the twentieth century, but they were fundamentally concerned with economy, not sensibility; their focus was on 'resource' conservation, not nature conservation.[27] Conservation had become linked with science, but was somewhat distanced from natural history. Professional resource managers saw science as a tool to solve the practical problems of primary industries, including irrigation, rabbit infestation, soil drift and forest fires. The early work of the federally funded Council for Scientific and Industrial Research (CSIR, later CSIRO) focused on these problems at the expense of the surveys of indigenous flora and fauna advocated earlier by the Australasian Association for the Advancement of Science.[28] Resource conservation leaders, especially in the 1930s and 1940s, were mainly concerned with promoting timber, water and soil conservation and improving bureaucratic mechanisms to implement programmes in these areas. Economics dominated the 'conservation' agenda, and the language of debate was supplied by the senior government officials who worked for land-management agencies.

Nature conservation, by contrast, was privately supported, popular and concerned with the reservation and interpretation of land for wildlife and recreation. Most community notions of conservation were not focused on elements of economic production (although there were exceptions; in 1909, for example, a schoolteacher, Miss Jessie McMichael, had argued for the establishment of the Gould League of Bird Observers on the basis that 'the thoughtless destruction of bird life would lead to an increase in numbers of insects, which would if left unchecked take a disastrous toll on crops of all kinds'[29]. For all its obvious popularity, nature conservation had yet to establish its right to be heard by government. Crosbie Morrison, with his magazine and radio programmes, provided a focus around which this movement flourished in Victoria. Its infrastructure came from the FNCV, particularly the hard-working secretary of the National Parks and National Monuments sub-committee, Ros Garnet (1906–98). When this sub-committee 'outgrew itself', the Victorian National Parks Association was established in 1952 to handle the considerable workload. Morrison became the VNPA's first president and Garnet its secretary.[30]

Until 1956 there was no arm of government specifically designated to manage nature reserves or national parks. The Fisheries and Game Department, as it was then known, had some role in protecting wildlife, but, as its title suggested, the commercially valuable species received preferential treatment.[31] Government commitment to the 'public interest' in national parks was the biggest and most important issue facing the new VNPA. The national parks that did exist in Victoria were managed by voluntary committees of management that had neither the power nor the resources to take on difficult commercial adversaries. It was left to the unpaid members of community groups to carry the burden of nature conservation work, including descriptive surveys ('stocktaking') and political campaigns for the preservation of habitat in particular places. The two went together, as A. D. Hardy had demonstrated in 1906. But there were no government resources to support 'nature' that was not demonstrably 'economic'.

There were many well-qualified scientists among the FNCV members, including quite a few from the National Museum of Victoria, but the FNCV was a 'hobby club', not a professional organisation. No one was excluded from membership, and many of the club's best experts on particular subjects had no formal qualifications. The FNCV conservation voice was sometimes scientific, but just as often nostalgic and personal. It was consciously concerned with creating a particular long-term future where the traditions of natural historians—bushwalking, observing nature and being 'at peace with the world'—could flourish. The emphasis on preserving personal associations with nature contrasted sharply with conservation as technology—as 'fixing up' natural systems that had been meddled with unwisely. This was the domain of the professional bureaucrat, the resource manager.

Interesting the Public in the 'Public Interest'

During the 1930s and 1940s attempts were made to find some sort of rapprochement between the nature conservation and resource conservation movements. The Forests Commission, a government agency that saw its future as intimately tied up with much of the potential national park land, sought to woo natural history enthusiasts. The chairman of the Forests Commission in 1935, A. V. Galbraith, expressed concern for both the interrelationships between wildlife and the forest, and 'the sentimental desire to preserve wildlife'.[32] Under Galbraith, the Forests Commission sought to balance the needs of the timber industry with wildlife conservation and 'increasing public recreational use'. The commission actively sought an alliance between its interests and those of the FNCV.[33]

There were many, both in government and in the community, who saw the management of national parks as a natural extension of the commission's duties, although some saw a conflict between the needs of the timber industry and natural history considerations. During the early 1940s the Forests Commission set out to establish a 'community face', a group that would support the wise-use conservation values dear to the forestry profession. Following a parliamentary inquiry into Victorian forest policy, orchestrated in 1943 by the Hon C. E. Isaac MLC, a Save the Forests Campaign was established in 1944.[34] This provided a focus for 'an intense educational campaign to save the forests, in which every tree-lover [should take] part'.[35] Isaac was also instrumental in persuading Parliament that a Royal Commission into Forest Grazing was needed, and in 1946 Judge L. E. B. Stretton, veteran of two earlier fire-related Royal Commissions, undertook the task.[36]

Stretton's brief was broad. The questions included under 'forest grazing' were the relationship between grazing and soil erosion, water catchment efficiency and, above all, fire.[37] In a dramatic single-sentence paragraph of his earlier Royal Commission report on the devastating Victorian fires of 1939, Stretton had declared: 'These fires were lit by the hand of man'.[38] The message of his 1946 report was similarly uncompromising:

> Amongst the many subjects which fill the field of this inquiry, three stand pre-eminent, in an inseparable trinity—Forest, Soil and Water. No one of them can stand alone. No one of them alone can be understood. No one of them without the others, can prosper. Each keeps the others in health. If one is injured, the three must share the injury. A cycle of destruction of all three may begin with any one of them . . . Destroy any one of them, and by the inexorable cycle which works for health or disease within this fundamental syllogism of the productive physical world, you destroy the well-being of your people . . . Civilizations have perished, leaving only the monuments of man's pretentiousness to mock their memory, because in ignorance or wantonness man's impious hand has disturbed the delicate balance which nature would maintain between forest, soil and water.[39]

Stretton's words became the language of the Save the Forests Campaign, and thence of the community. The campaign republished extracts from the report, and distributed 5000 copies of them in brochure form.[40] Cyril Isaac, who had instigated the inquiry, took 'an inseparable trinity' as the theme of one of his regular radio broadcasts in 1955.[41] The first history of the campaign, published in 1950, took its title from Stretton's words. The Stretton Commission served to direct conservation interests toward resource conservation, and perhaps distracted the community from national parks.[42] Stretton did, however, mention in passing that

> all grazing and other harmful activities should be excluded from [national parks], some of which are being ruined in the quest of a miserable revenue won at the expense of their beauty and well-being.[43]

Stretton deplored the fact that the Forests Commission had been 'ousted from national parks and similar reservations', and recommended that it be responsible for all forests. He felt that ad hoc committees of management were not sufficiently strong to manage national parks, which should therefore return to the stronger control (especially against fire) of the Forests Commission. Stretton was also concerned about water and soil. He suggested the foundation of a land utilisation authority, perhaps instead of the Soil Conservation Board. This Authority 'should enjoy a large measure of freedom from political control'. It would oversee the management of land, ensuring justice for all the resources of the 'trinity' and guiding the Department of Lands and Survey, which was to continue to administer the alienation of Crown land, 'on broader issues', implicitly including nature conservation.[44]

Stretton's recommendation for a land utilisation authority was not adopted by the government of the day, although it influenced the decisions that were eventually taken with respect to soil conservation in 1950.[45] The period after the release of the report was a particularly unstable one in Victorian politics, with nine governments being formed between 1946 and 1956. It has been said that Theodore Roosevelt was able to force a showdown on conservation in America in the first decade of the twentieth century 'because it was a relatively dull and uneventful period of history with no great external events to dictate his agenda'.[46] Victoria in the decade from 1946 to 1956 was anything but dull and uneventful. It was reeling from the effects of World War II and the sudden influx of repatriated soldiers. There was intense pressure on resources, especially land and timber. Long-term conservation philosophies were well down the political parties' list of priorities, and none of them stayed in power long enough to reach lower priorities. These same pressures helped to keep the community campaigning for good management of national parks, but the process was slow, and was constantly impeded by changes of parliamentary personnel.

The Campaign for a National Parks Authority

The FNCV was one of the thirty-seven organisations that had supported the foundation of the Save the Forests Campaign. It acknowledged the important work to be done in the resource conservation sector. It also pressed on independently for better management of national parks. Following Morrison's initial remarks about Wilsons Promontory, a public conference was called in June 1946. Backed up by the considerable research of the club's National Parks and National Monuments Sub-committee, the conference resulted in the publication in 1948 of *National Parks and National Reserves in Victoria*. This document was widely disseminated, and received coverage in the metropolitan press.[47] There were then two further public conferences, in July and December 1948, and a deputation in 1949 to the Minister of Lands about the reservation and management of national parks.[48] The central contention was that all Victoria's national parks and monuments should be under the control of one authority. The FNCV proposed that this central authority should consist of representatives of the various interests involved, including major government departments, scientists (specifically, the National Museum, the National Herbarium and the University of Melbourne's Faculty of Science) and representatives of the natural history societies in the State.[49]

The government called for the State Development Committee to report on the subject. It received submissions throughout 1950 and 1951, and handed down a report in November 1951.[50] The format of the report drew heavily on the FNCV's 1948 document. It endorsed many of the FNCV recommendations, including the establishment of a statutory authority to control all the State's national parks and national reserves, a point noted with satisfaction by the FNCV Council at the time of its release.[51]

In March 1952 the FNCV called another public meeting, and the Victorian National Parks Association was established.[52] Nature conservation was supported by a rather different group of organisations from those concerned with resource conservation, as can be seen by comparing the initial supporters of the Save the Forests Campaign in 1944 with those of the VNPA in 1952.[53] Six major State government departments threw their weight behind the Save the Forests Campaign.[54] In addition, the campaign received support from the University of Melbourne, six other government agencies, seven 'industry' groups and eleven 'citizen organisations', including the Boy Scouts Association, the Housewives Association, the Country Women's Association and the Returned Soldiers', Sailors' and Airmen's Imperial League of Australia. Forest, water and soil conservation attracted a broad range of interest groups, many of them with large memberships.

By contrast, the VNPA's support was closely identified with natural history groups and recreational clubs, especially walking clubs, which were absent from the list of official supporters of the Save the Forests Campaign.[55] The VNPA's lively and active excursion programme was a great attraction for its members, and in its early years this was significantly shaped by the secretary of the Federation of Victorian Walking Clubs, Eric Stewart (1902–82), and his wife Ena. The Stewarts were such enthusiastic members and office-bearers in the VNPA that they were granted honorary life membership in 1973.[56] The only government group supporting the VNPA was the National Museum, which was not involved with the Save the Forests Campaign.

There was no industry support for the national parks movement until 1955, when the VNPA found an unlikely partner in the Australian Primary Producers Union (APPU), which co-sponsored another conference on national parks. The APPU became involved because it had a forceful and maverick leader in Dewar Goode (1907–), a grazier and a passionate conservationist.[57] Goode had travelled widely overseas and decided that Victoria needed national parks urgently as destinations for international visitors to the 1956 Melbourne Olympic Games.[58] This fresh line of argument may have been the catalyst that was needed. On 30 October 1956, just a month before the Olympic Games, the Victorian Parliament finally passed the National Parks Act 1956, which established a government authority to protect and develop Victoria's national parks.

The passage of the Act brought to a close a decade-long, bitter and personal campaign. Crosbie Morrison's name was so closely linked with the campaign that he was mentioned disparagingly in Hansard during debate on the reading of the National Parks Bill. Morrison, now working again for the *Argus*, used his column to rebut gently:

> May I be permitted a personal word? Several speakers in Parliament have mentioned my name, one going so far as to call the Bill the 'Crosbie Morrison Pension Bill'. This has been very embarrassing. I

have never sought for myself nor have I ever authorised anyone to seek for me any position connected with the National Parks Administration. I am very comfortable where I am.[59]

The closure of the 'great national parks campaign', as Graham Pizzey called it, was achieved by the creation of a new bureaucracy, the National Parks Authority (NPA). The public credibility of this new body was vested in the appointment early in 1957 of its first director. Despite his earlier protestations, this was Crosbie Morrison.

Morrison, as director of the small and poorly funded National Parks Authority, soon realised that his appointment was not the end of campaigning but the beginning of a fresh campaign. He chose to draw clearly and directly on American-style nationalist literature in the framing of the conclusion to his first (and only) Annual Report as director in 1957. Morrison made a direct appeal to politicians for more funding, using a 'big picture' argument about the importance of national parks to national character:

> The National Parks of this State are reserved as samples of the Victorian countryside as Nature made it. They are the living and only true portrayal of the National Character . . . Our parks and the unique living things they contain are the show windows of the Australian bush, and as the years pass, with the advances in soil science and technology, the unspoilt bush will become confined more and more to the places which, in the words of the Act, we 'protect, preserve and maintain'.[60]

The use of 'national character' derives clearly from the Roosevelt tradition, including a view of wilderness as a morally improving force, essential to national 'virility' and greatness.[61] The fact that it was years before the NPA received funding commensurate with such a vision (if indeed it ever did) suggests that neither the populace nor the politicians could be persuaded to identify natural places with national character or the 'national interest' as they had in the USA. When conservation returned to the political agenda in the late 1960s, it was an internationalist, not a nationalist vision that prevailed.

Unfortunately, Morrison had little time to shape his senior public service position or to sell his 'national parks for national character' philosophy. Barely a year after his appointment, he suffered a cerebral haemorrhage and died at the age of fifty-seven. Nature conservationists were left stunned and leaderless. Morrison had been able to inspire, to communicate a vision. But one of the difficulties for the movement was that without the visionary leader, the vision did not readily translate into progress. The NPA remained under-funded, and very much junior in status to the other big State bureaucracies, especially Lands and Forests.

Morrison's successor was Dr Leonard H. Smith (1910–), a forest products chemist and experienced industrialist.[62] Smith had a considerable personal interest in the lyrebirds of Sherbrooke Forest, and had written and photographed for Morrison's *Wild Life* magazine and other natural history publications, but he did not have the high public profile that Morrison had brought to the job. The public (including the VNPA and the FNCV) was not fully aware of the authority's parlous state. Exhausted by the long campaign, and without the leadership provided by Morrison, the national parks movement in Victoria went into hibernation.

3

The Local and the Global

Don't for a moment believe the conservation movement started with us ... Those of early generations were just as active as we were, but there were fewer of them. I got to know quite a lot of them later on as old men in the Field Nats when I was a young feller and they were still battling on.

Ros Garnet

The Little Desert campaign of 1969 was the first major national parks dispute in Victoria since Crosbie Morrison's death. It revived the conservation movement and took it in new directions. The concerns about agricultural development in the Little Desert and at Kentbruck Heath in south-western Victoria were not just about saving nature, they were also about introducing a moral sense of 'limits to development'.[1] The Little Desert campaign was quickly followed by campaigns focused on other developments, especially those proposed by the Tasmanian Hydro-Electric Commission (HEC). The most important of these were the unsuccessful bid to stop the inundation of Lake Pedder in 1973 and the successful stand in 1983 against building the Franklin Dam. The Pedder and Franklin protests pushed the global–local frontier further, with major campaigns for both conducted on the mainland. Furthermore, the positive resolution of the Franklin dispute depended on intervention by the federal government, which invoked its international obligations under World Heritage agreements to justify using its external affairs power to protect the area. Federal powers had previously been used to resolve a dispute over sand-mining on Fraser Island in Queensland during the mid-1970s, in which the local activists of the Fraser Island Defence Organisation (FIDO) were supported by national conservation groups. State government support for the mining companies was unbending, but sand-mining was prevented through a federal ban on export permits.[2] In the late 1990s a similar alignment of forces emerged over proposals for three dams on the Fitzroy River in north-western Australia, with business interests and the State government pitted against national and international conservation interests.[3] The local and the global are now inextricably entwined.

The Little Desert dispute was the last of the big conservation campaigns to be resolved within a State framework. It was a local antecedent of the 'think globally, act locally' environmental movement. But it was run by an older conservation movement drawing its traditions from the Morrison 'parks for people' era, with an emphasis on the public's right to nature and natural bushland.

Ever-expanding chemically dependent agricultural development had become an international concern during the 1960s, following the publication of Rachel Carson's *Silent Spring*. City people in Australia who had no other reason to think about the farming sector were beginning to take an interest in reading books and newspaper columns by agricultural economists such as Bruce Davidson and Alan Lloyd. They were also aware of growing global campaigns against the population 'explosion' by Paul Ehrlich and others.[4] These did not translate into instant action, but provided a background against which activism made sense on a different level.

City conservationists 'blew the whistle' on proposals for agricultural development in two different areas in the west of Victoria, the Little Desert and the Lower Glenelg River and its environs. Although at first these were just typical local campaigns, by the end of the 1960s the two protests were conjoined, and the local campaigners of western Victoria were given new strength by a groundswell of urban opinion based on global ethical concerns.

The 'limits to development' campaign depended on city muscle and city-based ethics, which were drawn from the international and cosmopolitan arenas. The 'global' view in turn depended on the local for effective action. The persistence of local campaigners with a personal stake in the territory under dispute made the bigger campaign possible. The linchpins of the campaign were the groups that facilitated communication between the local and the metropolitan, bridging the country/city divide. The background information that fuelled metropolitan rage had been garnered carefully over many years by a small number of tireless local naturalists and publicised through natural history societies. The FNCV had branches in Portland, Ararat and Horsham, and individual members in places such as Kaniva, right on the edge of the Little Desert. But it was not simply a matter of city 'philosophy' and country 'fact-finding'. There was a constant two-way interchange sponsored and supported by the natural history groups throughout the post-war years.

Sometimes the tradition of respect for the local infuriated metropolitan interests more concerned with the bigger picture. Professor John Turner, who chaired meetings of the VNPA in the late 1960s, and who was committed to finishing them before 10.30 p.m., found Ros Garnet, the secretary, to be rather too interested in what Turner termed 'putting out minor fires':

> There are little urgent matters that cannot [wait]. Developers start knocking over a building or somebody wants to put a road through a favorite heath and you spend ages fighting theses little conflagrations. And you can't get onto the problem of looking ahead a bit.[5]

But the respect and energy that Garnet gave to each little local campaign did much to maintain rural–urban links. His long-windedness perhaps put some people off attending meetings, but the fact that 'minor fires' were respected in the metropolitan centres was crucial to keeping faith with a wide range of supporters. And it was always possible that a 'minor fire' could suddenly burn out of control.

Noel Learmonth, Fred Davies and the Lower Glenelg

The campaign for the preservation of the area around the Lower Glenelg River began in the 1940s, when Noel Learmonth (1880–1970), a Portland grazier, invited members of the FNCV to examine the region around the river with a view to creating a 'national forest sanctuary' in the area. Learmonth was seeking 'a permanent reservation administered by the Forests Commission yet possessing most of the advantages that national parks are intended to possess'.[6] At Easter in 1947, five FNCV Committee members (Ina Watson, Ros Garnet, R. D. Lee, A. Burke and F. A. Cudmore) went to Portland and camped out in the Lower Glenelg area, hosted by local experts from the Portland Field Naturalists' Club (established 1945). A lengthy report on the excursion was published in the *Victorian Naturalist*. The FNCV's annual report for 1947 signalled support for Learmonth and the Portland Field Naturalists' Club in their efforts to secure a reservation for 'a tract of country on the lower reaches of the Glenelg River'.[7]

In 1949 the Lands Department agreed to cede control over 'nearly all' the land under discussion to the Forests Commission.[8] The State Development Committee visited the Portland/Lower Glenelg area in 1951 as part of its general review of the State's national parks, and was reportedly 'impressed . . . with the potentialities of the region as a national park'.[9]

Learmonth, a keen ornithologist and naturalist, was a confident campaign leader. He was a well-known local identity and came from an establishment family that had held property in the Portland area since the earliest days of white settlement.[10] As early as 1948 there was local and metropolitan support for naming the Lower Glenelg Forest Reserve in his honour, but it did not eventuate because of a general decision taken by the National Parks Authority in 1968 that national parks should not be named after people.[11] Learmonth's work for the national park was eventually commemorated by giving his name to a track ('Noel's walk') near Mount Richmond, a decision that did not require the formality of State government assent.

Learmonth was successful because he was knowledgeable about the workings of government. He had worked as a government surveyor, and had been private secretary to the Minister of Lands between 1899 and 1905. In 1951 he retired from his property at Tyrendarra and moved into Portland.

In Portland Learmonth was joined by Fred Davies (1908–94), another farmer who had moved to the town from Deniliquin in New South Wales. Davies' conservation work was inspired by a nostalgia for the wild country of his early childhood at Pine Hills (later called Mayrung), New South Wales. By contrast with Learmonth, Davies was from a family of rural battlers. There was not enough work to pay him on his father's two farms, so he had spent the depressed 1930s shooting possums (for an average income of £4 per week) and building dairies and rough mud-brick houses for people living around Deniliquin.[12] In 1938 he returned to his father's farms to 'wait for the water'—the irrigation scheme promised for the area, which it was hoped would take the farms into 'a more profitable era'. But the scheme was seriously delayed by the war, and there were many years of worry before the water finally arrived. When it did, Fred Davies quickly became aware of the problems of dairying in very hot, semi-arid country. 'Far too much water had to be used to keep the place viable.'[13] After a few years Davies switched to fat lambs, and then in 1950 he sold up to move to a place where rainfall was better and more reliable. He was convinced that flood irrigation 'was wasteful of water and wasteful of land; it was an extremely expensive way of producing protein for both human and animal well-being'.[14]

Davies' interest in the stewardship of land and natural resources continued to develop in Portland. He joined the Portland Field Naturalists' Club in 1954 because he saw it as a way to 'do conservation'. Davies recalled that 'at the first meeting I found the idea of a national park at Mount Richmond already in the air'.[15] Learmonth and Davies worked tirelessly through the Portland FNC for nature conservation in the region, Davies taking on the secretarial work, especially the preparation, writing and circulation of documents. They worked as a team in Portland much as Crosbie Morrison and Ros Garnet worked in Melbourne.

Having made conservation his mission, Davies also determinedly pursued international environmental literature.[16] He was not a typical field naturalist, in that he did not express a passion for botany, ornithology or some other natural history speciality, but rather was interested in the environment in a broad sense. His later interest in natural history developed because of his passion for conservation, the reverse of the experience of most field naturalists. Davies learnt about birds from Learmonth and vegetation from Cliff Beauglehole, a distinguished amateur botanist who lived nearby. Davies used to accompany Beauglehole on his botanical field trips—'caddying' for Beauglehole, he called it—and in the process he felt that he 'caught just a glimpse of the web of life'.[17]

Davies' written words betray a knowledge of scientific matters far beyond what one learned at school in the years before 1922, when he had finished his formal education at the age of fourteen. When I interviewed him in 1989 and asked him which books had influenced his views, Davies mentioned Bruce Davidson's books, *The Northern Myth* and *Australia: Wet or Dry?* and Francis Ratcliffe's *Flying Fox and Drifting Sand*. He still had well-thumbed copies of various nature conservation books: *The Last of Lands*, edited by Leonard J. Webb and others, *Conservation*, edited by A. B. Costin and H. J. Frith, Judith Frankenberg's *Nature Conservation in Victoria* and also several technical scientific treatises on his local region. But he acknowledged that his ideas had also been shaped by a broad range of international environmental literature including *Silent Spring*, *The Population Bomb* and Max Nicholson's *The Environmental Revolution*, which was a particular favorite. Some of these he found more quickly than others: he had read A. J. Marshall's compilation, *The Great Extermination*, and was quoting from it very soon after its publication.[18] Davies' arguments for the preservation of the 'complete ecological unit' of the Mole Creek catchment show an excellent understanding of science and its political uses. It was not only the city people who thought globally. This country leader had seized the nettle of internationalism.

Mount Richmond National Park was gazetted in 1961, and both Learmonth and Davies were appointed to the committee of management, Davies as secretary. In the following year Davies was appointed as Mount Richmond's first ranger, a position he held for three years until park rangers were brought under the Public Service Act and he was obliged to retire because of his age. After retirement, Davies continued to serve on the committee of management.

Establishing and managing Mount Richmond National Park had fully occupied the Portland Field Naturalists' Club from the late 1950s until its establishment, but as soon as this was achieved, the earlier issue of a more extensive Lower Glenelg national park arose again. The FNCV chose Portland as the venue for its New Year excursion from 26 December 1961 to 1 January 1962, when it was joined by members of Ballarat, Bendigo and Hamilton clubs, as well as the host group, the Portland Field Naturalists' Club.[19] This was the first of many co-operative ventures orchestrated by the field naturalists' clubs of western Victoria. Recognising the importance of working in concert, they later formed the Western Victorian Field Naturalists' Association and, in 1968, the politically active Western Victorian Conservation Committee (WVCC).

The WVCC was presided over by a Casterton grazier, Claude Austin (1929–88). Austin was a generation younger than Noel Learmonth, but like him in many ways. His family had also been among the first Europeans to settle in the Western District. Like Learmonth, Austin was an enthusiastic ornithologist and naturalist with very good personal knowledge of the bushland of western Victoria.[20] The WVCC also had the advantage of having as its secretary Fred Davies, now retired from his ranger's job and free to invest effort in political causes again.

While Learmonth and the original Lower Glenelg campaigners of the 1940s had been satisfied that the Forests Commission offered the area better protection, especially against fire, than a small, under-funded local committee of management could hope to achieve, the establishment of the National Parks Authority sparked the hope that good management could be combined with a high priority on nature conservation values. By the mid-1960s there was much less local confidence that the Forests Commission could manage the area for nature conservation objectives in the way the specialist National Parks Authority could.[21]

In the early 1960s the Land Utilization Advisory Council, which was the government's major interdepartmental committee dealing with land-use management, had set up a scientific study group on south-western Victoria. Its report, published in 1964, reminded nature conservationists that the 1959 Land (Plantation

Areas) Act had empowered the Forests Commission to seek out suitable land for pine plantations.[22] After 1966, when the Commonwealth government established a generous subsidy scheme for pine plantations, the commission actively sought all suitable land for this purpose, including native bushland. The area around the South Australian border not far from Portland was already producing profitable crops of *Pinus radiata*. In the latter half of the 1960s, the Forests Commission was moving steadily into the area that Victorian nature conservationists had hoped would be reserved, on the lower reaches of the Glenelg River.

The Portland Shire Council also had a scheme to develop part of the area for farms. This scheme was supported by the Lands Department, which was preparing to alienate the necessary land. Conservationists were outraged when the line drawn on the map (allegedly by the Minister of Lands himself) to mark the edge of the alienation cut straight across the watershed of the Mole Creek, an important tributary of the Glenelg River. This watershed area, a wet heathland called Kentbruck, became the symbolic centre of the conservationists' campaign for the Lower Glenelg. Those who knew and loved the area, who had compiled species lists of its flora and fauna since the 1940s and earlier, were affronted that Sir William McDonald and his bureaucrats in Melbourne should show such disrespect for the boundaries of nature, the patterns of water flow and the ecology of the region. The decision was also an affront to the painstaking scientific work of the Land Utilization Advisory Council's study group in the early 1960s.[23]

The Western Victorian Conservation Committee compiled and published a report, *The Case for a Lower Glenelg National Park*, and took it to Melbourne in 1968 to gather support.[24] The VNPA meeting of 27 November 1968 was addressed by Dr Frank Moulds, Commissioner of Forests, on the subject of Forest Reserves. The VNPA president, Gwynnyth Taylor, wrote to encourage FNCV members to attend, and announced that copies of *The Case for a Lower Glenelg National Park* would be available at the meeting at $1.00 each.[25] It was in Melbourne that the campaign for the Lower Glenelg met that for the Little Desert.

The Little Desert Campaign

The Little Desert first appeared on the FNCV's agenda in July 1951, when the Council minutes record that Ros Garnet 'spoke of areas [in the Little Desert] that should be reserved and advised that a survey of flora . . . has been made'.[26] Garnet knew the area personally and had earlier been responsible for persuading the FNCV to support the cause of a small flora and fauna reserve near Dimboola.[27] The flora survey of the Little Desert had almost certainly been undertaken in conjunction with the Kaniva botanist and farmer Alec Hicks, who joined the FNCV at the meeting where Garnet first raised this matter.

In Kaniva, local pride was given a fillip in 1952–53 when the area received a visit from Dr Ronald Melville, Curator of the Australian Section, Royal Botanical Gardens, Kew.[28] When I spoke to Alec Hicks in 1989, he dated his concern about conservation in the Little Desert from the visit of that senior British scientist.[29] Though he clearly already knew the botanical value of the area and had been collecting and pressing specimens (especially grasses and sedges) in the 1940s, the fact that an 'international scientist' had been prepared to travel to Kaniva to see it impressed its value on him differently.

Hicks became one of the leading local campaigners for the western Little Desert, especially in the 1960s, the other two being P. L. Williams and Avelyn Coutts, who were also farmers in the area. 'P. L.', the spokesman for the group, recalled that pro-development locals had dubbed them 'the Three Blind Mice', because 'they reckoned we were retarding progress. Well that didn't disturb us at all. We really appreciated it and now . . . we refer to ourselves as the Three Blind Mice!'[30]

The central Little Desert had an advocate in Keith Hateley, the store-keeper in Kiata, a small town near Nhill, and later the first ranger of the Little Desert National Park.[31] Hateley led efforts to preserve the area as habitat for the mound-building lowan from the mid-1950s. In 1955 he received support for the establishment of a 'Kiata Lowan Sanctuary' from the Nhill Progress Association and local farmers. Among them was K. W. Jordan, who offered to donate adjacent land on condition that the government agreed to the reserve.[32] The VNPA was also involved.[33]

Ros Garnet used this example to encourage Noel Learmonth in his Mount Richmond campaign. In his correspondence with Learmonth, Garnet revealed his strategy for getting national parks reserved by the Lands Department:

> Quite recently the Nhill Progress Association—supported by Dimboola, Stawell and Lowan Councillors—urged the reservation of over 500 acres in the Little Desert near Kiata. This is for preservation of the Lowan and I think the Department [of Lands] will agree to it being reserved. As soon as the folk up that way get this project settled they intend to work for a bigger one—a wildflower sanctuary in the Lawloit Range and, I hope, extend the Lowan area to a more adequate size.[34]

It is quite possible that the earlier reservation at Dimboola (supported by the FNCV in 1946) had inspired the Nhill Progress Association to support the sanctuary. Garnet was a master of strategy.

The Kiata Lowan Sanctuary was gazetted in 1955, a total of about 700 acres (300 hectares), comprising 537 acres (217 hectares) of Crown land and the balance donated as promised by K. W. Jordan. A committee of management comprising three Dimboola Shire councillors was duly appointed. To finance the fencing of the sanctuary, Keith Hateley arranged an exhibition of wildflowers and a museum of natural history in the Kiata Hall in September–October 1955.[35] This 'Kiata Nature Show' became an annual event, and often involved people from Melbourne and other parts of Victoria.[36]

The 'Three Blind Mice' campaigned for the west of the Little Desert, Keith Hateley for the central area, but the east did not need a specialist spokesperson. It was never really under threat because its very low rainfall and poor soils made it an unattractive proposition for agricultural development. It was in the eastern Little Desert that Sir William McDonald offered a national park as a 'sop' to the conservation lobby, in an area unsurveyed and previously unconsidered by the National Parks Authority.[37]

The natural history societies provided a forum for multiple community voices in conservation issues at the local level. But Sir William McDonald's settlement proposal stirred up another style of community campaigner, one more concerned with democracy than with natural history.

A 'Lone Campaigner'

Valerie Honey was not a member of any natural history society. She lived in suburban Melbourne and had done so since she was a child, but her family had their roots in the Wimmera, on the southern edge of the Little Desert:

> I was born in Natimuk, so was my mother . . . I used to go back when we moved to Melbourne . . . for school holidays. I would borrow old bicycles and I would ride out to . . . the scrub . . . [It was] just the change in terrain . . . to realise that there was more than wheatfields.[38]

Honey's personal association with the Little Desert was just a distant memory of twenty years earlier, but when McDonald proposed agricultural development it began to stir. The part of the Little Desert she remembered, the eastern end, was never seriously under threat from any McDonald scheme, but by the time letters started appearing in metropolitan newspapers in 1969 about the 'Little Desert' the whole area was acquiring a unity in the mind of Melbourne people.

Honey's childhood memory was sufficient to galvanise her into what she described as an 'obsessive' eight-month campaign about the Little Desert. She researched her subject thoroughly and sought a hearing with the Premier via her local Member of Parliament. She joined the VNPA in order to campaign, and enlisted the support of its president, Gwynnyth Taylor, for her deputation to the Premier. Taylor was one of the founders of the Save Our Bushlands Action Committee, a very experienced campaigner who was active in eleven different conservation and natural history societies at the time.[39]

By the time the Acting Premier received Honey and Taylor with their well-researched case for the Little Desert in July 1969, Honey had single-handedly gathered a petition with 4000 signatures. She wrote to conservation organisations and set up a little stand with information about the Little Desert wherever local traders would tolerate it. Honey also used the media, regularly contributing to talkback radio programmes, despite the fact that she did not have a telephone at home. Anxious 'not to impose too much', she borrowed two different neighbours' telephones. By sheer persistence, she persuaded two key radio announcers, Gerald Lyons of 3DB and Ormsby Wilkins of 3AW, to look at the material she had prepared about the Little Desert. Honey also approached Stephen Downes, a journalist at the *Age* office, because 'he was the son of somebody on the Land Utilization Advisory Council and had written a few things about the Little Desert'.[40] The *Age* duly covered her deputation.[41]

By the time Honey actually visited the Little Desert in September 1969, she was a well-known campaigner and something of a celebrity. She was shown around the Little Desert by local activists, including the 'Three Blind Mice'. While she was there, she happened to meet Sir William McDonald himself: 'He strode across to us, shook hands and said "McDonald's the name". He obviously thought we were prospective farmers, and then I said "Valerie Honey's the name" and the smile went off his face immediately'.[42]

Honey's effectiveness as a lone campaigner was based on her ability to tap into the resources of the natural history societies. She borrowed mailing lists from the Bird Observers' Club, the VNPA and the naturalist and journalist Graham Pizzey.[43] The case she prepared about settlement in the Little Desert was a synthesis of expert opinions from diverse sources, including natural history societies, much of it drawn from the VNPA and FNCV archives, which had been meticulously maintained over many years by Ros Garnet. The authorities she cited were impressive: the Australian Academy of Science, the Australian Conservation Foundation, the Wimmera Regional Committee, and a number of key individuals: J. R. Garnet; W. G. D. Middleton; Alec Hicks; Avelyn Coutts; Claude Austin; R. J. Newman (an agrostologist); Sir Samuel Wadham, Emeritus Professor of Agriculture at the University of Melbourne; A. D. Butcher, director of the Victorian Department of Fisheries and Wildlife; R. G. Downes, chairman of the Soil Conservation Authority of Victoria and J. H. Willis of the National Herbarium.

Because Honey was outside all interest groups, she was able to infuse the information with her personal passion. 'Who knows what scientists will discover in the ability of plants to flourish in this harsh climate, or what drugs may be available from them?' she asked.[44] She was angry that reserves for national parks were not a primary consideration of government. 'When land is recognised as useless for any other development, then it will suffice for a national park'.[45] Although she was aware that 'emotional arguments just don't carry water with the people who pull the strings',[46] she articulated the rights of nature to exist, and angrily addressed those in power who would destroy it. Her energy and commitment permeated the rational face of her document:

> Economic arguments must be overwhelmingly strong before they justify the extinction of any species of animal or plant life. Therefore I feel it my duty to object to what a great number of people consider gross misuse of natural resources, in this case, unnecessary alienation of rapidly diminishing Crown Land, for extremely doubtful end-results, and offer herewith the signatures of some 3,600 persons objecting to the State Government's land development scheme for the Little Desert.[47]

She spoke for all those with no 'authority' (and perhaps less preparedness to undertake rigorous research than herself). To the politicians she portrayed herself as 'the ordinary voter'.

Because she was not a long-standing member of the FNCV or the Bird Observers' Club, she could not be written off as a 'birds-and-bugs fanatic'. Fanatic she perhaps was, but she was a new sort. She represented an emerging class of citizens concerned about 'quality of life' issues, who looked to the bush as, paradoxically, an important part of urban culture.

The campaigns for the protection of the Little Desert and Kentbruck heathland were joined around the 'rights' of people (and their unborn children) to enjoy the pleasures of the bush. It was a public right to seek 'relief from the stresses and strains of everyday life' in bushland and national parks. This notion of escape from the metropolis, of an 'other' that counterbalanced life in the city, was part of the larger international conservation movement of the time, especially the American wilderness movement.[48]

The Save Our Bushlands Action Committee document, *Outline for a Bushlands Magna Carta*, carried an extract from 'A Creed to Preserve our Natural Heritage', President Johnson's message to the US Congress on February 1966. In it the President spoke of the citizen's rights to water, air, and places of beauty where nature can be enjoyed. The notion of people's 'rights' to national parks suggested a positive dimension for the campaign. The conservationists concerned about the Little Desert and Kentbruck heath were not just against marginal development; they were *for* a particular vision of bushland preservation through national parks. It was this new, more strident voice, calling for another sort of democratic right, that emerged with the Little Desert dispute and became the basis for later environmentalism.

4

The Ecologists

[The] public expression of interest [in the environment] engendered, in bureaucratic circles, a craving for experts ... It was to the universities, citadels of expertise and scientific management, that the bureaucrats turned. And there, as if waiting for discovery, was an obscure biological specialty called 'ecology', which was to become a household word.

Neil Evernden

On 14 October 1969 the Honourable J. W. Galbally moved in the Victorian Legislative Council that a Select Committee be appointed to inquire into and report on the proposal to open the Little Desert to settlement. The committee was required to have special regard for the suitability of the land, the economics of the proposed farm units and 'the value of the area as a sanctuary for native flora and fauna'.[1]

The Little Desert Settlement Committee (LDSC) was a political exercise, instigated by opposition politicians who held a majority in the Legislative Council. It was never supposed to be a 'balanced' inquiry, and all participants recognised that. Once the government lost a proposed amendment that would have given it equal representation on the committee, it refused to participate. Sir William McDonald declined to appear before the committee, leaving his Secretary of Lands, Alan Judge Holt (1912–93), in the difficult position of having to defend the scheme at a hostile inquiry.[2] Galbally saw the way clear for his final report to heap maximum discredit on the government scheme to develop the Little Desert. He also saw the three-pronged approach through agricultural science, economics and conservation values as the best means for achieving his ends. The LDSC inquiry provided evidence of a particular form of scientific citizenship that had been building throughout the post-war period. The inquiry was a significant political moment in a situation where the public craved the 'solid evidence' of ecological science, and where the ecologists were prepared to go out of their way to offer their science for political purposes. The scientists who spoke at the LDSC inquiry had volunteered their services—as part of scientific citizenship—and their offer had been gratefully accepted by Galbally.

The two ecologists to give evidence at the Galbally inquiry were Dr Peter Attiwill (1935–), a forest ecologist, and Dr Malcolm Calder (1933–), a pollination ecologist and reproductive biologist. Both came from the University of Melbourne's Botany School. This was no coincidence. The Botany School had participated significantly in public scientific matters in the decades leading up to the 1960s. The Professor, John S. Turner (1908–91), was a great supporter of conservation and outreach endeavours by his school. If he had not been in England on sabbatical leave at the time of the Galbally inquiry, he would almost certainly have given evidence himself. The younger scientists knew that their appearance at the inquiry would be endorsed by the 'Prof'.

The School of Botany at the University of Melbourne had long enjoyed strong links with public service professionals. Turner's own special leadership role in education, conservation and ecological science provided the structure for the platform from which Attiwill and Calder assembled their evidence. Botanists taught and controlled aspects of the curriculum for foresters and agricultural scientists, and participated in co-operative research ventures with a number of government departments, including the Soil Conservation Authority. Other university departments had similar interests. In the Monash University Zoology Department, for example, the ecologist Dr E. H. M. (Tim) Ealey actively involved senior scientifically trained public servants in teaching his honours students. It was a lecture given by Frank Gibbons of the Soil Conservation Authority that was responsible for enthusing key members of the Monash University Biological Students' Society to take an active role in the campaign against the agricultural settlement of the Little Desert.[3] In 1973 Ealey established an Environmental Science master's degree programme at Monash.[4] He was, in a sense, building on the work of his foundation Professor, A. J. (Jock) Marshall (1911–67), whose edited book, *The Great Extermination: Anglo-Australian cupidity, wickedness and waste* (1966), had played an important role in making scientific arguments about conservation available to the concerned public. Turner worked with Marshall on this book, contributing a chapter entitled 'The Decline of the Plants'.[5]

J. S. Turner and the University of Melbourne's School of Botany

John Stewart Turner was appointed to the Chair of Botany and Plant Physiology at the University of Melbourne in 1938. He came from Cambridge University with an academic background in plant physiology. Turner's doctorate had focused on respiration and photosynthesis, 'biochemical physiology', as he called it.[6] He was not trained as an ecologist, but he brought from England some knowledge of ecology, gained in his spare time, because of his twin loves of rambling and landscape art. When he arrived at the University of Melbourne, he sought to build a very broadly based Botany School modelled on his old department in Cambridge, which 'covered every aspect of botany from physiology and biochemistry right across to fossil botany and field botany and plant pathology'.[7] He was also required to undertake 'service teaching' for agriculture and forestry courses, and served on the board of the university's Forestry School at Creswick.

In Britain and Australia ecology, like other field sciences, was frequently undertaken as a labour of love by enthusiasts whose professional concerns were elsewhere. Ecology was not seen as 'enhancing' physiology, as it was in America, but rather as a distraction from it. When Turner reached Australia, where there were so few scientists that they were forced to be 'jacks-of-all-trades', he realised the importance of his broader interests. 'Getting to know the new plant communities' was an immense task, in which he depended heavily on people with local knowledge. He was painfully conscious that in Britain, in an area similar to Victoria, there were fifteen professors of botany, whereas in Melbourne he was the only one and he knew nothing of the local plants. He tackled the task of acquainting himself with Victoria immediately, with significant help from two local professional botanists, Dr Ethel I. McLennan (1891–1983) and S. G. Maisie Fawcett (1912–88), and national parks campaigner Sir James Barrett.[8] Soon after Turner's arrival, Victoria was devastated by the massive fires of 1939. Turner later regretted that he had not had sufficient background to seize that opportunity to study 'forest fire ecology'.[9]

The fires caused extensive erosion, and made soil conservation a vital concern for the State. A Soil Conservation Board was established in 1940, but because of the wartime labour shortage it had no staff to undertake the urgently required ecological study of water catchments in the Victorian Alps. The State Electricity Commission took a particular interest in the Kiewa catchment area because its hydro-electricity scheme was located on the Kiewa River. The Department of Agriculture and the State Rivers and Water Supply Commission were concerned about silting in Lake Hume from the Mitta Mitta River, which rises in the Alps. Lake Hume was vital to irrigation farming. The particular concern was whether summer grazing of sheep and cattle in the high country was affecting other water catchment uses.

In 1941 the soil erosion campaigner and senior Lands Department surveyor Charles T. ('Bull Ant') Clark took Turner on a survey tour of the eastern high country around Omeo, where surface soil erosion was evident.[10] The survey convinced Turner of the urgent need for detailed research into the ecology of the high country. He recommended that the work be undertaken by Maisie Fawcett, a mycologist with some ecological expertise.[11] The Soil Conservation Board initially did not wish to appoint a woman to a research officer's position, but accepted a compromise whereby Fawcett continued to be employed by the University of Melbourne (until 1944), but her research expenses were met by the Soil Conservation Board. Turner and the School of Botany therefore remained more closely involved with her Soil Conservation Board research than might otherwise have been the case. In the years from 1941 until 1948, Maisie Fawcett worked on a succession of ecological regions in the various alpine catchment areas. Early in 1945, at Fawcett's request, the State Electricity Commission fenced a 7.7-hectare area at Rocky Valley to exclude grazing stock and begin an ecological survey of the Kiewa catchment. Fawcett evaluated the effects of cattle on the vegetation by comparing plots in the closed area with plots of matching size and similar vegetation in the grazed areas. Other 'paired plots' were pegged out on the slopes of Pretty Valley late in 1946 to look closely at the effects of grazing on sub-alpine *Poa* grasslands not represented in the Rocky Valley sites.

The concept of an enclosure (or what later became known as an 'exclosure') was not new to ecological science. Soon after World War I the British ecologist Dr A. S. Watt used enclosures to exclude rabbits in oak woods near Cambridge, and later in beech woods on the South Downs and in the grasslands of the Breckland.[12] Professor Frederic Clements used a similar technique in the American Midwest grasslands to investigate 'processes' such as trampling, burrowing, erosion and burning. In Australia enclosures to examine the effects of cattle on vegetation had been used by Professor T. G. B. Osborn on the Koonamore Vegetation Reserve in South Australia in 1925. Dr Dick Roe, a pasture researcher with CSIR, also used them in northern New South Wales and south-west Queensland in the late 1930s and 1940s.[13]

What was significant about the Rocky Valley and Pretty Valley plots was the free labour that enabled Fawcett's study to be exhaustive, at least for the summer period. The staff and students of the University of Melbourne's Botany School worked together on the plots, the university supplying transport and liaison to undertake the intensive study every summer for a decade from the mid-1940s to the mid-1950s, and on a less frequent basis since. The analyses were extraordinarily detailed, despite the short season. In 1949 and 1950 more than 1000 sites were sampled.[14] Such detail was only possible because of the willing 'holiday' labour of many botanists, agricultural scientists, members of the Soil Conservation Board and their friends, including Turner himself. Academic visitors, including A. S. Watt from Cambridge, also participated in the summer trips and offered practical hands-on advice.

Dr David Ashton, one of Melbourne's most eminent ecologists, found the high plains trips invaluable, and felt indebted to the vision of Watt, in particular. Ashton's own work focused primarily on forest ecosystems, but the methodology he learnt on the Bogong High Plains became part of his style. The historian and botanist Dr Linden Gillbank has described the convivial atmosphere of the parties undertaking the alpine research, which 'provided an important cohesive force for research students and staff in Turner's department'.[15]

The plots were also providing key information to government departments, and formed the basis for continuing co-operation between the School of Botany and government. Both science and bureaucracy benefited from the relationship.[16] The influence of the high country 'team' on ecological science in Australia is subtle, pervasive and difficult to quantify, but the Fawcett–Turner ecological studies were significant in shaping networks between ecologists and other botanists, and also between university scientists and those working for government agencies.

The Little Desert Field Trip

Before 1969 neither Peter Attiwill nor Malcolm Calder was particularly acquainted with the Little Desert area. Both had arrived in the School of Botany in 1966. Calder was an agricultural biologist, originally from New Zealand, who had been Senior Scientific Officer at the University College of Wales at Aberystwyth. The Welsh Plant Breeding Station where he had worked was internationally renowned for its expertise in agricultural science, especially plant breeding and pasture ecology. Attiwill had trained at Melbourne, initially as a forester, then had completed a doctorate in soil fertility and plant nutrition. From 1964–66 he was Visiting Fellow and visiting assistant professor at Cornell University in New

York State. He arrived back in Melbourne three months after Calder had joined the school. Both brought international practical as well as theoretical knowledge to the Botany School, where they taught the Agricultural Botany courses for final-year agriculture students. They were very different personalities, but in 1969 they were both under the strong influence of Professor Turner, and were united in their condemnation of the Little Desert Settlement Scheme.

The central research on the Little Desert was undertaken in a single week-long field trip held as an educational exercise for agricultural botany students in August 1969. The preparation for this trip had involved a careful search through the scientific literature for information about the Little Desert, and good advice from local Kaniva contacts, particularly P. L. Williams, Alec Hicks and Avelyn Coutts.[17] The destination for the trip had been chosen because of the continuing controversy about whether the Little Desert should be developed for agricultural purposes. It offered a topical botanical task for agricultural science students, more 'relevant' than the destination of previous years, Wilsons Promontory, where there was little of agricultural interest.

The stamp of the Turner school could be seen in the careful choice of pedagogical exercise and the strategy adopted for approaching the task. First, Turner always encouraged newer staff to tackle unknown plant communities in a range of areas. He had come from somewhere else himself, and understood the need to be exposed to fieldwork as soon as possible. He often personally took new staff members and visitors to the Botany School's field station at Wilsons Promontory. Secondly, Turner encouraged team fieldwork, a practice reinforced since the 1940s by the work on the High Plains plots. Attiwill arranged the trip, but he was supported by Calder and Dr Tom Neales, a plant physiologist whose teaching also centred on the agriculture students. All staff were expected to 'pitch in' to make field trips a success.

Plant communities were examined using the 'point quadrat' method. Quadrats (plots) of increasing size—1, 2, 4, 8, 16 and 64 square metres—were placed randomly throughout a plant community. The number of species in each quadrat was then counted, and vegetational diversity evaluated by graphing the number of species versus the size of the plot. In areas where there was great diversity, the number of species would continue to increase with the plot size, but in vegetationally uniform areas the line on the graph would flatten out. This was a standard international procedure, but it was introduced to the High Plains study by Botany School bio-statistician Dr D. W. Goodall, who set out to find a technique for reducing the labour-intensity of the work on the Fawcett plots.[18]

In the Attiwill–Calder survey of the Little Desert, the students were required to study the nature of selected plant communities. The task was not to make an exhaustive list of species (something that would be impossible in a week's fieldwork, because not all species flower at once), but to study how plants co-exist in a range of physically different environments. The general areas were identified with assistance from local amateur naturalists Alec Hicks, P. L. Williams, Avelyn Coutts and Keith Hateley. The particular study sites were random within these areas. The students were encouraged to think about whether it would be possible to develop part of the Little Desert without losing too many plant communities. At the time it was a practical pedagogical exercise in 'development versus conservation'. Only later, with the Galbally inquiry, did the data assume a new importance.

Ecology and the General Public

How did 'ecology' gain a space in the public arena in Victoria? It was known to scientists from around the turn of the century, but did not really emerge as a discipline until the 1920s. Ecology entered public consciousness through reforms to the science curriculum in secondary schools, and through the activities of field naturalists' clubs in publicising their concerns about the vulnerability of habitat. The ecological studies undertaken for the purposes of soil conservation were important in making public servants aware of the value of ecological science. The Turner Botany School was not solely responsible for any of these developments, but it left its mark on many of them. Turner was uniquely positioned to foster connections between the public service, the secondary schools and universities, and the national and international scientific community. He was also passionately committed to landscape conservation and gave generously of his own time to further 'aesthetic' ends.

In the mid-1940s the science educator F. G. Elford explained the science of ecology in terms of understanding the 'web of life'— the interdependence of natural systems—a concept that was familiar to biologists but new to the general public.[19] Ecology was important in the new post-war secondary subject of 'General Science'. At the 1935 conference of the Australian and New Zealand Association for the Advancement of Science, the education authorities had been urged to begin teaching biology in secondary schools. This challenge spurred radical changes in the teaching of science in Australian schools. The shift was part of what the educational historian Rod Fawns described as the 'scientific restructuring of the culture'.[20] At the forefront of this field were Turner and Sir Samuel Wadham (1891–1972), Professor of Agriculture at the University of Melbourne. Turner also fostered interest in science education among scientists; in 1940, for example, he organised a discussion for the Australian Association for Scientific Workers on the subject of biology in schools.[21] Soon afterwards, Turner joined the Victorian Curriculum Board (Melbourne University Schools Board) and remained a member for more than two decades, chairing its General Science Standing Committee from 1943 to 1967.[22]

While other tertiary teachers were more concerned with university entrance standards, Turner's involvement began where science first entered the school syllabus, at middle-school level. He was keen to ensure that all science students were introduced to biology at year ten level, where previously many took only physics and chemistry. In 1943 Turner worked with international textbook author Frederick Daniel to produce *General Science for Australian Schools*, a local adaptation of an international textbook. The narrative style of the book encouraged pupils to explore for themselves rather than learn by rote. General Science was no 'soft option'. Turner located it firmly in the new scientific age: 'The young inquisitive mind is disappointed with an advanced nature study course when the magic words Physics, Chemistry, Astronomy, Biology, Geology and so on beckon. In this scientific age, General Science should be science and not merely popular science'.[23] In an ironic twist, this high valuing of the scientific probably helped to popularise science. If science was indeed 'an essential humanity', then it became natural for a new generation to express its humanity in scientific terms.[24] The natural place to look for a word to express 'life balance' was in the science of 'nature's balance', ecology.

Turner sought an extension of General Science in a biology course for years 11 and 12 (the final two years of school). He encouraged the Australian Academy of Science (of which he was a Fellow) to employ David Morgan to edit what became known as the *Web of Life* textbooks and programme for upper secondary schools. Work for the *Web of Life* began officially in 1965 with the proposal that an American upper secondary biology course be adapted for use in Australian schools.[25] By the early 1970s the academy was producing large print-runs of the textbook and its companion student manuals and teacher's guide. Turner commented that:

> *The Web* came at a most appropriate time when the revolution in biology and the concern for the environment combined to steer youngsters into biology courses at school and university ... No doubt the success of the course and its texts was in part responsible for the swing to Biology from Physics and Chemistry.[26]

Morgan, as co-ordinator of the project, explicitly used 'an ecological approach' and sought to educate 'the average child as a future member of society' rather than as a future tertiary-level biologist.[27] In the 1990s the academy took this vision further with a science programme for primary schools, launched in 1994, and a programme for upper secondary students, *Environmental Science*.[28]

The mission to make science part of ordinary life, or to cultivate a universal 'citizenship' in science, operated on a broad front, the formal education system being only one prong of its attack. The general public was wooed by books, newspapers, magazines, radio and, after 1956, television. All these media gradually began to carry scientific and documentary information (and at times, propaganda) in the optimism of the 1940s and 1950s, sometimes termed the 'New Atomic Age'. The popularity and positive valuing of science had been around earlier, but it built to a crescendo in the period following World War II.

Crosbie Morrison's *Argus* articles of the 1930s, his magazine *Wild Life* (1938–54) and his radio broadcasts of the same name were part of this genre. Earlier writers such as Donald Macdonald and Charles Barrett had enjoyed enormous success with nature study columns, but it was Morrison with his Master's degree in zoology who introduced a consciously scientific note into nature-study writings and broadcasts.

As general levels of education rose and a basic knowledge of science became more common in the population at large, science writers in the 1960s began to move away from selling the virtues of science towards writing material that was critical of science, technology and their products. Perhaps the most internationally significant work in the new genre of popular scientific literature was *Silent Spring*, by the American marine biologist Rachel Carson, published in 1962. In Australia, the publication in 1966 of Marshall's *The Great Extermination* marked the beginning of the new era of local scientists as 'whistle-blowers'.

The British–Australian biologist Francis Ratcliffe wrote in both the earlier and the later periods, for very different audiences. Ratcliffe's *Flying Fox and Drifting Sand* was a personal account of his time working as an 'economic biologist' for CSIR in the 1920s and 1930s.[29] He called it a 'scientific travel diary'.[30] It offered a general audience an insight into science in the field, grappling with practical problems. Its fame rests on its brilliant descriptions of the people, places and nature of the Australian outback. At the same time, Ratcliffe was critical of those 'who read newspapers and pretend an interest in world affairs' but had no practical experience of the limits of the Australian inland country.[31] He was also cautious about what science could achieve in these remote parts:

Those who regard land policies as sacrosanct . . . can only suggest that the forces of science should be mobilised to grapple with the problem of the inland. In handing the task to the scientist, these people are really asking him to improve the native vegetation, to make it better, more productive, less tiresomely vulnerable. Botanists might be able to do quite a lot . . . but they have not the magic to refashion the vegetation of a vast and varied region to withstand the demands of an arbitrary and over-exacting system of exploitation.[32]

The audiences of the 1940s read these words, but they perhaps did not fully appreciate Ratcliffe's sobering assessment of the limits of pastoralism in Australia. His book was set as a school textbook in the 1950s for its stories of outback heroism, and perhaps because of its message that science could be part of that heroism. The book would never have been given to schoolchildren to read if the pastoral industry had been fully conversant with its subversive dimensions.

Ratcliffe's last works, produced when he was working with the Australian Conservation Foundation between 1965 and 1970, are written with a greater certainty that there is an audience wanting to hear 'whistle-blowing' from scientists. The young Ratcliffe confronted the question 'Was there *any* system of stocking and management, workable and economic in practice, that would preserve the vegetation of the semi-desert country, and thus ensure the survival of human settlement in these areas?' He could find only one answer 'and it was not the answer I wanted or had hoped to find'.[33] The older Ratcliffe no longer apologised for expressing his deeply felt conviction that there should be some limits to economic development. 'People in highly industrialised countries are beginning to feel a desperate need for escape from a crowded and too often ugly environment', he wrote.[34] Ratcliffe felt that the natural world provided an important balance to the built environment, and that human beings were not yet evolutionarily adapted to an unnatural (urban) setting. Within a single working lifetime, the role of science in society had shifted significantly, and Ratcliffe's writing is indicative of that shift. His work also suggests a widening of the range of themes admissible to scientific discussion in the 1960s. The integration of scientific, philosophical and aesthetic concerns created a new holistic 'conservation genre'.

The public often became aware of ecology through natural history. The term 'ecology' was increasingly used in field naturalist circles in the context of arguments for the conservation of the balance of nature, the web of life and, a little later, the preservation

of 'habitat'. Ecology was seen as a science that justified nature conservation, and as something that grew out of natural history and
nature study. By the 1950s, for example, Edna Walling, a well-
known Melbourne landscape gardener, regarded the science of ecology as an essential adjunct to conservation and landscape design.[35]

A Landscape Preservation Council was established under the
aegis of the National Trust in 1960. Its primary function was to
provide another 'track' by which conservationists could influence
government planning bodies, particularly those whose actions
affected rural and 'wild' landscapes. The council's aims were:

(a) to assist in the preservation of landscape, natural and man-made,
in country and town, from the dangers of over rapid agricultural,
residential and industrial development.

(b) to promote public awareness of such dangers and to act as a
rallying point for public opinion in such matters.[36]

The council distanced itself from other conservation agencies such
as the Soil Conservation Authority and the Natural Resources
Conservation League; these bodies, it stated, were concerned with
'material resources', while its own focus was primarily on the conservation of 'those things which nourish the spirit as well as the
body of man'.[37] It sought to place conservation in the category of
'high culture'. Its president was Professor John Turner.

Turner had shown a similar outlook in his work for the Save
the Dandenongs League, which he founded with Miss May Moon
in 1950. The League aimed to preserve the aesthetic appearance of
Melbourne's nearest mountains by preventing developments that
would detract from their natural beauty. Turner, who remained
president of the Save the Dandenongs League throughout the 1950s
and 1960s, used a radio broadcast to urge citizens to 'encourage
your local shire to take more interest in things like Beethoven's
sonatas, Shakespeare's plays or a grove of Manna gums with
Greenhood orchids'.[38]

But Turner did not adopt the aesthetic at the expense of the
practical. He actively sought to ensure that the results of the Fawcett
High Plains investigations were made available for both resource
conservation and ecological science. Fawcett, now working under

her married name as Stella G. M. Carr, was about to depart for Belfast with her husband, fellow botanist Dr Denis Carr.[39] The major scientific description of her work, 'The Ecology of the Bogong High Plains', was finally published in 1959, some fifteen years after the work was conceived, with Turner as co-author.[40] An important incentive to publish at this time was the fact that the Australian Academy of Science was interested in soil conservation in the Australian Alps, especially in the 'Kosciuszko Tops', where the major Snowy River Hydro-Electric Scheme was centred. Long before Fawcett's ecological work was finalised and published, she had given evidence at the Stretton Royal Commission into Forest Grazing in 1946. Her early findings were sufficient to provide Stretton with an ecological basis for his recommendation against grazing leases for sheep, a recommendation adopted by government in 1947.[41] Her work and that of A. B. Costin in New South Wales provided the basis for Turner's *Report on the Condition of the High Mountain Catchments of New South Wales and Victoria*, which was published in 1957, the first of the Australian Academy of Science's prestigious publications.

In the early 1960s ecology received an unexpected boost from outside Australia. The International Council of Scientific Unions launched an International Biological Program (IBP) to promote the science of ecology and to put it on a more quantitative basis. Turner was one of the two representatives sent by Australia to the IBP's preliminary meeting in Paris in mid-1964. He immediately sought to shape the Australian contribution in a way that would support urgent conservation objectives, nominating R. L. Specht, a member of his own department, as the Australian co-ordinator for the programme. This task would occupy Specht's time for two decades, long after he had moved to take the Chair of Botany at the University of Queensland in 1966.[42] The IBP effort was directed toward detailed surveys of the plant communities of every State, some groundwork on which had already been done for the Australian Academy of Science.

The idea of making detailed surveys was also taken up by the Victorian National Parks Association. Turner was a staunch supporter of the VNPA; he was a member of its council throughout the

1960s, and encouraged his staff to take an active role on its executive.[43] Among them was Specht, who was president of the association in 1963–64. Under his influence, the VNPA asked its members
to contribute £2 each to support a 'scientific survey' of the national
parks of Victoria. The appeal was successful, and as a result Judith
Frankenberg, a postgraduate student in the School of Botany, was
able to fulfil (and indeed extend) a cherished wish of Crosbie
Morrison, who had written in 1957 in his annual report for the
National Parks Authority: 'On the ecological side, I have begun
what will be a long piece of research, to obtain from the Victorian
scientific literature a list, as complete as possible, of all the flora and
fauna recorded from each of our National Parks'.[44] Frankenberg's
detailed study of the plants and animals of the national parks and
reserves of Victoria was published in 1971 as *Nature Conservation
in Victoria* (edited and updated by J. S. Turner, after Frankenberg
had left the department). Much of the literature on which it was
based came out of the journals of the scientific societies, professional and amateur, nineteenth and twentieth century. The
Frankenberg report was the product of a surprising but successful
liaison between professional scientists and popular conservationists. Scientific work had been privately funded before, but not
usually by public subscription. Generally big bequests or major
donors were involved, and funding tended to favour biomedical
projects. The VNPA pioneered a new sort of 'public science', funded
by small individual contributions given for what was seen as the
long-term public interest.

Turner was the architect of the union between conservation as
science and as popular concern. He was able to achieve this through
his dual status as a senior scientist and a local figure. By the late
1960s, after three decades in Melbourne, he had a pervasive influence, and all sorts of people sought his advice. Often he would go
out of his way to assist a truly local concern, while refusing offers to
take on what might have been regarded as a more prestigious role in
a national or international conservation programme.[45] In a letter to
an activist concerned about a proposal for the Warrandyte State
Park in 1969, Turner concluded by using his recent observations of
conservation movements in England to encourage the local group:

One of the very obvious things about active conservation movements in England is the close collaboration between local groups like yours and Government servants, and the results are quite magnificent. One of the most encouraging features of the Victorian scene in recent years has been the growth of local conservation groups, and I'm sure that without them there would be little movement by the Government.[46]

Turner was encouraging the local group, but he was also suggesting a particular mechanism for achieving conservation ends that he had personally found to be successful. Turner was first a scientist, but he was also a concerned citizen. He saw science, conservation and citizenship as inextricably linked. The ways in which he pursued these goals, individually and severally, were central to the popularisation of ecology in Victoria in the post-war years.

Turner's conservation activities were part of his life as a 'Renaissance gentleman', not an extension of his work as an ecologist. Turner's argument was that the urge to conserve was intimately connected with the scientific understanding of the countryside, but he did not believe that conservation itself was a science. In 1990 he reflected on the practical implications of this distinction:

In all the thirty-five years that I was in Melbourne I was occupied with conservation matters several evenings a week and at week-ends often. I never put on a course to my students at any level because I don't believe that is what we are there for . . . It's no good taking people out to save the countryside and telling them you've got to save it because conservationists tell you. You've got to know it to save it, to do any real good . . . I'm absolutely certain that when Dave Ashton takes his students out for a whole week to do ecology in some remote part of the countryside and they camp there and they work there all day long . . . it sinks into them that this is something that is interesting, delightful. And they see the countryside and they fall in love with parts of it and they . . . are quite interested in doing something about it. But to teach it . . . like teaching them how to calculate or something, it doesn't work.[47]

Turner saw the science as providing the fundamentals for knowledge, and conservation as born of the love arising from the knowledge, or the 'humanity' of the science. He did not see botany students as needing instruction in conservation, because they were sufficiently informed to develop their own notions of conservation. He did, however, see some value in the kind of conservation courses taught at Monash University by the zoologist Tim Ealey, because 'engineers and people who had never thought about this sort of thing' enrolled in it.[48]

Scientists in this period wanted very much to contribute to public debate, but they were often hampered by lack of specific ecological information for particular conservation concerns. They all at some stage felt the need for the big general survey that no one had time to do. The interconnectedness yet separateness of ecology and conservation was a difficulty that each scientist resolved differently. As the ecologist David Ashton put it:

> Ecology is the study of why plants and animals are where they are
> ... Conservation is an appreciation of what we have and want ...
> You can't conserve scientifically unless you know something of the 'why'.[49]

He saw conservation as overlapping with science, but involving something else, captured in the words 'appreciation' and 'want'. Conservation was a matter of negotiation rather than an absolute science. There was, however, unanimity among conservationists, scientists and utilitarian professionals that science, especially ecological science, was and should be a guiding principle in negotiating conservation goals. The generation trained in the science of the 'web of life' sought to weave that web beyond the scientific world, to interconnect the spiritual, aesthetic and rational elements of conservation issues. By 1969 even the politicians had noticed it. Scientific testimony played a key role in the Galbally inquiry into the Little Desert.

The Scientific Evidence

Galbally was a barrister, experienced at orchestrating the presentation of evidence before a court. When the scientists appeared before the Select Committee, he began by asking them about their formal qualifications. So, before the members of the Select Committee had heard any substantial testimony, they were supplied with a statement of the witness's academic qualifications, including a doctorate and distinguished international research experience.[50] This established the authority of Attiwill and Calder as representatives of 'pure science', despite the fact that Calder was speaking on behalf of the Save Our Bushlands Action Committee.

The centrepiece of Attiwill's testimony was his scientific argument for preserving the biological diversity of the Little Desert. In the 1990s 'biodiversity' is a familiar term, but in 1969 it was a new concept for the general public, and Attiwill explained it carefully. He described the 'point quadrat' method for evaluating biological diversity,[51] and reported the results of the Little Desert surveys. Many species were found at only one or two of the ten plots examined, and there were significant variations between the plant communities that supported the recorded species. The Little Desert was not just biologically rich, but also diverse.

This presented a particular problem for alienating even part of the area for farming. Given the diversity of the Little Desert's plant species, whatever the area chosen, it was statistically almost certain that some species would be lost, even if a substantial area were retained for a national park. On the evidence of Attiwill's survey, species did not occur throughout the region, but were often found only in particular pockets. Because the survey had been so brief, Attiwill could not state categorically which species would be lost in any particular place, only that it was statistically likely that some would be lost. This was a powerful argument, for it carried the implication that time-consuming and detailed research would be needed before any alienations could 'safely' occur.

In summing up, Attiwill called for the preservation of all remaining unalienated areas in the Little Desert. His closing statement moved away from his specific expertise to what he called 'a new morality':

[The] recognition of the need for conservation is part of a worldwide movement which, in essence, appears to be related to the problem of over-population and greatly increased mobility. We now recognise that a finite world can support a finite population. The goal of 'the greatest good for the greatest number' is simply not possible—we cannot maximise two variables at the same time. I believe we must maximise 'goodness', or the quality of life. It is the desire to maximise the quality of life—to make the world a fit place in which to live—that has brought to our attention problems of pollution, of contamination, and of conservation. The need to control the quality of our environment is, I consider, part of a new morality which is now man's urgent responsibility.[52]

Malcolm Calder's statement at the hearing on behalf of the Save Our Bushlands Action Committee was in a sense a culmination of all that the Turner Botany School had worked to achieve in the public sphere. The Save Our Bushlands Action Committee, Calder explained, was a forum through which the people of Victoria could 'express their concern over the failure of the government to recognise the social, scientific and even moral responsibility they have to conserve large areas of our natural environment'.[53] He emphasised the growing awareness that 'land is a finite resource', and that it therefore needed 'a far-sighted policy on land use, taking into consideration the needs of the rural industries and primary producers as well as the needs of society for national parks and wildlife reserves, housing, roads and communications, recreation areas and industry'. He urged that 'the Little Desert can only be considered in relation to other areas and within such a comprehensive policy of land use'.[54]

Taking the language of McDonald and filtering it through his new vision, Calder then boldly proposed an 'alternative development scheme'. The Little Desert was ideally suited to 'the establishment of a National Park in association with a field study centre along the lines of the Field Study Centres operating so successfully in Britain'. Calder argued that field studies along the lines of those that he and Attiwill had recently undertaken with the agricultural botany students were of value to the whole population. By helping to develop the practical skills used by ecologists, they provided 'a cultural and aesthetic discipline ... bringing an increasingly urbanised population into closer touch with natural phenomena and rural life'.[55] The government should redirect its efforts away from a 'high level of investment in doubtful primary production' toward research that would offer the general public greater knowledge and respect for the environment—and would 'assist to a similar level the policy of decentralization'.[56] Galbally commented that this was 'a most interesting and arresting suggestion'.

The ecologists were so confident of the public credibility of their science that they felt free to speak outside their discipline. Their arguments for a national park in the Little Desert appealed to all the conservationist traditions of their time, not just the discipline in which they could be regarded as expert witnesses. Attiwill's argument about 'quality of life' had utilitarian overtones, while Calder appealed to the urban population's sense of loss of things Arcadian, using the sorts of arguments traditionally presented by such organisations as the Landscape Preservation Council or amateur natural history groups. Both submissions were marked by the sense of social responsibility nurtured in Turner's School of Botany. The ecologists were conscious that they were contributing scientific expertise to a popular debate, but were also aware that other non-scientific arguments would hold sway with parliamentarians and the media.

It was perhaps easier for ecologists to accept social responsibility for their actions than it was for other scientists—nuclear physicists, for example. But the ecologists took the risk that, by making their science accessible to the general public for political purposes, they would in some sense lose control of the science. Dorothy Nelkin, who has analysed the role of the professional association of American ecologists in this period, concluded that by the early 1970s American ecologists preferred to return to the isolation of their laboratories rather than try to keep up with the mountain of socially responsible work that was accumulating for the few trained specialists in the field.[57]

In Australia there was certainly a trend in the same direction. The demands placed on qualified scientists to speak about environmental issues increased sharply in the late 1960s and early 1970s, to the point where they overtaxed the energies of the individuals involved. By 1971 even Turner found himself having to refuse requests for assistance:

I am now getting several letters a week requesting the assistance of my department on some conservation matter or another. I have a very full programme in the University and I am now becoming more and more occupied with the affairs of the L[and] C[onservation] C[ouncil] and the other conservation bodies to which I belong; the time has come when I simply cannot take any more work of this kind. I fully sympathise with the case you propose to present, and I know that you will have difficulty in finding people with sufficient ecological knowledge to speak in that field. However, everything is progressing so quickly that the burden on the few ecologists in the State is becoming almost intolerable.[58]

The social responsibility of ecologists was something each worked out according to his or her own lights. Australian ecologists had always worked closely with planners and managers, and co-operative work continued into the 1970s and beyond. Australian ecologists never had the vast resources for 'pure' research that they did in the USA, but perhaps this meant that they were less encumbered by the burden of defending a 'discipline'. The lower degree of professionalisation, and the nature of the opportunities to study ecology in Australia, meant that the notion of ecology as a 'management tool' was more readily and easily accepted in Australia than in America.[59] Australian ecologists, as represented by Attiwill and Calder, felt the moral imperatives of their science intensely and expressed them powerfully.

5

A Wimmera Perspective

> *There is tremendous interest being shown in the*
> *Little Desert . . . People are intrigued with the*
> *open country because the city is overcrowded. I*
> *can see the writing on the wall . . . In the next*
> *twelve or eighteen months that Little Desert*
> *will be invaded. City bus companies are waking*
> *up to this.*
>
> Len Graetz, Wimmera Promotion Officer

Before the 1960s the Little Desert was not a well-known place. It had acquired its name about the 1880s, but local people often referred to it simply as the 'scrub' country.[1] It was wasteland, 'desert', in the sense of having poor potential for agriculture. It was perceived as a dreary, impoverished landscape. Local farmers despised this lost tongue of white sand, leached of nutrients, invading the rich black-soil country of the Wimmera.

The ecological and tourist values of the drier north-western parts of Victoria had begun to gain popular recognition in the mid-1960s, particularly in metropolitan Melbourne. The centre of focus was most often Wyperfeld National Park, a large reserve of mallee country about 100 kilometres north of the Little Desert. Wyperfeld, famous for its mallee-fowl, was one of Victoria's earliest national parks, reserved in 1909 and enlarged between 1921 and 1937 as a result of steady campaigning by Arthur Mattingley, Sir James Barrett and the first National Parks Association.[2] The Wyperfeld arid-zone national park was the only one of its type in Australia for

many years, despite the fact that 70 per cent of Australia is classi-
fied as arid.[3] The experienced members of the park's Committee of
Management actively supported the idea of another reservation in
the Victorian mallee country.

By the 1960s the Academy of Science too was urging that
national parks and reserves should be more representative of the
different types of Australian ecosystems, and the notion of another
Victorian mallee park gathered pace.[4] Wyperfeld itself was gaining
in popularity, thanks in no small measure to Ros Garnet. In 1965
Garnet addressed the FNCV on his new book, *The Vegetation of
Wyperfeld National Park*, and showed an accompanying film made
by the Tourist Development Authority for the Council of Adult Education.[5] On the nomination of the Wimmera Field Naturalists' Club,
Garnet won the prestigious Natural History Medallion in 1966 for
this work and his other contributions to nature conservation.[6]

While a few key local preservationists promoted the natural
history value of the Little Desert, it was the city rather than the
country newspapers that discussed the merits of a national park. In
the country development, not conservation, made news, and local
preservationists such as the 'Three Blind Mice' were often regarded
as a bit odd. Local crusaders for conservation relied heavily on their
city contacts in natural history and conservation societies to further
their cause.

Among the Wimmera activists was W. G. D. (Bill) Middleton
(1926–), who was based at Wail, near Dimboola, at the eastern end
of the Little Desert. Middleton had grown up in Nhill, and as a boy
he often cycled as far as the Lawloit Ranges in the western Little
Desert in search of bird life and natural history.[7] He felt a strong
personal association with the region as a whole. He left the region
to pursue his education, but returned to the Wimmera in 1959 as a
qualified forester and Officer-in-Charge of the Wail Forest Nursery.
It was then that his childhood hobby of ornithology blossomed. He
became well known for his work in the community, and presented
a natural history programme on Wimmera radio for fourteen
years.[8] He joined the FNCV and the Colac Field Naturalists' Club,
which affiliated with the FNCV in 1957.[9]

Middleton, an excellent strategist, understood the importance of enlisting metropolitan activists in local campaigns. As a government officer, he was well informed about appropriate procedures and had access to crucial information, but he was seriously constrained in what he could do officially. He had been warned by the chairman of the Forests Commission, A. O. P. Lawrence, that he should avoid 'being seen to be going against the government'.[10] This was sound and carefully worded advice, probably based on personal experience, from a man who was broadly sympathetic with Middleton's objectives. It was not until he retired that Lawrence revealed his own conservation colours; somewhat to the surprise of many conservation activists, he became the first president of the Conservation Council of Victoria.

The Wimmera Regional Committee

Local government in the State of Victoria in the 1950s and 1960s was co-ordinated through thirteen regional committees consisting of representatives of all the shire councils in each region. The regional committees provided a bureaucratic track through which shires could gain access to the State government, and also could explore issues that affected adjacent shires. The Wimmera Regional Committee represented the shire councils in the vicinity of the Little Desert. It had first addressed the Little Desert issue in the context of the AMP Society's 1963 proposal to subdivide and develop the Little Desert. Clearly this was a regional issue, potentially affecting up to six shires.

In May 1963, not long before the AMP's proposal was put to the State government, the Natural Resources Conservation League, in conjunction with the Wimmera Regional Committee, held a Regional Convention at Horsham.[11] Inspired by the success of this event, the Wimmera Regional Committee organised a second convention in Nhill on 26 August 1964 specifically to canvass local and expert opinion on the AMP's proposed settlement scheme for the Little Desert. The papers of the convention reveal that both development and conservation issues were discussed openly by the local community. A large number of technical experts travelled from all over the State to attend. The FNCV also followed the convention's deliberations, calling on local FNCV members Keith Hateley, Ian McCann and Alec Hicks to represent the club and report back.[12]

The recommendations that arose from the conference were published (at the government's expense, Bill Middleton observed wryly) and set the agenda for later events.[13] The recommendations built on the earlier VNPA and FNCV suggestion of a national park in the Little Desert, but they were more rigorous in specifying the areas needing reservation and identifying their conservation values. In conformity with Lawrence's directive, Middleton had taken a 'behind-the-scenes' approach, collecting natural history data on the species in the Little Desert, identifying and locating key natural sites that should be spared agricultural development. (In his evidence to the Galbally inquiry, Peter Attiwill commented that the Wimmera Regional Committee Report's list of 600 species of plants for the Little Desert was exceptional in its thoroughness.[14]) Middleton then ensured that the information reached high-profile local ornithologist Claude Austin, a private grazier unconstrained by being in government employment. Austin was a shrewd choice. He was not only a well-informed and willing accomplice for conservation interests, but he was also a prominent Liberal Party supporter and a personal friend of the Premier. The battle for the Little Desert was fought loudest in the city, but local figures provided many of the bullets fired in the city campaign.

The View from Kaniva

Sir William McDonald's first announcement of his scheme for developing the Little Desert was made in June 1967 at a meeting of the Kaniva Jaycees, very soon after he took over as Minister of Lands. His last public function promoting the scheme was just over two years later, in November 1969, when he was speaking to the same group. Kaniva, almost on the South Australian border, at the far western end of the Little Desert, was seen by McDonald as the centre of his political support for the development scheme. Alec Hicks's brother, Councillor Bill Hicks, was one of those strongly in favour of the settlement scheme.[15] All the six shire councils that abutted the edges of the Little Desert were generally in favour of the scheme, which promised to bring them increased rates and State-funded road works.

Country newspapers were noticeably more supportive of the agricultural development proposal than their city counterparts. Some attributed city scepticism to a lack of understanding of what they saw as the virtues of development. The writings of J. J. Potts, the editor of the *Kaniva Times*, exasperated Alec Hicks, who remarked that 'our newspaper editor has been "brainwashed" by "Black Jack" McDonald'.[16] Potts made much of the success of farmers such as Mr D. James, owner of a South Australian farm close to the Little Desert, and the paper ran his story under a major headline: *Little Desert Responds to Development—2 Sheep per Acre No Worry—Even in Drought Year*. Potts commented:

> conservationists are prepared to make wild statements to 'brain wash' the public against the developmental proposal and thus keep the landless from securing the land that they want.
>
> Mr James thinks it is a shame that people who want farms should be brushed aside by old trogldytes [sic] and conservationists who want to keep young Australians from buying farms by reserving the whole of this area, which over 90% of them do not visit.[17]

Potts was following the lead provided by Sir William McDonald in setting up the development of the Little Desert as a 'rural rights' issue. City people were portrayed as out of touch (troglodytes), uncaring (do not visit), and seeking power at the expense of country people (especially the young, who were disappearing from Kaniva and other regional towns at an alarming rate). Melbourne folk and their concerns seemed very foreign to many Kaniva people. The town tended to look to Adelaide as its metropolis rather than Melbourne, which is slightly further away. McDonald, who had grown up on the border between South Australia and Victoria and had attended school in Adelaide, understood this ambivalence, and played on it.

At the turn of the century Victoria was a predominantly rural State, with about 60 per cent of its population living in the country and 40 per cent in Melbourne. In the first half of the twentieth century, political power in Victoria was shared in a three-way split between urban Labor, urban non-Labor and country interests. The combination of a relatively high country vote and the malapportionment of electoral boundaries ensured that country interests wielded great power in State government. Between 1930 and 1945 the State was governed by a Country Party–ALP coalition, with the Country Party leader Albert Dunstan as Premier.[18]

By 1944, however, the population percentages had reversed, and Melbourne had 60 per cent of the State's population. This forced a redistribution of electoral boundaries, which was followed by a series of rapidly changing, unstable minority governments until Bolte came to power in 1955. Despite the boom in agricultural commodity prices, Melbourne's population percentage continued to increase slightly in the 1950s and 1960s, partly because farmers were employing new, less labour-intensive techniques. The Bolte government was adept at exploiting country/city tensions; during the Little Desert dispute, it suggested that the city opposition to the scheme was simply self-interested, and denied that there was any real basis for concern about the McDonald scheme. Premier Bolte said he 'believed in developing the country [whereas] the *Age* seemed to believe in a policy of development in the city only'.[19]

But there were concerns about the scheme in the country too Between 1967 and 1969 country newspapers reflected an increasing uncertainty about the value of developing the Little Desert. The rural debate focused almost entirely on the carrying capacity of the land. On 10 July 1969 the weekly newspaper, the *Countryman*, publicised the concerns of the president of the Victorian branch of the Australian Institute of Agricultural Science in an article headed 'Many people have doubts about the future of the Little Desert'. After that, most country papers, like their metropolitan counterparts, were circumspect about the scheme. There was great concern about the idea of development simply for the sake of negative taxation arrangements for wealthy city interests. Such investment would do very little for the viability of local businesses and schools. The Nhill Chamber of Commerce had supported the McDonald scheme, and was criticised for this in the local press. Supporting the McDonald scheme was regarded as undermining a tourist opportunity rather than creating wealth for the town. The council's actions even featured in a debate between Dimboola High School and Nhill High School students; the Dimboola students won, arguing that 'Nhill Chamber of Commerce deserves adverse criticism over its stand relating to the Little Desert scheme'.[20]

By the time the Liberal Party lost the Dandenong by-election and spending on the Little Desert scheme was suspended, there were surprisingly few regrets expressed in the Wimmera papers. Shire councils had initially seen agricultural development as a possible way to stem the rural–urban population drift, thereby shoring up their local power base and the power they held in State politics. As the controversy about the Little Desert proceeded, however, they were quick to realise that it had produced a windfall business opportunity in the form of new tourist interest in the area.

The Little Desert dispute came at the end of the agricultural boom, not long after the severe drought of 1967–68. The years from 1970 to 1975 saw a 14 per cent increase in Melbourne's population—or one thousand people per week—much of it at the expense of rural shires.[21] J. J. Potts, the editor and proprietor of the *Kaniva Times*, felt he was the 'end of the line'. He watched his younger son learning offset printing, knowing that he would

> start up in a year or two—after I die I presume—in a city, and move with his wife and family from Kaniva. That is how the rot sets in in small country centres . . . We are one of the few papers in Victoria printed in a town of under 1000 population, and a Shire of 2137 odd people.[22]

Potts' pride in his town fed his fear of city people and their decisions. The different cultures of the city and the country were manifest in the perceptions of the outcome of the Little Desert dispute.

The national parks ideal was an overwhelmingly urban phenomenon, and there was much animosity in the country to the idea of 'locking up' land in reserves to accommodate the recreational needs of 'foreigners' from the city. The city/country division was an international phenomenon, and the movement 'back to nature' rather than 'back to the land' was an international urban response that valued nature's spiritual impact above its economic importance. As Peter J. Schmitt put it: 'Those who looked to nature for a living had categorically settled for something less than Arcadia; the man on the street, not the man on the land might better benefit from "natural" resources'. Many country people regarded themselves as business people, and felt they could understand city business people, but the idealistic 'Arcadians' who valued simply being in nature without 'improving' it, seemed totally incomprehensible, especially when they were known only as stereotypes rather than individuals.[23]

It was when the local people began to see the Little Desert as having tourist potential, and therefore an economic value other than as agricultural land, that they began to accept the idea that it might be left undeveloped. But before the businesses of the district began to advocate tourism, a very different group of locals saw its potential.

Breaking down the Barriers

The Aboriginal land rights activist David Anderson was one of the first Wimmera locals to seize the nettle of what we would now call 'eco-tourism'. Anderson not only protested against the 'destruction of the environment' that would be caused by the McDonald agricultural scheme, but in his 1970 speech to the Galbally Little Desert Settlement Committee he called for the development of tourism to benefit 'the people who have prior occupancy rights' so that they would 'have a viable economic weekly income that is just for all Aboriginal men and women capable of being employed'. He specifically advocated developments 'in the secondary and tourist industries' and called for the Little Desert to be declared a national park 'with a proviso that the Wimmera Tribes actually will always have prior right to freely hunt and fish there'.[24]

The notion of development through 'secondary and tourist industries' also had increasing appeal for non-Aboriginal locals. Many of these people were far less concerned about 'the destruction of the environment' through unsuitable agricultural development than Anderson, but business people in Nhill and elsewhere began to promote a pragmatic view of the national parks ideal. The *Nhill*

Free Press exhorted the town to 'get behind any move to promote tourism in an effort to attract as many people to the area as possible'.[25] The views of what Anderson described as the 'identifiable group of people' most in need, the traditional owners of the land, were quickly drowned by the clamour for secondary and tourist industries that would create jobs for the European Australians of the region.

The Kaniva Promotion Committee was established in 1969, at the height of the negotiations over the Little Desert. It enthusiastically sought strategies to attract 'the travelling public and commercial concerns to the Shire'.[26] It produced a tourist brochure, optimistically entitled *Desert Wealth*, 5000 copies of which were published in January 1971.[27] West Wimmera Tours, one of three companies licensed in the early 1970s to take tours of the Little Desert, offered discounted tours for 'local people', perhaps suggesting that some locals still needed to be persuaded of the benefits of tourism.[28]

West Wimmera Tours took up its licence just in time to benefit from an expected influx of tourists associated with an exhibition of Little Desert paintings in Kaniva by the well-known Melbourne artist Neil Douglas. Douglas, a conservationist, had painted twenty-two images designed to re-educate tastes and celebrate the positive aesthetic values of the Little Desert.[29] He gave away two of these paintings, one to Keith Hateley and one to the *Age*, for the part each had played in preserving the Little Desert.[30] The formal presentation of Douglas's 'Arid Garden' to the *Age* was made in Kaniva. The Kaniva Council also purchased a painting (through public subscription) for its chambers.[31] There were other art shows in later years, generally in the May school holidays, though none of the other artists were as prominent as Douglas.

The controversy also inspired R. C. (Wimpy) Reichelt to begin a tourist business near Nhill on the edge of the Little Desert. Reichelt was at a personal career crossroads because of a serious accident at work. He recognised that, while city people had become very interested in the Little Desert, there were no services in terms of tours or accommodation.[32] He applied for a permit, and at Easter in 1970 he went into the tour business on a part-time basis. The

Wimmera River near Dimboola

Ebenenezer Aboriginal Mission (1859–1904) was established on a former meeting site of Wotjabaluk people near the Wimmera River. The Crown land reserve remained home to Aboriginal people long after the mission station closed.

Typical open heath, Little Desert

operation grew steadily, and in 1976 Wimpy and Maureen Reichelt formed a company to establish an educational centre in the Little Desert, picking up on Dr Malcolm Calder's proposal at the Galbally inquiry for the establishment of a 'field study centre', which had been ignored by governments for the intervening seven years. The 'Little Desert Lodge' eventually grew into a relatively large centre, employing local people and providing motel and hostel accommodation, camping facilities, educational walks, aviaries and mallee fowl facilities.[33] The influx of tourists quickly compensated the Wimmera community for the loss of the agricultural development. According to the Melbourne *Age*, 12 000 people visited the Little Desert in the year following the dispute.[34] Numbers remained sufficiently high to ensure the viability of tourist businesses such as Reichelt's Little Desert Lodge in the 1990s.

The increasing emphasis on tourism in the Wimmera during the 1970s brought country and city people together, and some deep friendships developed, resulting in a much greater sharing of values. An outspoken city conservationist, Reg Johnson, who was active in the Conservation Council of Victoria, provided some of the initial capital for the Little Desert Lodge venture. Johnson also wrote a book about the Reichelt business, indicative of the long-standing and important friendship between the two men.[35]

More surprisingly, J. J. Potts of the *Kaniva Times* befriended Geoff Edwards, a young biologist and former activist in the Monash University Biological Students' Society during the Little Desert campaign. In 1970, as a direct result of the dispute, the Victorian Department of Fisheries and Wildlife employed Edwards and two others to undertake a survey of the Little Desert area. Through his friendship with the young biologist, Potts became very interested in the scientific conservation values of the Little Desert and the region generally.[36] From 1970 until Potts' death in 1974, Edwards and Potts maintained a lively and thoughtful correspondence, generally on matters of scientific concern to Potts, including the prediction of drought, tree-planting and land clearance. Edwards became personally interested in the Kaniva community, not just the 'wilderness' of the Little Desert, and became a subscriber to the *Kaniva*

Times. Potts' last letter to Edwards finished charmingly: 'I am glad you still enjoy the paper. I am very proud of my friendship with you. Regards, Jay Potts.'[37]

Such pride was testimony to the bridge-building that had played a vital role in breaking down barriers between city conservationists and the people who lived close to the Little Desert. The friendship changed city people from being unknown, foreign, even 'troglodytes', to known, friendly and perhaps more understandable individuals. City–country friendships also provided a human touch for wilderness visitors, reshaping city perceptions of an idealised place.

As conservation-minded city people (later called 'eco-tourists') came into the Little Desert, their attitudes to the 'scrub country' became local and acceptable. Many locals, keen to retain the interest in the area, sought to extend their natural history knowledge. It was no longer marginal or odd to know something of the flora and fauna of the Little Desert. The city people's views of the desert's heritage values became accepted, and within a few years even became the standard local view of the place. Local tourism depended on the desert, and it was a lone growth industry in an area of economic decline. Once they had lured visitors to the area, local tourist operators often sought to interest them in more conventional rural tourism through sheep-shearing displays and farm holidays.[38]

The continuing urban support for the conservation of the area throughout the 1970s and 1980s contributed to the Land Conservation Council's final recommendation to gazette most of the Little Desert as national park. Individual initiatives have also added to the conservation values of the Little Desert. The land around Broughtons Waterhole in the Western Little Desert, for example, was presented to the State government to be added to the national park by Percival Williams on behalf of his brother John, on 24 June 1989, some twenty-five years after his father, P. L. Williams, had first offered it for that purpose.

The concept of 'private' conservation has been taken up more broadly by the Trust for Nature—Victoria (first established in 1972 as the Victorian Conservation Trust), which facilitates conservation on private land by enabling landowners to 'covenant' the conservation-sensitive parts of their land so that when the land is sold these areas cannot be cleared.[39] One of the key fieldworkers in the Trust is Bill Middleton (in his retirement) who has worked toward covenanting large areas of land with high conservation values. The personal touch is still important. The Wimmera region has a very high proportion of Victoria's covenanted land.

Some time after the Little Desert campaign ended and the Save Our Bushlands Action Committee disbanded, another outer-suburban activist group, the Blackburn and District Tree Preservation Society, formed the Urimbirra collective. In 1973 it purchased private land near the edge of the Little Desert, adjacent to the prospective national park. Its initial aim was to purchase the land in order to defend conservation values, then eventually present it to the State to be added to the national park. The Urimbirra group saw the Little Desert as a conservation 'Mecca', and believed that as much of it as possible should be preserved. The collective comprised more than 120 families, a number of whom still make an annual pilgrimage from Melbourne in order to check the block and undertake conservation maintenance tasks such as pulling boneseed in the Bill's Gully area near by.[40] The Bill's Gully locals and the Urimbirra team have become friendly over the years, and meet in the Bill's Gully hall.[41] On Keith Hateley's retirement as ranger in the Little Desert National Park, a Urimbirra member, Clive Brownsea, left his long-time job working in the State Savings Bank in Blackburn in 1974, and moved with his family to Nhill to take over the job.[42] Another founding member of Urimbirra, the research chemist Les Smith, took on the task of establishing a 'Friends of the Little Desert National Park' group in 1988, soon after the legislation for the large national park had been enacted. He co-ordinates this group from his home in Melbourne's eastern suburbs.

In the 1990s the Urimbirra collective has reviewed its original plans to offer the aggregated holdings to the government. Because of continuing severe cuts to national parks management budgets, Urimbirra directors are no longer confident that the State can manage the land as well as the collective. They have placed a covenant on the land to ensure that it cannot be cleared. In 1995 they sought the assistance of rolling funds from the Trust for

Nature to purchase another block that is also privately managed.[43] Urimbirra represents the interesting paradox of 'private' conservation by a 'collective'. It is one of the unseen privatisations of the 1990s. Private conservation areas support and enhance the biodiversity of wild bushland on public land by offering 'buffer zones' for nature in an agricultural landscape.

Despite a growing interest in various forms of private conservation, there is still much land clearing in the region, and the Wotjabaluk people are very concerned about this. They speak anxiously of salinity-affected farmland and continuing dust-storms sweeping the topsoil to the city. Most of all they are angry about choked waterways, including the Wimmera River itself, where weirs are holding back the natural flow so that local councils can water parks and gardens in the town.[44] Concern about the continuing deterioration of the land contributed to the Wotjabaluk people's decision in 1993 to place a Native Title claim, through the Mirimbiak Nations Aboriginal Corporation, on the public lands of both the Little Desert and the Big Desert.[45]

Like the Urimbirra co-operative directors, the Wotjabaluk community of the 1990s is not convinced that the status of 'national park' provides sufficient protection for the environment of the Little Desert. Black and green activists alike are concerned that the pragmatism and economic rationalism of late 1990s government policies can only spell disaster for an environment they all value. A successful Native Title claim would open the possibilities for Wotjabaluk management or co-management of the public lands of the Little Desert, perhaps following models suggested by Kakadu and Uluru National Parks in the Northern Territory. This would offer the community, which has become increasingly visible since the formation of the Goolum Goolum Aboriginal Co-operative in Horsham, a way into that tourist industry mooted by David Anderson in 1970.[46] There is already a shop selling locally made Aboriginal art and artefacts in the main street of Horsham. Peter Kennedy, director of the Goolum Goolum Co-operative, reported that the Mirimbiak Nations Aboriginal Corporation had commissioned a 'tourism strategy' for the area 'so that local Aboriginals can start tourism out there and keep it going without wrecking the environment'.[47]

'Indigenous eco-tourism' is not part of the vision for the national park laid out in the 1996 *Little Desert Management Plan*. The management plan is heavily dependent on archaelogical surveys of pre-contact artefacts, and inadvertently portrays Aboriginal culture as dead on the land rather than living in the heart.[48] The values and stories of the living, post-invasion culture are not regarded as relevant. Peter and Cape Kennedy (now in their thirties) have been going out into the Little Desert from the time they were fourteen or fifteen, learning from Cape's father where to find the waterholes and soaks so that 'we knew where to get a drink and that', but they are relieved that the National Parks Service has not asked them to talk about it much, because they fear that the non-Aboriginal community 'could put it in all in books . . . [without] even going out there'.[49] Learning about culturally significant places must be based on personal experience and oral tradition. Visiting the desert country is an act of trust and sharing, of keeping culture strong. If the original Wimmera locals are given the opportunity to undertake their 'tourist strategy', to share some of their unique expertise with non-Aboriginal Australians and international visitors, the Little Desert's conservation values will be significantly enriched.

The Bureaucrats

I can remember the Chairman [of the Forests Commission] telling me one day—waving his finger at my nose and saying 'Bill, don't you get involved in that exercise, or at least don't let it be seen that you are getting involved'. So Bill, like a lot of other public employees, went underground.

Bill Middleton speaking at the handover ceremony
for Broughtons Waterhole, 1989

Bureaucratic activities and responses are an important component of any history of the conservation movement, because many of the key actors in conservation disputes have been bureaucrats, scientists or both. Yet, as Hugh Stretton has observed, historians have been slow to take on the challenge of writing about bureaucracies.[1] Historical geographers have offered leadership in this field. The history of the land-management and conservation bureaucracies has been researched by J. M. Powell, his students Ray Wright and Sandra Bardwell, and his colleague David Mercer.[2] By paying serious attention to bureaucratic mechanisms, and to the philosophies and styles of the bureaucrats themselves, such studies allow influential individuals to emerge as personalities, and bring to light the day-to-day constraints that have shaped various bureaucratic systems and departments. These processes were crucial in the case of the Little Desert, where the building of a conservation philosophy inside the bureaucracy largely set the parameters within which Sir William McDonald's settlement scheme was disputed.

Although McDonald was a believer in land development, a sizeable proportion of his electorate did not believe in it, or at least not in development at all costs. At the same time, the conflict was only partly about whether the Little Desert should be developed or conserved. The central concern was power—who should have power, how the power should be managed, and how those in power should account for their actions to the general public.

State public servants working in the several departments and commissions that dealt with land and natural resources were the group most directly concerned with the day-to-day management of power over land. These bureaucrats were the first to become really angry about the proposal to develop the Little Desert that emerged in 1967, after McDonald took over the portfolio as Minister of Lands. They were first because they were privy to information before it was released to the general public, and they were angry because they had not been consulted, or their advice had been ignored. They were probably also frustrated because, although they believed they had a strong case for not developing the Little Desert, there was no direct way for them to condemn government policy. The dispute over the Little Desert began with this group, and the issue could not be said to have been resolved until they were satisfied.

The complex and rather fragmented organisational and administrative arrangements associated with land-use planning in the Victorian public service in the 1960s make it difficult to determine exactly which bureaucrats—or even which bureaucratic institutions —were concerned about the Little Desert, but it is clear that concerns came from a wide variety of places, especially the departments of Agriculture, Lands, and Fisheries and Wildlife, the Forests Commission and the Soil Conservation Authority. Local government regional committees also commented on land-use proposals, and a parliamentary committee, the State Development Committee, had an interest in land development. The views of these men— they were almost certainly all men[3]—were influential, yet they remained faceless, obscured by the labyrinthine structures of the land-management bureaucracy.

In attempting to research the role of bureaucrats in the dispute I have met with significant silences, with records never made or quietly overlooked. Public service etiquette prevents senior bureaucrats from revealing their personal views on political issues, at least while they are in public office. Twenty years later, Bill Middleton was happy to admit a central role in condemning the Little Desert Settlement scheme, but at the time he and others had to go 'underground' to take a view contrary to government policy.[4]

The difficulty of finding out which individuals contributed and how they defined and shaped the controversy is aggravated by the need for bureaucracy to present a united front, irrespective of internal machinations. Neutrality and impartiality are the basis of an efficient bureaucracy. The calculability or predictability of the administrative system is what defines its rationality, and hence its success.[5] It is not in the interests of professional bureaucrats to reveal that the inside of the bureaucratic 'machine' is not a smoothly running, well-oiled engine, but rather a quirky organic struggle between individuals and putative systems, between egos and memoranda. Bureaucrats are particularly unwilling to reveal the nature of tensions between departments, because interdepartmental warfare is not part of their professional ideal.

In fact, the Victorian departments involved in land use were constantly at odds with each other, and had been for many years. Many of these tensions were played out at the meetings of the inter-departmental Land Utilization Advisory Council (LUAC), a small, powerful body involving the heads of the relevant departments. Without an understanding of this long-standing internecine warfare and the workings of LUAC, the Little Desert dispute could easily seem to have come from nowhere—as Sir William McDonald found, to his cost.

Despite the later interest of 'environmentalists', the framework of the Little Desert dispute was laid down by those who defined their missions in terms of 'wise use' (or utilitarian) conservation. The decision not to develop the Little Desert was the culmination of a long line of interdepartmental negotiations, based fundamentally on economic arguments. At the same time, what was defined as 'economic' and 'not economic' was shifting in response to growing recognition of the long-term cost of repairing the damage caused by overstocking marginal land.

The agricultural economists of the Department of Agriculture were vociferous in their opposition to the development of the Little Desert. Costing the development of marginal land was becoming increasingly complex as more and more new factors were woven into the equation—short-term factors such as soil erosion and drought, as well as long-term environmental considerations and non-money benefits. From the mid-1950s onwards, agricultural economists both in the universities and government departments were urging larger rather than smaller farms. They also advocated more intensive use of partially developed land in preference to the infrastructurally expensive 'opening up' of new areas.[6] Bruce Davidson's influential books *The Northern Myth* (1965) and *Australia—Wet or Dry?* (1969) highlighted the continuing economic failure of expensive irrigation schemes designed to bring arid land into production. In government circles, the Soil Conservation Authority and the Land Utilization Advisory Council were much quicker to seize on these understandings than the politicians.

The Heytesbury Dairying Scheme

When I interviewed him in 1990, Sir William McDonald remembered with pride his involvement in the Heytesbury dairying scheme during the 1950s and 1960s: 'The last period of Heytesbury development, it was my baby'.[7] He identified the scheme as a career 'highlight'. Yet agricultural economists regarded Heytesbury as a 'disaster'. Criticisms of the scheme rang within government departments from the 1950s, but clearing continued apace until Norman Wettenhall of the National Trust's Landscape Preservation Council spoke directly with McDonald in 1967.

Heytesbury, a big land development scheme in the southern part of Victoria's Western District, was criticised by agricultural economists and utilitarian conservationists alike. Agricultural economists argued that Heytesbury was undesirable because the State already had an export surplus of dairy products. The Forests Commission expressed concern that large stands of high-quality timber were lost because of the scheme. As Alan Lloyd, Professor of Agricultural Economics at the University of Melbourne, observed:

> [Heytesbury] was an inefficient use of natural resources, involving subsidised development of an area to increase agricultural output, when there was clear evidence that there was huge potential in the existing settled areas for cheap increases in productivity through pasture improvement . . . You can't . . . give farmers properties at a big discount on their market value, plus subsidised credit, and then . . . subsidis[e] their output as well. Nationally, the whole thing was loss-making—all over the place.[8]

Yet, if the economic case for development was no longer relevant, the 'dynamic developer' image still had political force. So while McDonald the politician basked in 'honour and glory', the economists were expressing serious concerns about 'inefficient use of resources'. 'Development', particularly in the 1960s, could still be portrayed as positive, irrespective of the economics. A politician who promised development could be seen to be 'doing something for the country'. Alan Lloyd did concede that Sir William had a right to be proud of Heytesbury 'because, given that it was going to be developed, he made sure it was developed efficiently'.[9] But the idea that 'non-development' could be positive was slow to emerge.

The Little Desert Settlement Scheme became Victoria's first public testing ground for the emerging agricultural economics. Alan Lloyd's arguments against the scheme were picked up on radio broadcasts and publicised in newspapers.[10] The costs of soil conservation and erosion repair had continued to rise. In the summer of 1967–68 Victoria suffered a particularly bad drought. The limits of the land were apparent even to urban dwellers, who were reduced to watering their gardens with buckets. The language of agricultural economics became newsworthy.

The officers of the Department of Agriculture felt they had a professional obligation to distance themselves from the minister's plans, yet they had no official way to do this. They therefore resorted to unofficial methods to publicise their personal competence and concern about the carrying capacity of the land. Rex Newman, an agrostologist from the Department of Agriculture, had been mentioned by McDonald as a supporter of the Little Desert Settlement Scheme. In fact, Newman had clearly cautioned against settlement in an article published in 1959. In the *Journal of the Department of Agriculture, Victoria*, he wrote:

> It is doubtful whether an attempt to maintain a leguminous pasture is warranted in country with an average rainfall of less than 17 or 18 inches per annum where soils are of such poor physical structure and low fertility as those over a large proportion of the Little Desert.[11]

Valerie Honey quoted these words in her submission to the Acting Premier in July 1969—adding a cheeky note that 'a copy of this Journal is in my possession'.[12] Newman's article was already in the public domain, but it was probably no coincidence that spare copies were circulating among conservationists some ten years after publication.

Sir William McDonald became angry about 'leaks' and gave formal instructions to the staff of the Department of Agriculture not to comment on the Little Desert Settlement Scheme. He was then outraged afresh when the information that he had issued the order was leaked. In November 1969 Alan Lloyd raised the issue at a public meeting in Kaniva, and described it as an attempt at 'gagging' the public service. When challenged by McDonald to 'name the source' of the story, Lloyd declined, saying that it might endanger the person's job.[13]

The Department of Agriculture's strong opposition to the scheme reflected the changing emphasis of the training of agricultural scientists in the 1950s and 1960s. In the early 1950s the opposition to development of remote country had been related to nature preservation and focused on preserving 'reserves' in the face of development. By the late 1960s, however, agriculturally trained public servants were advancing arguments against land development on economic grounds. The Little Desert was 'marginal land', not a wildlife reserve or potential national park.

Utilitarian Conservation in Victoria

Since the first decades of the twentieth century, the public resource managers concerned with Victoria's forests, soil, water and wildlife had been informed by scientific principles of utilitarian conservation. They defined conservation as a concern for the 'wise use' of resources. They also implicitly defined the resource professional as the person best able to judge the 'wisdom of use', so endorsing both the style of conservation and the professional nature of resource management.

Throughout the course of the twentieth century, most industrial societies have seen a proliferation in the range of professional occupations and in the number of professionals they employ. Some have even promoted professionalism as a panacea for the rampant individualism of acquisitive Western cultures.[14] Professionals, like public servants, are seen as being orientated to the needs of the community rather than to their own self-interest. Unlike many other bureaucrats, resource professionals are also 'experts'. Professionals often feel that they bear moral responsibilities in administering their areas of expertise, and this creates a particular tension for public servants who must also serve their political masters.

In Australia, as in America, the word 'conservation' was first used in a technical sense in relation to water conservation.[15] The Victorian Parliament passed a Water Conservation Act in 1881 that was concerned with means to 'conserve' (or save) water for times of shortage. It was some time before the term was generalised to refer to wise use of resources other than water. In Britain the term 'conservancy' was favoured until as late as the 1950s,[16] but Americans used the term with respect to multiple-purpose river development late last century.

Although the first utilitarian conservationists were water professionals, it was an American forester, Gifford Pinchot (1865–1946), who was probably most responsible for the popularisation of the term through the Conservation League of America, which he founded in 1908. From 1905 Pinchot was also responsible for the entire United States Forest Service. The Conservation League was established to arouse public support for 'progressive development' through the professional management and wise use of natural resources, especially water and timber. Pinchot's concern as Chief Forester was with the management of forests throughout America for sustained yield. 'Conservation' was for him the opposite of 'waste', and was not under any circumstances to be confused with 'preservation'.[17] His tactic of making forest management a public concern was influential throughout Australia, as evidenced in the quarterly national journal, the *Gum Tree*, established in March 1917 and 'devoted to the Conservation, Propagation and Utilisation of Australian trees'.[18] Professional foresters in Australia were also influenced by British forestry, particularly the Imperial Forestry School at Oxford. The first chairman of Victoria's Forests Commission, Owen Jones, was also experienced in imperial forestry in the wider sense, having come to Victoria from the Ceylon Forest Service.[19]

Because of the aridity of the Australian continent, there has been a public consciousness of the value of water ever since the beginnings of European settlement.[20] Large-scale irrigation schemes in Victoria were mooted as early as 1856 at the Philosophical Society (later the Royal Society) of Victoria. The Irrigation Act of 1886 enabled local water trusts to be supported by central funding for major capital works, but the economic depression of the 1890s left the irrigation trusts in deep financial trouble. In 1905 the State Rivers and Water Supply Commission was established to give centralised direction to embattled irrigation schemes and to support closer settlement initiatives designed to offer opportunities to the large numbers of unemployed.

The State Rivers and Water Supply Commission was chaired from 1907 by Elwood Mead, a leading American professional irrigation manager schooled in the ideals of the progressive conservation movement. The engineers working under Mead appreciated his sense of progress through conservation and developed a pride in their own professionalism. They became deeply disturbed when the problems of soil erosion became so serious that by the 1920s irrigation channels were silting up, demanding increasingly frequent dredging. As a result a number of the 'water professionals', particularly those who had worked in rural areas, turned their attention to soil problems.[21]

Soil erosion was also a concern of surveyors, many of whom worked in the Department of Crown Lands and Survey. The Victorian Institute of Surveyors arranged a symposium on erosion in 1939, probably spurred by the establishment of the Soil Conservation Service of New South Wales in 1938.[22] The symposium, organised by the energetic Charles Tate ('Bull Ant') Clark, a district surveyor and president of the institute, drew together twenty-six speakers, all but two of whom were senior and 'expert' public servants.[23] The symposium was tied closely to the work of the 1938 Erosion Investigation Committee, which had been chaired by W. McIlroy, Secretary of Lands. In 1940, following the Erosion Investigation Committee and the surveyors' symposium, an Act was passed establishing a Soil Conservation Board in Victoria. Its powers were extended in 1950, and it was renamed the Soil Conservation Authority.

Other important 'water professionals' were those concerned with urban water needs, which were managed through the Melbourne and Metropolitan Board of Works (MMBW). The distinctive 'closed catchment' water conservation policy that the MMBW had adopted since its inception in 1891 had to be justified to other potential users of water catchment areas of the State, especially forestry officials. Under the closed catchment policy, logging, camping and other recreational activities were not permitted in Melbourne's water-catchment areas. It was not only a source of conflict between foresters and water engineers, but was also unpopular with those advocating country settlement, who perceived the catchment areas as being 'locked up' for city use.[24] While the utilitarian conservationists had in common the notion of scientific management of natural resources, each of the professions involved had a narrow focus on its area of specialist expertise— forests, survey, water, soil—and this resulted in considerable conflict between them. Land management in Victoria was guided by technical expertise, but different experts contributed different visions of what 'wise use' meant. The difficulty was to bring the visions together and to control interdepartmental tensions in land management decision-making.

Bringing the Bureaucracies Together

At the national level, Australian land management policy has suffered serious fragmentation because the responsibilities for lands and natural resources (including national parks, nature reserves, forests, water and wildlife) have fallen under State jurisdiction. There have been few attempts to achieve uniformity across State borders. The sale of land and natural resources has been a major source of public revenue, and one jealously guarded by the States, with their limited taxation bases. Historical differences between colonies resulted in enormous variability in land management between States. For example, in 1964, Victoria had alienated (sold into private ownership) more than 60 per cent of the State's lands, and another 11 per cent were 'licensed or leased'. The remaining 28 per cent were either uncommitted, occupied by government agencies or 'reserved' (for example, 'reserved forests'). Contrast this with Queensland, where only 6 per cent of the land was alienated and more than 86 per cent was 'licensed or leased' (that is, publicly owned but privately managed), leaving only about 6 per cent of lands uncommitted or occupied by government agencies. Other States had different ownership patterns again, reflecting the differences in their land management priorities.[25]

At various times the Commonwealth intervened to suggest ways in which a national land management policy might be implemented. One important Commonwealth initiative was made toward the end of World War II through the Rural Reconstruction Commission. In ten volumes of reports produced between 1944 and 1946, the commission set the States specific (and uniform) land management objectives.[26] This review of land utilisation was motivated by concern about the settlement of returned servicemen on agricultural properties, a reward for war service that had also been offered after World War I. The Rural Reconstruction Commission was endeavouring to ensure that the post-World War II schemes would be more successful than the settlement schemes set up between 1915 and 1938, where the properties allocated were frequently in marginal country and were too small to be 'viable'—

that is, to offer a satisfactory standard of living to the soldier and his family.[27]

The Commonwealth Rural Reconstruction Commission recommended that each State establish a Land Utilization Council under the control of the Premier to co-ordinate policy 'on all phases of land use concerning the allocation of land for farming, forest development, water resources, national parks and reserves, and erosion control'.[28] The commission also recommended that each council be chaired by a full-time executive officer whose status should be equal to that of the head of a department, and that members should be the heads of the following departments: Agriculture, Forestry, Lands and Survey, Water Supply and Soil Conservation (if a separate soil conservation department existed in the State concerned).[29]

In Victoria, the Rural Reconstruction Commission's report was followed almost immediately by the report of the 1946 Royal Commission on Forest Grazing, in which Judge Stretton recommended that an 'extradepartmental authority, charged with the duty of protecting all land, be created'.[30] The juxtaposition of the two reports provided the impetus for establishing a Land Utilization Advisory Council in Victoria in 1950.

The Land Utilization Advisory Council, 1950–70

Both Judge Stretton and the Rural Reconstruction Commission drew attention to the need to plan land use in ways that a single department, even if it were the department of Crown Lands and Survey, could not do. Intelligent land allocations relied on a multiplicity of forms of expertise—including mapping and survey, but also a knowledge of forests, water catchments, soil conservation and agriculture.

There was an important difference, however, between the two sets of recommendations: the Commonwealth report specifically recommended that certain experts were to be gathered together, thereby limiting the membership to senior public servants and excluding certain others. (The Victorian Fisheries and Game Department, for example, had biological expertise not available

Sir William McDonald, architect and chief advocate of the Little Desert Settlement Scheme, with parliamentary colleagues, 31 October 1969

The border between Victoria (left) and South Australia, 1969

The Little Desert is not traditionally scenic. View from the highest of the 'Sisters' hills.

*Philip Crosbie Morrison
(1900–58)*

*Keith Hateley, campaigner
for the Kiata Lowan
Sanctuary and central Little
Desert area*

Mrs Valerie Honey and family, 1960s

Victorian National Parks Association stalwarts at a picnic, Steels Creek, 1991.
Standing (left to right): Geoff Durham, Budg Bleakley, Malcolm Calder, Stephen
Johnston, Dick Johnson. Seated: Gwynnyth Taylor, Ros Garnet, Joan Lindros.

through the other departments at that time.) Judge Stretton was more canny. He recommended an 'extradepartmental' authority, which would have been more flexible, able to call on a wider range of expertise and possibly—although Stretton was not explicit on this point—even provide for public representation.

The Victorian Parliament passed the first of many Soil Conservation and Land Utilization Acts in 1947, but as a result of delays and a change of government, a second version of the Act was passed before both came into operation on 15 February 1950.[31] As the name implied, soil conservation was its first concern, and its most important immediate effect was to upgrade the small and understaffed Soil Conservation Board, which had been established a decade earlier, to a full-scale Soil Conservation Authority with its own minister. The first Minister for Conservation was Henry Bolte, MLA, a junior minister in the conservative (Liberal) government.

The 'Land Utilization' part of the Act was manifest in the establishment of the Land Utilization Advisory Council (LUAC), which met first on 26 April 1950 with the Minister for Conservation in the chair. The composition of the LUAC was much as the Commonwealth Rural Reconstruction Commission had recommended: permanent heads of the departments of Agriculture and Lands, along with the chairmen of the Soil Conservation Authority, Forests Commission and State Rivers and Water Supply Commission. But its brief was much narrower: it concerned itself with land-use conflicts in water catchment areas. The LUAC did not deal with the allocation of land for farming unless that land fell within a water catchment area or, after 1959, in a plantation forestry area.

Despite the narrowness of its brief, the minister made it clear that this was to be a very senior council. Permanent heads were directed to attend its meetings in person.[32] This directive was followed over the years most consistently by the Soil Conservation Authority. The Forests Commission, the State Rivers and Water Supply Commission and the Department of Lands were also generally represented by their permanent heads, but the Director of Agriculture seldom attended until 1967,[33] leaving the task to his deputy, an indication that the Department of Agriculture did not regard the LUAC as central to its concerns. Throughout 1950 and

1951 the Minister for Conservation attended all meetings, but after that the meetings were presided over by successive chairmen of the Soil Conservation Authority—George T. Thompson until 9 February 1961, and R. Geoffrey Downes from 14 April 1961 to 17 December 1970, when the LUAC was disbanded. Apart from the first eight meetings, and eight consecutive meetings in 1968–69, the incumbent Minister for Conservation presided over only eight other meetings out of a total of ninety-two.

Throughout the 1950s, under the leadership of George Thompson, the LUAC travelled frequently, inspecting water catchments all over the State. Eighteen of the forty-one meetings organised by Thompson were held in rural venues outside Melbourne, often taking over a local court house or shire council office for the necessary formal proceedings after a session in the field. In the 1960s the council's business altered and field trips became rare. Geoff Downes convened fifty-one meetings over the second decade of the LUAC's life, and only two of these included 'inspection tours'. One other meeting was convened in 1966 at Wilsons Promontory National Park, but this was as a 'retreat' and did not include an inspection tour, much to the chagrin of the Director of National Parks at the time.[34]

Downes was more of a centralist than his predecessor. Thompson in his younger days had worked in the Mallee on irrigation projects for the State Rivers and Water Supply Commission. It was this work that had aroused his concern about soil erosion.[35] Thompson knew the value of regional consultation and was keen to allow local people time to express their concerns. Downes was much more a 'progressive conservationist', concerned to find genuinely scientific—and therefore centralist—solutions to technically defined problems, and to implement them as efficiently as possible. His two country 'field trips' were not at the behest of municipalities, but rather to see government science in action: at Reefton, to show the work of the Soil Conservation Authority's Experimental Station, and at the Werribee Research Farm run by the Department of Agriculture.[36] The changing role of the LUAC itself contributed to the reduction in the number of field trips, but there was also a steady decrease in the power delegated to regional committees in the 1960s.[37]

In 1959 the LUAC's brief was extended by the Land (Plantation Areas) Act, which required it to assist in the selection of sites suitable for softwood plantations. The LUAC's workload also increased from 1966, when the Commonwealth government, on the recommendation of the Australian Forestry Council, called for an endeavour to increase softwood plantations to an area of three million acres (1.2 million hectares) by the year 2000. The chairman of the Forests Commission of Victoria estimated that this would mean that the existing planting rate of 2400 hectares per annum would have to be increased by a factor of 2.5 by 1971.[38] The LUAC suddenly found itself seeking 6000 hectares of sites suitable for pine plantations every year. Without sites, Victoria could not obtain a share of the $20 million the Commonwealth offered in free loans each year from 1966 to 1971.

Although the LUAC's official brief was to deal with matters of land use within proclaimed watersheds and plantation areas, there was persistent pressure from the mid-1950s onward for its powers to be extended to cover other types of land and land use, as the Commonwealth Rural Reconstruction Commission had originally recommended. In June 1955 a conservative government came to power at the sixth election in five years. The Minister for Conservation was again Henry Bolte, but this time he had an Assistant Minister for Conservation, A. J. Fraser, as Bolte was also Premier.

Within a year the State Development Committee, in a bid to find new areas for agricultural development, advocated that the powers of the LUAC be extended, a recommendation rejected by the LUAC's members.[39] Yet the government persisted. The minutes record only that 'On 7 August 1956 the Land Utilization Advisory Council attended a meeting of the Cabinet Subcommittee which was appointed to recommend administrative procedures in the determination of land use'.[40] Cabinet refused to accept that the LUAC could avoid taking responsibility for a broader range of land utilisation decisions. Several closely spaced meetings in mid-1957 resulted in a report from the LUAC to the Minister for Conservation 'concerning the availability of land for settlement'.[41] The LUAC again expressed its reluctance to become involved with the tendentious issue of land settlement:

The submission is the considered opinion of the members of the Council as to the suitability for settlement of the land specified in the lists, but . . . this Council as constituted, refrains from expressing an opinion as to whether or not the land listed should be made available for settlement.[42]

The pressure to extend the LUAC's authority was not only coming from the politicians. The Wimmera Regional Committee had also recommended to the Central Planning Committee that the LUAC be empowered to consider the use of all Crown and undeveloped land, a recommendation rejected by the LUAC.[43] The matter did not rest with administrative procedures. But within a couple of meetings, the LUAC was called on to consider a proposal for agricultural settlement.

The Rocklands Catchment Area Controversy

In mid-1958 the LUAC received a request from the State Rivers and Water Supply Commission that the area above the Rocklands Reservoir in the Grampians in western Victoria be proclaimed a water catchment under section 22 of the Soil Conservation and Land Utilization Act. It appears from the minutes that the timing of this request was no coincidence, for the decision was unpopular with the Department of Crown Lands and Survey, the department directly responsible for land alienations.[44] Two meetings later, on 16 December 1958, the LUAC received a formal request 'that land to the West of the [Rocklands] Reservoir be made available for Settlement'. The request came to the Premier from the Speaker, Sir William McDonald, member for Dundas, on behalf of four shires in his electorate.[45] The Premier referred the matter to the LUAC for investigation. The Soil Conservation Authority and the Forests Commission prepared background reports for the LUAC, and a major tour of inspection was held in February 1959. The tour party comprised ten regional officers of the major departments affected as well as six LUAC members. Twelve criteria were used to guide the group in their land-use assessment task, including possible uses other than agriculture (timber, bee-keeping), costs of settlement (roads, clearing, possible erosion and siltation, supervision of settlement and so on) and other considerations such as economics and the preservation of native flora and fauna.

The council's report on the Rocklands catchment settlement proposal was written by Geoff Downes, the deputy chairman of the Soil Conservation Authority, who regularly attended meetings of the LUAC. His report, released in May 1959, recommended against alienating the land. Between the time of the tour of inspection and the release of the report, a new *Soil Conservation and Land Utilization Act No. 6372 (1958)* came into operation on 1 April 1959. The new Act gave broader responsibilities to the Soil Conservation Authority. As well as being responsible for dealing with soil erosion and the promotion of soil conservation, the Soil Conservation Authority was charged with 'the determination of matters relevant to the utilisation of all lands, including Crown Lands, in such a manner as will tend towards the attainment of' the prevention and mitigation of soil erosion and promotion of soil conservation.[46]

Downes used this clause to ensure that his report was not ignored. He pointed out that the area proposed for settlement only slightly overlapped the catchment area (making it only marginally the LUAC's responsibility), but that the erosion hazard of all the land was moderate, and would become severe if the land were partly developed and then abandoned. This neatly placed the land within the ambit of the Soil Conservation Authority and the LUAC, and left Downes free to comment that the low-fertility soils covered with scrubby timber would make settlement 'economically doubtful'. He also noted that the few patches of better soil were difficult to segregate from the less useful country, and under the circumstances were better left to timber.[47]

The next month Sir William McDonald and A. J. Fraser met the permanent heads of the Forests Commission and the Soil Conservation Authority to press for a reconsideration of Rocklands 'in the long range interests of the State'. The LUAC confirmed its previous opinion.[48] But the pressure to develop Rocklands would not go away. It reappeared again in May 1960 after yet another inspection tour, this time by Keith H. Turnbull, Minister for Lands, with Fraser and McDonald. 'As a result of an inspection of land . . . the matter was again referred to the Land Utilization Advisory Council by the Acting Minister for Conservation', the minutes recorded laconically. This time the council sent a firm reply to Henry Bolte expressing its unequivocal opinion that 'Crown areas within the catchment in the Cherrypool and Black Range Units should not be alienated under any circumstances, and pointing out the dangers inherent in the alienation of the land in the Tyar Unit'.[49] The Soil Conservation Authority had evidence that the potential siltation or salination of the Rocklands Reservoir could affect up to 70 000 people, which would make the scheme 'political suicide'.[50] The Rocklands scheme was dropped.

Rocklands was not a major issue for the metropolitan newspapers. It was seen as something only affecting country people—a mere 'parish pump' concern, of no interest to people in the city. It did, however, test the authority of the Land Utilization Advisory Council in State land management decisions, something that was also approved by the relevant regional planning committee. The Wimmera Regional Committee, in its 1964 document *Need for Reservations in Desert Settlement*, again advocated an extension of the powers of the LUAC, and also an extension of its membership to include the Directors of Fisheries and Wildlife and of National Parks, and a representative from the local Regional Committee.[51]

The LUAC was still reluctant to take on the political 'hot potato' of recommending on land development for the State. It had fought the Rocklands case and won by stretching a very narrow brief to its limit. It preferred to continue to work within those limits, to do the smaller job well, not expand to a point where it could not be so thorough or, perhaps, to the point where it could no longer present a united front. By maintaining a narrow and technical definition of its brief, the LUAC could continue to run under the chairmanship of the Soil Conservation Authority, one of the least powerful (and least controversial) of its member departments. If the LUAC had to make recommendations on the allocation of agricultural land, the Departments of Agriculture and Lands would be forced to play a much bigger role, and this would almost certainly have exacerbated tensions between those departments and the Forests Commission, which were an increasing problem at a time when expanding pine plantation programmes were actively competing with agriculture for land.

Ronald Geoffrey Downes

R. G. (Geoff) Downes took over the chairmanship of both the Soil Conservation Authority and the LUAC in 1961. He held a Master's degree in Agricultural Science, and was determined that the LUAC's work would be based on sound scientific principles.[52] At the same time he recognised that this sort of work was time-consuming and his professional soil-science staff was small. Downes was concerned not to extend his ambit so far that he would have to compromise scientific principles. He may also have recognised that, if the LUAC's brief became broader, the Soil Conservation Authority's key role might become less clear, and eventually he might lose the chairmanship to the permanent head of a bigger department such as Lands. By keeping the brief technical and narrow, the LUAC could stick to a strictly scientific approach, and the SCA's leadership would remain unquestioned.

Downes' solution to the Wimmera Regional Committee's recommendations, which were referred to the LUAC for comment by the Central Planning Committee, was simply to ignore the issue of extension of powers and to focus discussion on the concept of extending the membership. Downes felt that two new members were the most the council should have, and suggested that the Departments of Mines and of Fisheries and Wildlife would be appropriate. After some discussion, the Council decided to resolve the matter simply by co-opting relevant people for the discussion of particular items.[53]

Within a year a directive from the Premier forced the Council to reconsider the matter of its membership, and the Director of Fisheries and Wildlife and the Secretary of Mines joined its ranks on 21 December 1966.[54] The Wimmera Regional Committee's recommendations that National Parks and local shires be represented were sidestepped.

It was consistent with Downes' centralist management style that he would not see value in local representation on the council. It is not clear why the Director of National Parks was overlooked.

Perhaps it was simply a lack of recognition of the 'professionalism' or 'science' of national parks management. Downes had a rigid definition of what conservation was—and was not. He had little sympathy for the sort of 'emotional' conservation represented by many national parks activists. Downes' vision of conservation was entirely technical, and he probably felt that he himself was the best qualified technically to serve the interests of national parks.[55]

Downes regarded 'preservation' as an old-fashioned notion peddled by amateurs, and 'conservation' as the proper business of those with technical expertise. In 1969 he wrote:

> Conservation is a word which is being much more commonly used today, but it has a different meaning from what it had thirty years ago. At that time conservation of natural resources was interpreted to mean preservation. Today it means the proper understanding of our resources and how they can be used and managed to provide not only what the community needs now but also what the community will need in future.[56]

This could have been written by Gifford Pinchot for his Conservation League of America in 1908. Downes' history is patently wrong; thirty years before those words were penned, the predecessor of his own Soil Conservation Authority, the Soil Conservation Board, was established on exactly the principles he outlined. Utilitarian conservation had been fashionable in the Victorian public service for six decades. Downes' poor history rendered 'preservation' as 'old-fashioned' and 'conservation' as 'modern'. His rhetoric points to a growing rift in the conservation movement of the time. Downes used 'conservation' in contradistinction to 'preservation' to exclude amateurs, nature lovers and romantics, just as Pinchot did in the USA in the first decade of the twentieth century against John Muir and the Sierra Club wilderness lovers.[57]

The centrepiece of the scientific organisation of the LUAC in the Downes era was the concept of study groups. By the mid-1960s officers of the Soil Conservation Authority had undertaken detailed ecological surveys using a 'land system' approach, covering about half of the State of Victoria. These surveys formed the basis for published reports and interdepartmental inspections of regions under discussion.[58] The study group was an interdepartmental subcommittee that made recommendations directly to the LUAC, drawing heavily on those who had done ecological surveys.

On 19 April 1966 the Premier issued a new directive compelling the LUAC to evaluate all lands of the State for which information was available for potential new or alternative land uses.[59] Although this was directly contrary to the expressed wishes of the council itself, the study group mechanism made it possible to handle the extra work involved without losing any of the technical detail regarded as essential to providing the government with informed advice. Council members were quick to recognise that this was the way to develop a balanced picture of the areas under consideration. It also, incidentally, maintained a technical, scientific brief for the LUAC, shoring up the centrality of the Soil Conservation Authority and its specialist expertise. The Premier's letter made it clear that the LUAC's ongoing responsibility was to look towards further land development, echoing the views of the Commonwealth Rural Reconstruction Commission more than two decades earlier. The LUAC continued to be cautious about rushing into land development for its own sake, no doubt most strongly influenced by the soil conservation costs of such developments going wrong.

The LUAC and the Little Desert

The LUAC's efforts to resist taking responsibility for land development were dealt a further blow when the new Minister of Lands and Conservation appointed in 1967 turned out to be Sir William McDonald, the old adversary of Rocklands days. McDonald attended and chaired the first meeting of the LUAC after his appointment. At that meeting he praised the work of the LUAC's study groups because they 'allowed alienation of Crown Land to proceed on a proper basis'. He also signalled limits to the discretionary powers of the study group: it should advise on the use of which the land was capable and that to which it should be put. Economic considerations fell outside its brief. McDonald made it clear that he wanted 'Crown land [to] be put into production as soon as possible'.[60] He went on to chair eight further meetings of the LUAC, more than any previous minister had ever attended.

All seven meetings in 1968 were led by McDonald, who was determined that the Little Desert agricultural settlement scheme would succeed where Rocklands had failed. The Little Desert had been extensively examined by an LUAC study group that had begun its work at the time of the earlier AMP proposal to develop the area. After McDonald's appointment to the Lands portfolio, the study group's commitment to the evaluation of the Little Desert accelerated. It made its first major report at a meeting on 25 January 1968. Although 1969 was the year in which the general public heard most about the Little Desert, by March 1968 the LUAC had concluded its deliberations and turned to another controversial region, southwest Victoria, especially the proposal to develop Kentbruck Heath.

The author of the study group's formal report on the Little Desert to the LUAC was the Soil Conservation Authority's principal research officer, Frank Gibbons. Gibbons recalled that the council never released the study group's report, only an amended version of it that had been sanctioned by Sir William McDonald.[61] Even so, the LUAC's advice about the development of the Little Desert was that certain areas be reserved for national parks and wildlife reserves (in accordance with the recommendations made by the Wimmera Regional Committee in 1964), and that no alienation proceed until a full economic evaluation of the scheme had been undertaken.[62]

By the time the general public had begun to be concerned about the Little Desert scheme, Sir William McDonald had stopped attending meetings of the LUAC. The LUAC's minutes do not record discussion of the Little Desert area after March 1968, or of the Kentbruck Heath area after June 1968. The minutes of 1969 are brief and cryptic, until the last meeting, held on 26 November 1969, which records a directive from the Premier on 24 November 1969 disempowering the LUAC from making further comment on land-management decisions. Accordingly, the council resolved to 'disband all Study groups, notify all members accordingly, and thank them for the work done'.[63] The LUAC continued for another year with a much diminished brief, debating water catchment and plantation matters, and then lapsed.[64]

Bureaucrats and Posterity: the LUAC and History

The people involved with the Land Utilization Advisory Council were proud of its work. They subscribed to the notion of a bureaucrat as an impartial and rational guardian of the 'public interest',[65] and believed that the systems they had set up for the management of land through science were the most efficient possible. Although the individuals were content to be 'faceless' to some extent, they wanted the work of the council to be recognised by posterity. This was first expressed in early 1963 by Sir Ronald East, chairman of the State Rivers and Water Supply Commission, who commented that the LUAC had then been in operation for twelve years and that a comprehensive report on its activities 'would be of general interest to all concerned'.[66] Downes's pamphlet, *The Land Utilization Advisory Council: Its functions and responsibilities* (1966) was a response to this request, published at a time when the council's responsibilities were growing rapidly, and were clearly stepping beyond the bounds of bureaucratic liaison into public policy-making.

Downes recorded that the council provided 'a regular forum for the heads of land-use departments, not previously available', and described it as 'a unique government organisation in Australia and possibly the world'. The key to its success, Downes claimed, was 'the attitude of its members who consider problems put before them on the basis of what is best in the public interest and not their own departmental interests'.[67] The document was, of course, an internal assessment of the LUAC's role, very much designed to act as publicity for its current work rather than as a balanced evaluation of its history. The document made no attempt to review the LUAC's activities or to reconstruct its brief.

The LUAC was by definition top-heavy. Its members regarded themselves as experts in their fields, obviating the need for consultation with 'independent' experts from outside the public service. The club-like atmosphere precluded the possibility of public representation. The model of the 'Wisconsin idea', in which independent citizens (especially academics) contributed to policy-making processes, was not possible within the LUAC's framework.[68] There was even less chance that a non-technical representative would be consulted under Downes, with his strong preference for a narrow technical definition of the LUAC's brief. The council also had 'blind spots' even within its own terms: for example, there was no trained biologist until the end of 1966, when the director of Fisheries and Wildlife, Alfred Dunbavin Butcher, became a member.

The LUAC's closed decision-making processes had disadvantages, even for its participants. As the director of the Forests Commission, A. O. P. Lawrence, commented when he retired in 1969, the LUAC's 'work did not receive sufficient recognition'.[69] On the other hand, much of its success rested on its insularity and elite structure. The case of the Little Desert scheme tested its authority and apparently resulted in its demise. The Premier's withdrawal of its power to comment on public policy in 1969 was, ironically, perhaps the greatest tribute paid to its work.

7

Public Participation and New Bureaucracies

*The achievement of a political goal by an
interested group leads to claims for more of
the same kind of benefit and not to contentment. Only through symbolic reassurance that
'the state' recognizes the claims and status of
the group as legitimate is quiescence brought
about.*

Murray Edelman

The campaign for the Little Desert did not end when the proposal
for agricultural development was stopped, nor even with the unseating of the problem minister, Sir William McDonald, although
this was very important to conservation campaigners. The campaign
was not 'closed' until the protagonists had been satisfied that mechanisms were established that would give continuing legitimacy to
the various groups representing 'conservation' interests. Bureaucrats were prime movers in ensuring that new bureaucratic processes were part of the campaign closure. In the course of closing
the dispute, both the conservation lobby and the government set up
new bureaucracies.

The importance of formal co-operation between conservation
groups had been emphasised in broad terms in 1968 by a visiting
American wildlife biologist, Gustav Swanson, who commented in a
radio broadcast:

The shooter is just as interested in the preservation of natural
environment as the bushwalker or the national parks association.
All of these types of organizations should be banded together and

113

pooling their influence, for there are important decisions being made every day which concern the environment in which they are interested, and without unity they will not have the needed strength to influence these decisions.[1]

The broadcast was a commentary on the national rather than the State-level conservation movement but, for as long as national parks and natural resources in Australia continued to be administered on a state-by-state basis, it was the State conservation groups that were best positioned to respond. In the 1950s the Victorian National Parks Association had provided a forum for the interest groups Swanson mentioned, but with a focus specifically on national parks. The notion of decisions that concerned 'the environment' had a new breadth that was emerging only in the late 1960s. In Victoria the Little Desert was a case of a decision about 'the environment' because the campaigners concerned themselves politically with the processes of land-use planning as well as with their goal to reserve a national park.

The Conservation Council of Victoria

The Conservation Council of Victoria (CCV), since 1995 known as 'Environment Victoria', was founded in October 1969, and was a key instrument in 'closing' the dispute, in creating an official or legitimate forum through which the public could express concerns about conservation. The CCV was an outgrowth of the unofficial Save Our Bushlands Action Committee, the natural next step for campaigners who had witnessed the success of that committee and also the Western Victorian Field Naturalists' Clubs Association, where district field naturalists' clubs had joined forces in order to have 'a greater influence on those in authority'.[2]

    The CCV had a stronger awareness of bureaucratic practice than the single-issue or local action groups that preceded it. It was a centralising force, drawing regional issues to Melbourne. It was an advocacy group, distinct from groups such as the Field Naturalists' Club of Victoria (FNCV) and the Victorian National Parks

Association (VNPA) in that its sole purpose was political. It did not have the natural history or the bushwalking interests that were essential to the character of the other clubs.

The director of the Natural Resources Conservation League and former chairman of the Soil Conservation Authority, George Thompson, was the first convenor of the Save Our Bushlands Action Committee, and was one of the architects of the CCV. The CCV's charter reflected Thompson's expertise and bureaucratic understanding of the machinery of government. The CCV was to provide 'a single channel of communication for the exchange of views' for all levels of government, local, State and federal.[3] The political wisdom of a joint group to represent conservation concerns to government was clear: instead of multiple negotiations, politicians and government officials needed only to consult one group. That group would, in principle, provide 'expert' advice representative of the interests of its members.

The Natural Resources Conservation League was particularly influential in shaping the proposed umbrella conservation society. It put itself forward as an organisational model, suggesting 'The League of Victorian Conservation Societies' as one possible name.[4] The CCV was not an organisation of individual members but a collaboration of societies. In this sense it was like the NRCL, and unlike the other societies it represented.[5] The NRCL took responsibility for the CCV's first secretariat. Lewis Godfrey, a former Supervisor of School Forestry, was seconded from the NRCL staff to undertake the duties of secretary to the CCV. The NRCL also provided the new organisation with office space and basic administrative facilities. As a result, the way the CCV operated for its first five years was to some extent dictated by the NRCL's mode of operation.[6] The NRCL also provided the CCV with regular space in its quarterly publication, *Victoria's Resources*, until 1980, when the CCV established its own publications and sought to distance itself from a magazine that had accepted sponsorship from mining interest groups.[7]

The CCV created a new level of hierarchy in government negotiations, a typically bureaucratic solution to a communication problem. In this sense, the CCV was the conservation lobby's own bureaucracy. On the subject of the Little Desert, conservationists of various persuasions had been united, thus providing a moment in which a joint umbrella group made philosophical as well as political sense. The bureaucrats (especially those in the NRCL) seized the opportunity to create the CCV and its new level of hierarchy, and in so doing they somewhat disenfranchised the traditional lobby groups of the natural history societies, though they did this with the support and encouragement of both the FNCV and the VNPA.

It is an indication of the fervour inspired by the Little Desert dispute that the concept of a unified group encountered no recorded dissent in 1969–70. The blending of conservation voices into a 'united political front' disguised diverse cultural and pragmatic perspectives. The singular reconstruction of the conservation lobby vested considerable power in the hands of conservation 'experts', particularly retired bureaucrats and resource managers, and a few university scientists. The quasi-professionalisation of the conservation movement occurred at some cost to the conservation interest groups concerned with issues for which power mechanisms were poorly defined (for example, wilderness preservation), or 'junior' in the bureaucratic hierarchy (for example, national parks). These 'dissatisfied elements' emerged later, creating serious tension within the CCV by the mid-1970s.

The Establishment of the Land Conservation Council

When the Little Desert scheme was shelved in December 1969, Sir William McDonald promised legislation for a new Land Resources Council.[8] Many conservationists were sceptical about this, especially those with links to government bureaucracies. The CSIRO scientist and editor of *Victoria's Resources*, Sibley Elliott, summarised the fears of many conservationists when he wrote:

> Will this really be a new era? Has Victoria, for example, entered a commitment of genuine, unbiased planning for the wisest long-term use of land as yet unalienated? Will the Land Resources Bill at

"An Inseparable Trinity"

In the 1940s Royal Commissioner Stretton's words, 'an inseparable trinity', became the language of the Save the Forests Campaign (NRCL Archives)

Agricultural Botany students investigating biological diversity, Little Desert, 1969

The 'McDonald Highway': a track bulldozed for the Little Desert Settlement Scheme. This photograph was part of the Little Desert: Conservation Victory *exhibition displayed in the School of Botany, University of Melbourne, 1970.*

present before the Victorian Parliament . . . really achieve what conservationists want, or will it supplant an existing potentially valuable Land Utilization Advisory Council with a potentially impotent Land Resources Council?[9]

The proposed Land Resources Council was to comprise eleven members, no more than five of whom could be government employees. McDonald appears to have been determined to punish the bureaucrats of the LUAC for failing to support him. The McDonald legislation was before parliament in March 1970, but the opposition parties used their majority in the upper house to block it. Opposition to the Land Resources Council was given strength and credibility through the well-timed release of the condemnatory report of J. W. Galbally's Select Committee into the Little Desert Settlement Scheme. It was obvious that the Galbally report was a political document, crafted by opposition forces to discredit the McDonald scheme, but it had amassed a large amount of data to this end. The Land Resources Bill was lost and the Bolte government turned its energies to the coming May election.

When Sir William McDonald lost his seat in that election, the government was freed—even obliged—to negotiate afresh with conservationists. In accordance with the Premier's election promises, a new round of consultations began. The Bill that formed the basis for the Land Conservation Act was drafted after extensive and explicit consultation with conservationists, especially those associated with the CCV.

The conservationists suddenly found themselves needing negotiating skills to work with a sympathetic government, rather than exercising their talents to 'whip up media fervour' in opposing an intransigent and autocratic minister. Gwen Piper, a conservationist active in the negotiations for the Land Conservation Bill, commented that she 'liked the business approach of the politicians'.[10] She was concerned that the conservationists by contrast were 'long-winded' and lacked 'conciseness of thought and speech'. Suddenly the ability to sway a crowd, or to express an emotional response, had become inappropriate, time-consuming and counterproductive. A different style of campaigner was needed, one who, in Piper's words, could 'research well and present our opinions systematically and concisely'.

Part of the problem for many conservationists was that most of their public speaking was to like-minded people, people who were happy to indulge speakers with more time than was strictly needed to make their point. The Field Naturalists' Club meetings, for example, were generally long, with many speakers making comments. Such a meeting style was undoubtedly democratic, but not 'business-like'. There was also an element of the sermon about many conservationists' speeches. The moral imperative of conservation would drive the speaker to quasi-religious rhetoric. Piper's delight in the fresh 'business' approach of the politicians was no doubt a reaction to sitting through some rather evangelical conservation meetings.

The ideal representative of conservation became one who knew how to 'do business' with bureaucrats. This accounts for the selection of Lawrence, the former Chief Commissioner of Forests, as the CCV's inaugural president. Lawrence retired from his official position in July 1969 and took up the job of CCV president the following October. The Forests Commission was already unpopular with many conservationists, especially those concerned about the Lower Glenelg National Park, where the Forests Commission was proposing to establish pine plantations. The appointment of the former Chief Commissioner to this key conservation job provides insight into the power relations between the various groups that joined forces to establish the CCV in 1969. It is strong evidence that the conservation movement in Victoria, despite various qualms about particular issues, still regarded forestry officials as 'on the side of conservation'—perhaps because of the significant conservation work done by Bill Middleton, the local forester for the Little Desert region. It is interesting to note too that when the CCV received some small government grants, these were administered through the Forests Commission.[11] The Kentbruck Heath activists, especially Fred Davies, had expressed concern about the cavalier forestry practices that were causing erosion on the banks of the Glenelg River, but broader criticisms of forestry practices emerged later.

The first challenge the CCV set itself was to ensure that the legislation for a Land Conservation Council was drafted in such a way that conservation was properly represented along with other resource interest groups. This negotiation process was perceived by conservationists at the time as a resounding success. The final legislation provided for a twelve-member Land Conservation Council, including two members representing conservation interests.

W. A. Borthwick's Vision for the Land Conservation Council

The new Minister of Lands, Bill Borthwick, was keen to show just how different he was from his predecessor, both in vision and in style. Whereas McDonald felt obliged to pursue the development ethic to its limits, Borthwick's Land Conservation Council was constituted to provide advice on land usage in Victoria in the post-pioneering era.[12] Borthwick recognised the plurality of the demands on land, and did not rate agricultural development above all other interests, as McDonald had done. The LCC's charter was explicitly tailored to cope with the conflicting demands of different interest groups through consensus and discussion rather than through autocratic decree. The legislation for the Land Conservation Council was the first plank in a new political platform based on pluralism and 'values planning'.[13] In the period between 1970 and 1973 this platform expanded to include a (senior) Ministry for Conservation, a Ministry for Planning and an Environment Protection Authority (EPA).[14]

In introducing the Land Conservation Bill, Borthwick explicitly named science as a critical value system on which his vision depended: 'The important task of land use decision making should become less of a political and parochial wrangle, and more of a scientific assessment and decision'.[15] Borthwick recognised science as an acceptable common ground for people of vastly different persuasions. Science was crucial to his pluralist vision for land-use management, and he applied it to the broadest possible range of conservation values. In his first overseas trip to look at conservation issues in 1973, he was impressed by what he dubbed a 'total department of natural resources' in Michigan. He wanted to create the opportunities for 'a multidisciplinary approach to resource management' in Victoria. 'If it was a fish problem, it wasn't just the fish fellows that stood around and debated it . . . the soil farmers had their say, the foresters had their say'.[16] Borthwick saw the approach as vital not only to the LCC, but also to the EPA, and indeed to all 'conservation'.

The term 'conservation' was chosen carefully because of its multiplicity of meanings, and was specifically contrasted with 'preservation'.[17] Borthwick was keen to distance himself from the view that 'conservation was national parks'.[18] The LCC regarded its task as 'resource allocation' rather than 'conservation' or 'preservation'. In some cases, the LCC's processes resulted in the alienation of land that would otherwise have remained in public ownership.[19] The LCC was required to assess and balance 'community land needs'—terms that allowed for a range of interpretations.

The Independent Chair

The crucial difference between the Borthwick model for the LCC and earlier models was that the new organisation was to be chaired by an 'outsider', someone independent of all government bureaucracies who could therefore find that elusive balance between their needs. If McDonald's proposal for a Land Resources Council had been passed, it would have been chaired by a nominee of the Secretary of Lands.[20] Downes actively sought to have the chairman of the Soil Conservation Authority continue to chair the LUAC's successor. He was particularly opposed to the appointment of an independent chair: 'Although this sounded nice politically, in his opinion the present Chairman had no vested interest in the use of land for any particular purpose and could be therefore said to be independent'.[21]

While it was understandable that Downes would not want a McDonald 'plant' nominated by the Secretary of Lands chairing the council, his personal investment in the LUAC over the previous ten years blinded him to the virtues of a chair who came from outside the bureaucracy. The proposed independent chair harked back to Judge Stretton's 1940s vision for 'extradepartmental' representation to keep the deliberations above simple horse-trading, but it went further, offering the main leadership position to an outsider.

The new Land Conservation Council, as it was finally constituted in 1971 under the independent chair of Mr Sam Dimmick, was closer to Stretton's proposed body than the LUAC. The LCC was able to adopt and expand the scientific process pioneered by the LUAC through its study groups, but the LCC's administrative model was entirely different. After the politics of the Little Desert dispute, natural resources and land-use policy-making were not just matters of sound scientific assessments, but also required demonstrable public accountability. The independent chair gave the LCC a distance from government and government departments that was essential to its political credibility.

The first chairman of the LCC, from 1971 to 1984, was Samuel G. McL. Dimmick (1922–84) BA, B.Com., Dip. Soc. Stud., who came to the position from outside the Victorian public service. Dimmick had a strong background in international relations, having been warden of International House at the University of Melbourne (1960–71) and Australian cultural attaché to Jakarta (1956–59), but he had no formal qualifications in science or land management. He was regarded, however, as formidable and effective in setting up networks within the various bureaucracies to ensure that the LCC could fulfil its charter.

John Turner, a member of the first LCC, commented that Henry Bolte chose Dimmick as a good organiser of people, and someone who could be regarded as 'neutral' on conservation claims. Turner went on to remark that within a relatively short time Dimmick developed considerable interest in and sympathy for the conservationist position in land management.[22] Dimmick was proud of his independence from all conservationist positions.[23] Although senior bureaucrats were initially unhappy about the appointment of an outsider to chair the LCC, they quickly learnt to work effectively with Dimmick. After his death, the chair of the LCC was filled in 1985 by David Scott, BA, a senior minister of religion with experience in a broad range of community work, who, like Dimmick, brought outstanding organisational skills to the LCC chair. Scott was also like Dimmick in having no formal qualifications in science or land management. The third chair, Don Saunders, appointed in 1994, was the first to have 'conservation qualifications', coming to the job with experience as head of the National Parks Service.

Public Representation

Borthwick's design for the LCC responded to the concern about 'public consultation', both in the conservation lobby and in the wider electorate. As part of this, two LCC members were appointed to represent conservation interests, although the conservation lobby was not given absolute power to elect its representatives. The Act specified that the two be appointed by the Governor in Council (in effect, the Premier) from a panel of five names submitted by the CCV. This protected the government of the day to some extent from having 'unsuitable' or politically unpalatable LCC members foisted on it.[24]

The other 'outsider' appointed to the LCC in 1971 was 'a person with experience in the conservation techniques used in developing land for primary production', who was appointed directly by the Governor in Council. This position was filled by the LCC's longest-serving member, Claude N. Austin, who remained in the position from the establishment of the LCC until his retirement in March 1987. Austin's initial appointment was regarded particularly favourably by members of natural history societies, because in addition to his knowledge of primary production, he was known as an ornithologist and an active campaigner for the preservation of both the Little Desert and Kentbruck heathland.[25] In effect, the Little Desert campaigners felt that they had three representatives on the LCC.

The scope for outside representation on the LCC gave its structure more flexibility than a council comprised entirely of heads of government departments could achieve. For example, Joan Lindros became the first female member of the LCC in 1979 and served until 1983, at a time when all the *ex officio* positions were filled by men because of the male-dominated structure of the Victorian public service. The flexibility provided by the 'outsider' category also allowed the LCC to adjust its membership to accommodate new interest groups such as industry and commerce (from 1981) and local government (from 1990) without altering its fundamental structure and procedures. The local government representative was appointed by the Governor in Council from a panel of

three names submitted by the Municipal Association of Victoria—
that is, the opportunity for community input into the selection was
similar to that for the nomination of conservation representatives.

Community Criticism of the LCC

The arrangements for election of 'conservation representatives' to
the LCC worked well for as long as the community had faith in the
CCV's choice of members, but in 1979 the geographer David
Mercer mounted an attack on the LCC's methods, describing its
work as 'shrouded in tight-lipped bureaucratic secrecy' 'notwith-
standing the veneer of public consultation'.[26] An examination of his
critique, which focused on land use in the Victorian alpine region,
reveals that the problem lay less in the LCC's methods than in the
fact that the CCV (and its 'older-style' representatives on the LCC)
no longer represented 'the views of the more politically active
younger conservationists of the state'. The Mercer critique was
a thinly veiled attack on the CCV as a community conservation
bureaucracy. All the flexibilities that Borthwick had engineered into
the design of the LCC became problems for Mercer because of what
he saw as poor representation of environmental interests.

The design of the LCC, which had worked so well with a
unified conservation lobby, failed to win the confidence of the new
radical environmentalist lobby of the late 1970s. The mutualism of
the LCC and the CCV was exposed in this critique as a problem for
the 'new' conservation lobby, a problem the CCV resolved to some
extent in 1979 by unceremoniously dumping John Turner and John
Landy and replacing them by nominees deemed to be more acceptable to the new movement: Bill Holsworth, a biologist, and Joan
Lindros, a pharmacist. The CCV wanted representatives more
prepared to keep it abreast of LCC developments, and felt Turner
and Landy added to the 'secrecy' by making executive decisions
without consulting the CCV regularly enough.[27]

The purge of the CCV nominees was perhaps necessary to
separate the conservation lobby more clearly from government. The
two bureaucracies born almost simultaneously in the turbulent
times of the Little Desert dispute needed to be separated, seen to be

representative of different ends, for each to function effectively. It should be noted that this separation was probably not a 'debureaucratisation' of the conservation lobby, but rather a takeover by the next, more radical generation of bureaucrats. Mercer states that his stinging critique relied 'quite strongly on information provided by anonymous past and present public servants as well as the "official line" [Land] Conservation Council documents'.[28]

The call for more public accountability and procedural openness was taken up by the CCV in the early 1980s under the leadership of its director, Geoff Wescott. The CCV also co-published an attack on the LCC by Gerard McPhee, president of the Federation of Victorian Walking Clubs.[29] This occurred at a time when there was great antagonism towards the Forests Commission of Victoria on the part of both the CCV and its co-publisher, the Native Forests Action Council. McPhee portrayed the LCC as the servant of the Forests Commission, and used a hypothetical example to show how the commission could potentially misuse its power and capitalise on the LCC's closed, cabinet-style decision-making processes.[30]

The LCC's annual reports reveal that it realised its public accountability was fundamental to its credibility, and took the criticisms of Mercer and the CCV seriously.[31] From the 1983/84 report onwards there was an explicit statement of 'Procedures Followed By Council' and a section on public participation.[32] That annual report also contained an appendix on public sources of information used by the LCC in its deliberations. From 1985 to 1990 the annual reports also included the number of Freedom of Information requests received by the LCC.[33]

The LCC could never entirely fulfil all possible public interest needs, but its flexibility of membership and regular elections allowed it to move with shifting public opinion. Its processes also allowed public submissions to be made at two different stages. The participants in the Little Desert dispute, land managers and members of the public alike, indicated a general satisfaction with the LCC.[34] Even those who disagreed with its recommendations on particular issues indicated satisfaction with the processes it used to reach its decisions. The LCC's design generally brought 'quiescence' to the 1960s conservation lobby in exactly the terms expressed by Edelman in the quotation at the head of this chapter. Later environmentalists expressed dissatisfaction with the LCC, but even the most radical were generally willing to participate in its processes.

Industry Criticism of the LCC

The LCC also received criticism from non-conservationist interest groups. Such criticism often focused, at least overtly, on the values the LCC processes omitted rather than on the effectiveness of the processes themselves. In a mid-1970s paper on forest-use conflicts, J. B. Dargavel and I. S. Ferguson, both foresters, were critical of the omission of economic data from the LCC's processes.[35] They advocated the use of cost-benefit analysis and other conventional economic techniques as a 'salutary discipline upon the planner'. They sought the economic quantification of supply and demand, as 'a more objective and consistent basis for choice . . . and an essential component of rational planning'.[36] Their fellow forester, John Taylor, a research officer for the LCC, had anticipated this type of criticism and noted that the use of economic techniques to calculate 'net social benefit' was limited by the 'number of intangible values which the Council must consider and the lack of data and time'.[37] Reading between the lines, one can only assume that the introduction of cost-benefit analyses would have been a decided advantage to the forest industries interest group, and would have reduced the credibility of the LCC with the 'quality of life' and conservationist interest groups, whose concerns were less easily quantifiable.

In 1981 the LCC's membership was expanded to include an additional outsider 'with experience in industry and commerce', a move that went some way towards recognising the needs of industry. Later the LCC took to commissioning economic studies of the value of public land, including the economic and employment consequences of proposed changes in land use. According to its chairman, David Scott, the LCC favoured using new economic models that assessed 'the money values of non-economic characteristics of parks, conservation areas, landscapes and waterways'. Scott also maintained that 'cash values are guides and not the final determinants of how land is to be used or conserved'.[38] The centrepiece of the council's work was its broadly based and non-quantitative paradigm of decision-making through negotiation and consultation.

Bureaucratic Criticism of the LCC: the Bland Report

In 1974, a few years after the LCC was founded, it was the target of a powerful attack by a senior federal public servant, Sir Henry Bland, who had been commissioned to head a Board of Inquiry into the Victorian Public Service. In the course of its review, the board came to the conclusion that 'the organizational and administrative arrangements relating to conservation, environmental and land-use planning matters were unsatisfactory'—so unsatisfactory that a fifty-page report was devoted exclusively to this section of the public service.[39]

Bland's report focused on what he perceived as inefficiency in the functional division between the management and planning of land in Victoria. It criticised the 'fragmentation of activity among agencies' and expressed the view that 'extensive powers and a high degree of independence were given some agencies and they were not conceived in any broad conceptual framework'.[40] In a recommendation that foreshadowed the amalgamation of the various natural resources and Lands departments in the 1980s, Bland recommended that all such agencies be housed under one roof to facilitate the sharing of resources.

In Bland's eyes, the LCC was a powerful and independent agency whose work duplicated that of others. His report noted that the Land Conservation Act, which created the LCC, was one of twenty-seven pieces of legislation bearing on conservation, environment protection and land-use planning.[41] Bland made the criticism that the legislation in this area was piecemeal, and that this led to issues in these fields being the responsibility of several agencies. The division between management and planning was 'inefficient', and although the LCC was acting as a co-ordinating body, its brief did not cover 'agencies operating under the Town and Country Planning Act', that is, those that dealt with private land.[42]

An *Age* editorial described the Bland report as 'a blueprint for some very good bureaucracy and some potentially bad conservation'. The *Age* was particularly critical of any threat to the LCC, which it perceived as necessary to prevent further 'debacles' like the Little Desert scheme.[43] In a sense, 'defending the Little Desert' had become defending the principles of land-use planning established the wake of that dispute. In defence of its position, the LCC argued that there was value in its being housed away from the Ministry of Conservation: as 'an independent body reporting to the Minister', the LCC required staff who were 'objective and not influenced by too close an association with the Ministry of Conservation'.[44] Furthermore, Dimmick, the LCC's chairman, sought the power to make 'more appointments from outside the [Victorian Public] Service, particularly in the case of scientific officers', as the number of trained land-use planners within the Victorian Public Service was very limited, with 'most of those being found in the Forest [sic] Commission'.[45]

Although Bland was not a Victorian public servant, he was an experienced bureaucrat. His vision for the organisation of conservation agencies within the State was very much a public service insider's view, concerned with maximising efficiencies and minimising interference from outsiders. Dimmick, by contrast, was well aware of the limitations of the resources at his disposal within the public service, and sought access to more outsiders (like himself) who could bring to the LCC new skills, especially in ecology and other scientific fields, and would also enhance its credibility as an independent body.

The LCC also argued that the concept of amalgamating the resources devoted to public and private land-use planning through closer liaison with the Town and Country Planning Board, although apparently structurally efficient, was not particularly helpful in a climate where the critical and time-consuming issues concerned public land. The proposal for an alpine national park and the forestry practice of clear-felling were among the issues attracting attention and discussion.[46] The LCC argued that there were considerable efficiencies in directing the LCC's limited resources to the key public land issues of the day rather than covering all land 'even-handedly'.

Bland was, in many ways, correct. The land-use management and planning agencies of the State had an organisational structure that had grown up ad hoc over a legislative period of more than a hundred years. His vision for the land-use planning agencies, however, was at odds with what government and indeed the bureaucracies themselves wanted. It failed to come to grips with the genuine desire for pluralism and public consultation that was so important both to the Minister for Conservation, Bill Borthwick, and the Premier, Dick Hamer. Bland had underestimated public servants' personal loyalty to their own departments and agencies. As Dimmick observed, 'many officers have no desire to move from one department to another'; and, he added, 'the idea that a person has to move from the office to achieve promotion is . . . inefficient and wasteful of experience and training'.[47] Borthwick and many of the bureaucrats had a personal stake in both the LCC and the Ministry for Conservation, which had only just been established at the time of the Bland review.[48] Both were predicated on 'the concept of understanding the resources available to the community and of making the best possible use of those resources for the benefit of present and future communities'.[49] The conservation community, through the CCV, also expressed opposition to the Bland report.[50]

It was unlikely that the LCC would be abolished or the Ministry for Conservation substantially restructured while Borthwick was minister. Within a matter of weeks, the Premier reassured the people of Victoria that the LCC would go ahead with its important work 'at full blast'.[51] The government passed legislation amending minor details such as extending the role of the National Parks Service to manage other types of parks 'where recreation, education, preservation of historical features or some other activity may be the primary use'.[52] It staunchly defended the LCC as 'one government organisation that everyone looks up to', and described it as 'the envy of every state in Australia'.[53]

Yet the Bland report continued to have repercussions long after it was presented. It was Bland who first proposed a 'superministry', a Department for Conservation and the Environment, a form of which was picked up by Labor in government and implemented in 1983. Successive Victorian governments have agreed that the organisation of conservation, environmental concerns and land-use planning needed streamlining. The 1980s and 1990s have seen massive amalgamations and restructuring of these bureaucracies and their reporting relations with ministers. There have been so many organisational and structural changes that at times staff have found it difficult to do their routine work. In the wake of yet another management restructure, one wag dubbed the DCNR (Department of Conservation and Natural Resources, established October 1992) 'the Department of Constant Name Readjustment'. At the time of writing, its name was Department of Natural Resources and Environment.[54]

Bland had suggested that the government establish a Commission for Conservation, the Environment and Land-Use Planning to subsume the role of the LCC and several other agencies. He had also recommended that provision be made for 'public involvement in the final determination of environment protection policy proposed by the Commission'.[55] This was never implemented, perhaps because Bland's concept of 'refining controversy'[56] was so different from Borthwick's notion of negotiation based on partnership between government and the wider community. The only immediate effect of the Bland report was that the LCC's annual reports from the mid-1970s onward included a one-line reference to its consultation and co-operation with the Town and Country Planning Authority. Even without major bureaucratic reshuffles, it took twenty-two years to review land use in Victoria region by region, a task that had initially been expected to take about five years.

The Little Desert was part of one of the last regions to be surveyed by the LCC. A number of issues arose in the time before the LCC had begun its evaluation, including fire control, army manoeuvres and a proposal to subdivide 3200 acres near Kaniva into fifty-acre holiday-home blocks.[57] Each of these issues caused the government of the day some passing embarrassment, but all were resolved in a way that did not pre-empt the LCC's deliberations. The faith that the activists of 1969 placed in the LCC was finally realised in 1988, when the national park was declared.

The LCC Survey Processes

The State was surveyed on a region-by-region basis, but the LCC also had the power to initiate reviews of its earlier work (which it did, for example, in relation to the alpine region). When its regional work was nearing completion, the council extended its brief beyond 'lands' to consider rivers, the marine and coastal environments, and various key ecosystems, including box–ironbark woodlands.

Advocates promoted the LCC's processes as progressive, flexible and more cost-effective than the approaches adopted in other States. While Victoria has had many disputes over public land use, they were resolved through negotiation and public consultation, giving a maximum of certainty with a minimum of conflict and cost, according to David Scott. Conflict was minimised by publishing a descriptive report on the region under consideration that in turn 'sets the scene and also the tone of the ensuing debate'.[58] The principal disadvantage of such extensive consultation is that it is time-consuming.

The LCC process allowed for public comment, submissions and lobbying at two stages: following a descriptive report of the area or ecosystem concerned, then following the publication of a set of proposed recommendations. By the time the final recommendations went to Parliament, they had thus already taken into account two rounds of negotiation with the general public and interest groups. Furthermore, all LCC publications—descriptive reports, proposed recommendations and final recommendations— were available very cheaply to interested parties. Even after recommendations went to Parliament it was generally some time before legislation was enacted, so there was space for further direct lobbying of the government after the LCC's processes were completed. Democracy was well served by the openness of the process. There was, however, a vulnerability in the system: in the interval between the LCC's published final recommendations and the legislation, it was possible for individuals or organisations to engage in 'asset stripping' (for example, logging or mining) without legal penalty, something that deeply concerned many in the conservation community.

One of the incidental side-effects of the LCC processes was that they sometimes provoked the emergence of an organised sectional opposition. An example was the Grampians Fringe Dwellers' Association, which was formed at the time of the LCC's deliberations on a proposal to make the Grampians into a national park.[59] The Mountain District Cattlemen's Association of Victoria, established in November 1969, also deliberately opposed itself to urban environmentalists seeking an alpine national park, and achieved media attention with its conspicuous and vociferous opposition to the LCC's recommendations.[60] Such groups appear to contradict Scott's claim that the 'consultative advisory process is enlightening and educative rather than polarising and constricting'.[61] Throughout all opposition, however, the LCC maintained control over the agenda to be disputed, and this in itself facilitated the possibility of negotiation.

Scott noted that 'visitors from Canada, the United States, the United Kingdom, and other Australian states . . . commented on the uniqueness of the process'.[62] The public participation elements of the LCC conformed to models that are described as desirable in recent literature. For example, in a different context, the American sociologist of science Sheldon Krimsky advocated in 1984 that the head of a government agency 'could request nominations of individuals from the important constituencies involved . . . [to] ensure that the interests of key populations are represented in the policy process—that is, if the agency director actually selects advisers from the list of suggested names'.[63] Krimsky saw this as part of the process necessary under the National Environmental Policy Act (1969), which required government agencies to 'avail themselves of commentary from various sectors of society on their policies before final decisions are made'.[64]

As David Scott observed, the final decisions to be made about appropriateness of land use are 'political, and must be made by elected governments'.[65] Whether such decisions are acceptable and accepted, however, depends on the public consultation involved in the advisory process. The LCC model for a balanced vision in land and natural resource uses was very successful. Over the twenty-seven years from its foundation until its sudden demise in June 1997, 96 per cent of its recommendations were accepted by the government of the day.[66]

The Environment Conservation Council

In 1997, without consulting the community or the bureaucracy, the Kennett government replaced the LCC with a new Environment Conservation Council (ECC). It remains to be seen how this body will be received. Will it cost the State more in the long run to abolish its independent arbiter of decisions on land use and environmental management? Under the 1997 legislation, only the government can initiate and pursue a long-term review, but it is not clear that the new council can do more than produce environmental effects statements on development proposals. The Environment Conservation Council will therefore be driven by proposals to 'use and develop'. The government appears to have legislated to take over a function for which developers have traditionally footed the bill, while abandoning its commitment to a holistic public State plan.

The LCC comprised both professionally qualified public servants representing different land uses and non-government members with specific expertise. The ECC, by contrast, consists of only three members 'appointed by the Governor in Council on the recommendation of the Minister'.[67] None of them are necessarily public servants; they are merely required to have 'the experience and knowledge necessary to enable the Council to carry out its functions'.[68] The capacity for the public to advise the minister in the choice of members was abandoned without notice.

Both in the environment movement and in the corridors of bureaucracy, there had been dissatisfaction with the structure of LCC membership. Because of the extensive restructuring of the public service in the 1990s, many *ex officio* positions specified under the old Land Conservation Act no longer made sense. Nevertheless, the decision to use the restructurings to abolish the idea of *ex officio* positions, and simultaneously to dismantle the mechanisms for public participation, created a body without credibility either within the public service or in the environment movement.

The new structure vested enormous power in the minister, eliminated the institutional memory of the public service and reduced public input. The Environment Conservation Council Act offered an open period of only 60 days (instead of a total of 120 days) for public comment and eliminated the important 'draft recommendation stage' that had kept the public informed of LCC processes.[69] Even more seriously, the ECC was not granted an independent budget. The chairperson was required to argue for resources on a case-by-case basis with the Director-General of the Department of Natural Resources and Environment (or its equivalent), and had to specify all expenses in advance of the investigation in question.[70] This would inevitably compromise the council's work.

The lessons of the Little Desert dispute have already been relegated to 'history', yet the question of the quality of democracy is not going to go away. Under the Environment Conservation Council Act, it is again possible for an autocratic minister to impose an unworkable scheme on the Victorian public. Even the fact that there was no opportunity to debate the ECC legislation was sinister. The members of the existing LCC were simply told at their meeting on 1 May 1997 that an Environment Conservation Council Bill had been initiated in the Legislative Assembly the day before and that the LCC would cease to exist from 30 June. Similarly, Environment Victoria, the successor to the CCV, was not consulted before the tabling of the Bill.[71] The community groups that had given time and energy to make nominations and submissions to the LCC were given one day's notice of the legislation. While the environment lobby had not always been satisfied with LCC decisions, it had recognised the value of the process, and had invested enormous, often voluntary expertise in making it work. If the ECC is perceived as only being interested in the environment in so far as the latest development scheme requires it to be, the environment lobby will inevitably resort to more confrontational ways of making its views heard, to the cost of all Victorians.

8

Conservation and Environmentalism

When the history of conservation in Australia comes to be written I am quite certain that the twelve month period to June 30 1970 ... will be viewed as a most significant one in the gradual evolution of new attitudes by Australians to their environment.

Sir Garfield Barwick

In Australia the five-year period from 1968 to 1973 embraced a significant change in self-perception. The nation moved from the height of a national minerals boom to the depths of an international petroleum crisis. These events dramatically affected the perception of the role of conservation. In 1968 Francis Ratcliffe wrote of the boom-time development fever and bemoaned the fact that 'any suggestion of restraint, or request for second thoughts on some local development guaranteed to provide a quick and sure economic pay-off, is only too easily brushed aside as unrealistic or even unpatriotic'.[1] It was assumed that patriotism and development were synonymous. Conservation was not part of nationhood.

Five years later the *Sydney Morning Herald*'s finance and business page carried the comment that 'virtually all the leases held by Mineral Deposits Ltd are threatened by conservationists'.[2] The financial sector still perceived development as essential, but conservation was no longer marginal. Establishment forces were adopting a siege mentality in the face of emerging environmentalism. Conservationists too were changed by these external events and came to eschew the co-operative tactics used by their predecessors of the 1950s and 1960s. Their political power and the centrality of their cause gave them confidence to adopt the confrontational stance characterised as radical environmentalism.[3]

Ratcliffe's document spoke of conservation as one of the three 'important issues facing the human race today'. The others were 'an atomic world war' and 'the need for *Homo sapiens* to find a way of living harmoniously in dense multi-racial communities, to which his ancestral behaviour patterns do not help him adapt'.[4] Ratcliffe argued that conservation should be based on a reconciliation between what he called 'economic conservation' and 'nature conservation'. It should include the wise use of economically important natural resources and the preservation of 'the less tangible things . . . for a full and satisfying life', including wildlife and the natural beauty of the landscape.

This document, written before the world had come to hear terms like 'green' and 'environmentalism', espoused exactly the same agenda as those 1970s movements. What dates it to the 1960s is the choice of vocabulary and the separation of the issues. Environmentalism forced those issues together under the umbrella term 'green'. Green issues included global destruction (as in the nuclear debates of the 1970s and the greenhouse debates of the 1980s and 1990s), urban living (with concurrent concern for multi-culturalism, heritage and urban space preservation) and 'wilderness' (or perhaps more generally 'escape from urban living', which includes rural and pastoral sensibilities), but they merged and blended, at least loosely, because the word 'green' bracketed them together.

In the 1990s concerns for 'environmental justice' also became part of the 'green' agenda. The lineage of these issues can be traced to older concerns about global destruction and urban living, but the political ripples from the renaissance of indigenous cultures created more complex, less ecologically 'pure' forms of environmental management. Internationally, threats to indigenous lifestyles posed by rainforest destruction and the deteriorating quality of air, water and land in traditionally poor industrial zones were brought together under the banner of 'environmental justice'. In Australia, the 'green' and the 'black' began to negotiate shared ground as the movement for Aboriginal land rights gathered pace in the wake of the Mabo judgment.

In terms of ecological consciousness, Ratcliffe's biological turn of phrase was ahead of its time. While clearly concerned with the quality of *human* life, he overtly recognised the place of other species in nature, and the role of the natural in human life. This is very different from the 'engineering' model that concerned itself with 'Man's Role in Changing the Face of the Earth', or 'Man, the Earth and Tomorrow' (to use the titles of two well-known books of the 1950s and 1960s). The concern with humans in nature has tended to lead away from technical solutions to problems, and toward new ways of living and cultural critiques. The ecological critique that had emerged and established itself in Australia by the mid-1970s was indeed deeply 'subversive'.[5] But, had Ratcliffe lived a little longer (he died at the end of 1970), he would have been comfortable with many of its values, though perhaps would have preferred science to have a more positive and central role.

In the late 1960s the conservation movement did not yet offer a new cultural critique, a new 'factor' to be added to the analysis of the issues of the day. There was some consensus that 'science' should guide conservation decisions, and that economic factors were also crucial, in the tradition of scientific utilitarianism. The social and political dimensions of conservation were recognised, but were seen as subordinate to science and economics. 'Nature' was not itself a factor, but rather was treated as something passive, caught in the cross-fire between advocates of the economic, the social and the political. The conservation movement, following Rachel Carson's lead with *Silent Spring*, was just beginning to come to terms with 'techno-pessimism', the view that not all conservation problems were amenable to a technical 'quick fix'. Herein lay the beginning of the suggestion that the existing regimes of knowledge in science and technology were built on values that were not entirely acceptable to 'conservationists'.

Judith Wright, a distinguished poet and an activist with the Wildlife Preservation Society of Australia, wrote in 1969:

> Nature is much to wreck, but man can do it
> (his last and greatest proof of power and will)
> and, part of what we ruin, we shall rue it
> Yes, man can do it, and he is doing it.
> Not only as proof of his power
> and his will, but as a by-result
> of his will to power . . .
> He too often seems through ignorance and greed
> to end up making the world, for us all
> . . . more perilous.
> And poorer.
> And uglier.[6]

Wright does not quite suggest a new world-view here, but certainly questions the old one. Her poetry reflects a loss of faith in the conservation 'solutions' of the day.

The politicians' sudden discovery of environmental concerns—from Henry Bolte's inclusion of 'conservation' in his election speech of May 1970 to US President Nixon's declaration on 22 April 1970 that the 1970s were to be 'the decade of the environment'—was a sign that 'something that had been happening for a long time suddenly became highly visible'. Almost simultaneously, Bolte, Nixon and other politicians throughout the Western world began to pay serious lip-service to the environment because of the efforts of the campaigners of the 1960s and earlier. The full cultural critique offered by environmentalism, however, is still emerging. The baby-boomer generation did not invent environmentalism, nor will they have the last word on it. As Neil Evernden has commented, there is 'no assurance that even such reforms as have occurred will long endure if economic indicators seem to point elsewhere'.[7] Most environmentalists are not on the radical fringe. The moderates or 'light greens' of the late 1990s have been slow to challenge the ascendancy of deregulationist rhetoric and a global 'free market' regime that is fundamentally at odds with the preservation of the earth.[8] The rest of this chapter examines some of the tensions and links between conservation and environmentalism, and considers historical continuities and discontinuities between them.

The 'Watershed' of the Little Desert

The activists of 1969 were unanimous in their delight about saving the Little Desert. They gloried in their new-found political power, in unseating the Minister for Lands and winning a place for conservation views at the negotiating table of the new Land Conservation Council. They were also delighted and perhaps a little surprised at their own unanimity. Philosophically and politically, those who joined forces to work for the Little Desert cause came from very different backgrounds. There were utilitarian conservationists, nature lovers, preservationists. There were also agronomists, economists and Aboriginal land rights activists. They voted Labor, Liberal and Country Party. Their only common ground was their certainty that the Little Desert should not be developed as sheep farms. This sense of consensus was the 'watershed' of the Little Desert, a term widely used in the media of the day. More than twenty years later the same term was used by almost every conservation activist that I interviewed, irrespective of their age, their political views or their definition of what conservation entails.[9]

The watershed concept was used metaphorically in its American sense to mean a catchment zone. It was about the confluence of ideas, ideas running as rivulets and streams from different points toward the valley floor, the political arena, where their total volume was sufficient to topple a Cabinet minister and close friend of Sir Henry Bolte, the Premier of Victoria. It was a rare movement indeed that united the voices of communist sympathisers and Liberal Party campaign managers. It was hardly surprising that such an alliance proved to be temporary.

The watershed notion also has appeal for those who analyse the Little Desert story nearly three decades later, but in a different sense. The watershed of the Little Desert for the conservation movement was like a dividing line between river systems. The Little Desert dispute was the last great campaign for many of its protagonists, the high point of the older conservationists' campaigning careers. Soon afterwards, many felt themselves marginalised. The 1970s environmentalists used a different language, had a different world-view—and, significantly, they failed to recognise their predecessors' achievements. Alfred Dunbavin Butcher bemoaned 'the inability of [new] environmental activists to recognise a victory when they scored one'.[10] Butcher regretted that his generation no longer set the parameters for what counted as a 'conservation victory'.

This analysis of the Little Desert campaign suggests that we should be cautious about focusing exclusively on the successful radical movement of the 1970s as if it were the culmination of all that went before. This is often the tendency of historians and sociologists writing of social movements such as environmentalism. For example, one group of European sociologists led by Andrew Jamison identified the following 'phases' in the movement's trajectory: beginning with the 'critical wave within the scientific community' (specifically mentioning Rachel Carson and Barry Commoner) in 1962–68, it ascended through 'the age of ecology' (1969–73) to 'the highpoint of environmentalism' (1974–80), followed by a denouement in 'the fragmentation of environmental concerns' (1980–90).[11] This periodisation may usefully reflect baby boomers' activism, but it fails to capture the contribution of other environmentalists and conservationists older and younger than the baby-boomer generation.[12] The long history of nature conservation concerns among Australian scientists, and the considered efforts of the Australian Academy of Science in the 1950s, have no place in the Jamison model. In fact, the Academy's experience of conservation was the opposite of that suggested by the model, with 1974–80 being a period of comparative inactivity.[13] Similarly, younger environmentalists would dispute the 'fragmentation' label for the later period. New concerns such as 'environmental justice' have become as much a focus as earlier 'green' issues. Perhaps the fragmentation has rather been in the baby boomers' commitment to the movement. It is important to recognise that, because of their greater numbers, writers of the baby-boomer generation are in a position to dominate the literature. As they have moved out of activism, they sometimes re-enter the discourse through history, where they tend to salute their own 'halcyon days'.[14]

Other generations have different halcyon days and different conservation victories, and they must not be overlooked in an analysis of the relation between conservation and environmentalism. The history of the Little Desert campaign and its activists (most of whom were at least one generation older than the baby boomers) provides insight into another conservation movement, the concerns of which have been overwhelmed or discarded by its more famous successors. The Save Our Bushlands Action Committee comprised experienced campaigners, most of them middle-aged, approaching retirement or recently retired at the time of the dispute. The young activists associated with environmentalism in the 1970s were largely absent from the 1969 scene, apart from a small scientific group, the Monash University Biological Students' Society.[15] But this does not mean that the earlier movement was not, in its own way, 'radical'.

Conservation and Environmentalism: Continuities and Discontinuities

The motivation for conservation shifted in the post-war years. In the natural history societies before 1945, there had been concerns about the loss of individual species and the loss of recreational nature. By the 1960s the concern for the loss of 'habitat' captured both earlier concerns. In the 1970s this developed into a fear that all of 'nature as we know it'—or, if you like, 'human habitat'—was about to disappear.

The field naturalists generally had an intimate knowledge of the nature proximate to their homes or favourite camping spots. It was their ownership of and intimacy with nature that was threatened, rather than nature itself. Nature was still passive, a resource for human refreshment. Urban environmentalists, however, began to display a concern for a nature they had never seen, for a wilderness that needed to 'be there', unused, to make sense, paradoxically, of their urban lives. This 'wild' nature—untamed, untouched—was part of a new view of nature as active subject, not merely passive resource.[16] This was also the nature of the 'ecologically pure' (human-free) scientific reference areas that became a part of national parks during the 1970s and 1980s. In the 1990s, while biodiversity is a catchword, the complexity of 'wilderness' is also being explored. In the interpretation centre at Nitmiluk Gorge in the Northern Territory, one of the national parks co-managed by Aboriginal and settler Australians, the visitor is welcomed to Jawoyn land and reminded that 'Nitmiluk is not a wilderness. It is a human artifact, constructed through the ceremonies, kinship ties, fires and hunting of countless generations of our people.'[17] National parks *are* about biodiversity, but not only about biodiversity. Ecologically minded environmental managers, especially those working in Northern Australia, are having to come to terms with the fact that 'biodiversity is a whitefella word'. Environmental preservation cannot be isolated from its cultural construction.

Back in early 1970 David Anderson, a descendent of the Wemba Wemba (Wembawemba) and the Waigira (Wergaia) people, speaking for Aboriginal interests at the Galbally inquiry, had to draw attention to the prior rights of Wotjabaluk people to the Little Desert and surrounding areas. It was difficult for him to give 'relevant evidence', in that the terms of the inquiry were too narrow for his purposes. But he took the opportunity to remind the European community of the continuing Aboriginal presence in the area under discussion. He described the way he felt about the McDonald scheme as being similar to the way his listeners might react if they saw him 'going up to St Kilda Road and running a bulldozer through the Shrine'.[18] In 1996 the *Little Desert Management Plan* includes a section on cultural heritage which identifies the local Goolum Goolum Aboriginal Co-operative, established in the early 1980s, as the interpreters of that heritage. It also states its 'aims' as being to encourage more Aboriginal cultural site management, and 'to increase awareness and appreciation of local Aboriginal culture'.[19] The management plan continues, however, to divide nature from culture in a way that betrays the western scientific underpinnings of national parks management.

The bush has always been important to the identity of settler Australians, but by the late 1960s their notions of the 'bush' were shifting. Graeme Davison has argued cogently that urban Australia invented the Bush with a capital 'B', the glorified view of the country encapsulated by Henry Lawson that has been so central to the mythical singular Australian identity.[20] Lawson's 'Bush' was Australia's pastoral frontier:

> We'll ride and we'll ride from the city afar
> To the plains where the cattle and sheep stations are.[21]

The pastoral frontier was still the Bush of the nation that Sir William McDonald envisaged in the 1960s. But the Bush of Henry Lawson had no resonance for the Save Our Bushlands Action Committee, although they too explicitly allied the 'bush' with national and personal identity.

For the Save Our Bushlands Action Committee, 'bushland' was public land, free of agricultural development. The conservationists were already beginning to reinvent and revise Russel Ward's 'Australian Legend' through a new understanding of the idea of the Australian bush.[22] Within a decade of Ward's book locating the source of Australian identity on the pastoral frontier, settler Australians were beginning to locate their nationhood in national parks, in biodiversity and in a legislatively protected frontier. For one generation bush-bashing meant heroism, for the next vandalism.

The Little Desert dispute was one of the first 'wilderness' battles that did not focus on a scenically remarkable area. Indeed, one of the challenges faced by the campaigners was to raise the consciousness of the general public to see beauty in the Little Desert's landscape, to create the sense of loss that agricultural development would bring to the region and to the city that depended spiritually on it. Both Lawson's Bush and the wilderness movement's 'bush' had their origins in the city. Both meant 'other', 'not the city'. They tell us a great deal more about city-dwellers' aspirations and identity crises than about those who dwell in and with the bush itself. Suburban Australians of the 1960s, like Lawson in the 1890s, needed to 'go bush' from time to time. But they no longer meant by this that they wished to retreat to the rural-based economy of a yeoman farmer ideal, or even to the nostalgic landscape of their childhood.[23] They saw the Little Desert as a place to commune with nature, not to overpower it. The frontier had become fragile, rare, in need of defence, not conquest. Peter Attiwill has commented that the name 'Little Desert' was important to the appeal of the campaign—the fact that it was 'little' implied a special need for protection.[24]

Perhaps 'desert' too, was important. The desert was seen as stereotypically Australian, but it was not the harsh, forbidding landscape of waste, but rather the land that is deserted, free of people and their problems. The Little Desert's human past was forgotten by many 'wilderness' campaigners. It was reimagined without its former roles as a home and a hunting ground. Its European history was also overlooked: travellers' tracks, early pastoral ventures and clearance for military purposes[25] were brushed aside in the creation of an idealised 'national park'. For many wilderness advocates, the opposite of the city was still the bush, but by this they no longer meant the 'country', but rather the non-human ecosystem. And often those who defended this position most vehemently did not want to choose between 'the city or the bush'; they wanted both. They wished to escape economy and history and to relocate themselves in nature rather than society, if only part-time.

Several Australians have been among the foremost advocates of ecocentrism, the philosophy that the earth should be managed in ways that do not privilege humans above other species.[26] This 'deepest green' philosophy has also been pursued by Americans and Norwegians, but much less enthusiastically by other Europeans. Where the wilderness ethic is part of national identity, ecocentrism seems both more 'natural' and more culturally acceptable.

It could be argued that what happened in 1969–70 was simply the making of national parks into commodities to be traded in a market-place. The traders were restricted to those who were members of the old system (land management bureaucracies) and those who represented another respected system, 'scientific conservation', acting in accordance with rules hammered out in the process of disputation and shared by both bureaucrats and community groups. Radical environmentalism, when it emerged a little later, argued that 'nature' had been sold out. As Ratcliffe had recognised, its spiritual aspects were simply not commodities. Spiritual values and quality-of-life issues were inexplicable in the scientific–technical language agreed on as the medium of communication by bureaucrats and conservation leaders of the late 1960s.

The techno-pessimism expressed by Judith Wright heralded another round of discussion and attempts to forge a new language of dispute. The pain of the fresh disputations, this time between 'life-world' groups, was manifest in the Australian Conservation Foundation in 1973 and in the Conservation Council of Victoria in 1978. Many of the proud and successful protagonists of the Little Desert found themselves stranded on the side of the bureaucratic system against the new greens. Nature, the object of scientific and technical world-views, was gradually emerging as subject and demanding a new epistemology.

The Green Environmental Movement

The first greenies—and the diminutive is an Australianism—were building workers.[27] Members of the New South Wales Builders Labourers Federation (BLF) used their collective power to institute 'Green Bans' (a variant of the union term 'black ban') prohibiting work on projects endangering areas or buildings of historic or environmental significance. The first and most famous of the 'green bans' prevented a housing development in urban bushland at Kelly's Bush in Sydney, beginning in 1970. In Melbourne too there was action in the form of BLF black bans on demolitions in the historic inner-city suburb of Carlton. The local residents' group, the Carlton Association, inspired the action in 1969, but the campaign did not become as famous as the Kelly's Bush fight. It lacked the special label, 'green ban', and it defended heritage, not nature.[28] It was only later, when the charter of the Australian Heritage Commission was drafted in 1975, that built and natural heritage were conjoined in the notion of 'National Estate'.[29]

In the late 1960s and early 1970s, after two decades of relatively full employment, Australian unions were in an unusually strong position to pursue overtly political causes, and 'the environment', redefined to include such issues as uranium mining, was one cause they pursued vigorously throughout the 1970s.[30] The first 'green' activists were concerned more with urban environmentalism than nature conservation. The union activists, in particular, flexed their political muscle in the interests of 'quality of life'.

It is significant that the first green environmentalists emerged with a political agenda out of the radical end of the trade union movement. They abhorred the old networks—the 'Old Boys' Clubs' and the elitist organisation of power that professionals in the early twentieth century had worked to build up. Their organisational style was participatory and egalitarian, anathema both to patriarchal community elders and to bureaucrats who had 'served time' to build up their seniority. It was a style entirely unsuited to the existing conservation movement. A left-wing model that gave voice to the 'little people' was foisted on a conservation movement that had run for more than two decades on a 'who-knows-who' basis. The obvious advantage of the 1950s and 1960s organisational style, to those in the system, was its 'efficiency'. A second advantage was that, because the networks of field naturalists were apolitical, the movement was free to lobby all political parties. At the time of the Little Desert dispute, the 1960s conservationists concentrated their efforts on unseating the problem minister, not toppling the government.[31]

At least in some cases, however, organisational structure was a symptom of deeper fractures in the conservation movement. Environmentalists were influenced not just by politics but also by philosophy. Philosophers concerned to give voice to oppressed minorities looked anew at the relationship between humans and nature. Environmental philosophers argued that the biota itself was oppressed by the human world. The 'liberation' of nature was a new moral obligation. This radical view percolated down to more moderate thinkers. Utilitarian conservation views became unfashionable. 'Wise use' and 'intensified production' came to be seen as exploitative concepts.

New environmentalists were anxious to distance themselves from an anthropocentric view of natural resources. In the 1960s 'ecology' was rescued from the relative obscurity of a sub-speciality within biology and popularised as a more general interdisciplinary science of the interaction of all biological species in an ecosystem. Gradually the term was adopted and adapted by a range of social scientists. Anthropologists with an interest in psychiatry wrote of the 'ecology of mind', anthropological linguists about the 'ecology of language' and historians of ideas about the 'ecology of knowl-edge'.[32] Each group was concerned with the relation between an abstract 'organism' (mind, language, knowledge) and its 'environment' or context. Ecology was fashionable, but it meant rather different things in different contexts. This fluidity led the popular meaning of the word to drift further from its scientific roots to refer to a new world-view, an alternative epistemology.

Many of the 1960s campaigners found the developments of the 1970s and later exciting. For example, Gwynnyth Taylor, founder of the Save Our Bushlands Action Committee, remained optimistic about attitudes to the environment in the twenty-first century. When I spoke to her in 1990 she believed that there was still a need for a broader consciousness of what 'saving the environment' means, a fuller understanding of habitat, not just concern with saving a few species. Although she did not altogether adopt their vocabulary, Taylor expressed a confidence that the new activists were 'on the right track'.[33] Similarly, Ros Garnet, a veteran of the 1950s campaign for national parks, commented that they perhaps did not go far enough in the 1960s, although he thought they were doing the right thing at the time.[34]

On the other hand the new greens have antagonised many committed older conservationists. Some of the latter still refuse to acknowledge that conservation could mean anything other than the wise use of resources by humans. Many of these were conservation professionals. The group most seriously alienated by the new environmentalists was the forestry profession. Foresters were at the heart of the conservation movement from the 1940s to the 1960s, some working very hard behind the scenes to block the McDonald scheme for the Little Desert. The 1970s shift in ecological consciousness left professional foresters stranded on the 'other' side of conservation debates.

Australian foresters became seriously disenchanted with environmentalists following the publication in 1973 of a book by Richard and Val Routley entitled *The Fight for the Forests*. The Routleys were highly critical of what they termed 'the takeover of Australian forests for pines, wood chips and intensive forestry'.[35] They were even more critical of the forest services and their failure to recognise a conflict of interest between their position as protectors of forests and facilitators of the timber industry, which was committed to maximum profits from forests. The forest services resisted the suggestion that forests might be managed 'in ways other than those best suited for wood production'.

The Routleys were philosophers, not foresters. Until that time the forestry profession had been particularly insular. Foresters in Australia were trained either in Victoria, at Creswick and the University of Melbourne, or in Canberra, at the Australian National University School of Forestry. In Victoria, almost all forestry undergraduates were sponsored by the Forests Commission and bonded to serve the commission at the end of their studies. Some later transferred to the timber industry, the other significant employer of foresters.

Foresters were surprised to discover that the public was dissatisfied with their management practices, and felt that all could be smoothed over with a 'public education' campaign They were slow to acknowledge that they might *learn* from the public. The Routleys argued that a campaign to educate the public was not what was required. Rather, foresters needed to address the 'genuine disagreement over values' between their profession and many members of the public.[36] The Routleys were not satisfied that the public interest was being served by the forest services: 'While forest services and professional foresters remain so closely identified with the timber and paper industries, the view that they resent so strongly, that forests are too valuable to be entrusted to foresters, is surely correct'.[37] The forestry profession responded to *The Fight for the Forests* by closing ranks. The book itself was published with some difficulties and included a disclaimer that the views expressed had 'not been considered by the Forestry Department of the [Australian National] University and must not be taken as necessarily representing the views of members of that Department'.[38] After record sales of the first edition and two further revised editions in 1974 and 1975, a decision was made not to republish or reprint again. The authors also claimed that the acting head of the Forestry School banned them from using the Forestry School library.[39]

The wider effect of the book was to make the profession more inward-looking and defensive. 'Pity the Poor Forester' was the title of one paper at the 1977 Australian Institute of Foresters conference in Adelaide.[40] In another paper at the same conference, L. M. Duffy stated: 'Forests and timber industries are criticised in pro-rata terms to a much larger extent than other comparative land-users. So much so, that they appear to rate only a little behind mining industries in popular censure'.[41] The antagonism felt by foresters had an impact on people working in cognate fields, especially ecologists. Peter Attiwill, who trained originally as a forester, claimed that he and a 'lot of good scientists' left the conservation movement in the early 1970s because it 'became a ratbag lot'—when it 'became political and taken over by the powers of the Left'.[42] Attiwill was referring to the shift to radical environmentalism, which was marked by a major split in the Australian Conservation Foundation (ACF) in 1973. The ACF had been established as a primarily scientific group in 1965, but in the early 1970s there was a grass-roots revolt by members who felt that changes were not happening fast enough. The issue of the flooding of Lake Pedder in Tasmania was the force behind the radical push. Activists still hoped that the lake could be saved even in 1973, when the water levels had begun to rise. The urgency of the Pedder situation gave radical environmentalists the edge over the pragmatic negotiators who had dominated the ACF until then.[43]

Attiwill is an interesting example of the shift in elements of scientific opinion. When I interviewed him in 1991, he denied the political dimensions of his statement to the Galbally inquiry, saying: 'I think my role in the Little Desert dispute was as a scientist, not as a political lobbyist'.[44] Attiwill's 'scientific' statement was nevertheless presented at an incontrovertibly political forum. The Little Desert scientific research was politically as well as scientifically motivated. Attiwill had wanted his Agricultural Botany students to undertake something 'relevant'. His students were enthusiastic about the political dimensions of their work—enthusiastic enough to write to the *Age* about the need for biological survey work in the area before they even began the work.[45] But in 1969 the science and the politics were both working in the same direction. In the 1990s Attiwill was expressing frustration with a decade of anti-forestry politics with which he had no sympathy. It was not a question of 'science or politics', but rather a change of the relation between them. In 1969, it was (for Attiwill) 'science *for* politics'. From the 1980s onward it was increasingly 'science *against* politics', something that discomfited him greatly.

Some foresters felt the profession itself had been betrayed in 1983, when the newly elected Victorian Labor government absorbed the Forests Commission into a larger Department of Conservation, Forests and Lands, and the designation 'forester' was discontinued. Bill Middleton, a stalwart of the Little Desert campaign, is one retired forester who continues to work actively for conservation. I asked him to define a 'greenie', since he clearly felt such antipathy towards them. His response was:

> a radical—people with radical views who . . . in case of the forest, for example, their aim is ultimately to stop all utilisation in all native forests. Now that is impossible and it is ridiculous and it is just not on. They're the ones that have been listened to and they don't know what they are talking about—if you see them interviewed on television they just don't know what they are talking about. And they're just bloody ratbags to my mind. But they're the ones that governments are listening to.[46]

This statement clearly reflects anger about loss of power. But its tone is, in a sense, borrowed from the new environmentalism Middleton wants to see discredited. Environmentalists assume an aggressive stance, identifying 'enemies of conservation'. Friends of the Earth, for example, has blacklisted products that are made by companies with what they regard as environmentally unsound policies.[47] The environmentalists of the 1990s were confident of having wide popular support, and therefore felt that they could afford to exclude some potential supporters, to create outcasts. In the 1960s there was no such certainty, and more embracing alliances were both necessary and possible.

It is important, however, not to stereotype individuals into polarities such as 'old style' and 'new style', 'utilitarian' and 'spiritual'. The environmental movement is dynamic, as are the participating individuals. Some utilitarians have embraced the new developments with a fervour enhanced by their scientific knowledge of the environment. In 1991, when I interviewed Frank Gibbons

(1923–94), a Soil Conservation Officer for more than twenty-five years, he confidently described himself as a greenie—but 'light green—with a social conscience'.[48] He commented that the disputes over the Little Desert and the Franklin River were critical to his personal outlook on life. Gibbons visited the Franklin in the summer of 1982–83 at the height of the environmentalist campaign to 'save the wild rivers':

> I went down to the Franklin River. [But] I wasn't game enough . . . to get arrested . . . My rationalising of that was that . . . I'm relatively old. I was probably the oldest person there, [or in] the oldest half dozen. Nobody of my age would take any notice of my opinions back here if I said to them 'I've gone and got myself arrested' . . . It wasn't appropriate [for my generation]. But I'll tell you what, it was a very emotional experience for me. We went up the river . . . I remember looking out of that tent into this green wilderness, beech trees with moss all over them . . . It wasn't a wilderness, it had been logged, but it looked like it . . . It was raining and I looked out of the tent and I [felt part of it].[49]

Gibbons' time at the Franklin made him look afresh at his soil conservation work. 'I [had been] so concerned with the relationship between vegetation and soil and climate that . . . the extent of the devastation . . . hadn't come back to me'.[50] Tours of New South Wales and Queensland in the 1980s reinforced his horror at the extensive devastation of the land.

Gibbons' spiritual encounters with the earth were part of his 'ecological consciousness', yet, because he was a committed Christian, he expressed his concern in terms of 'stewardship'. Judaeo-Christian traditions have been said to interfere with the possibility of equality in the relations between humans and nature by promoting a model of 'dominion over all creatures'.[51] Yet Gibbons' notion of 'stewardship' of the land was not one of domination or self-promotion, despite years of working in utilitarian conservation. In his retirement he worked on rates of soil movement and addressed Christian gatherings about the social responsibility of soil conservation. But he also developed a spiritual sense of the earth, a sense that he was 'of nature', not above it. The new environmental movement touched him personally.

The Little Desert as a Cultural Icon

The Little Desert story has elements of both the local and the international. While 'ecological consciousness' is an international phenomenon of the late 1960s, consciousness must also be personal and particular. It is an abstraction located in one's own known world. For many people involved in the Little Desert dispute, ecological consciousness was simply a realisation that wilderness was finite, not an imperative to change their world-view. For other participants, the sense of a 'last wild place' invoked by the Little Desert marked the beginning of a long personal odyssey, forcing a re-evaluation of their whole relation to nature, or 'being in the world'.

The 1960s were the years when terms like conservation and ecology were 'fleshed out' and began to evoke political and emotional fervour in the general public. The Little Desert dispute became part of the struggle for new meanings and new understandings. Concern about 'wilderness' has often begun in centres far away from the wilderness itself. As Roderick Nash has commented: 'Appreciation of wilderness began in the cities. The literary gentleman wielding a pen, not the pioneer with his axe, made the first gestures of resistance against the strong currents of antipathy.'[52] In Melbourne in 1969 there were, in addition to the long-time campaigners for national parks, other city-dwellers who were prepared to fight for a 'wilderness' they had never seen. They just wanted to know it was there.

The term 'conservation' continues to have multiple meanings. Conservationists may be 'light green', environmentally conscious consumers, or 'dark green' radical deep ecologists. Some conservationists have eschewed the designation 'green' altogether. But for all these shades of opinion the Little Desert scheme became a cultural icon. The *Macmillan Dictionary of the Australian Environment*, which is predominantly a dictionary of technical terms, has a listing for 'Little Desert Scheme'.[53] It is there because it was abolished 'by public pressure'. The Little Desert dispute contrasts with the contemporaneous controversy over the flooding of Lake Pedder in Tasmania by the Tasmanian Hydro-Electric Commission. Seven years' campaigning did not 'save' Lake Pedder and its distinctive sandy beaches.[54] While 'Lake Pedder' is an icon of loss for Australian conservationists, the 'Little Desert' is a symbol of hope, a reassurance that political pressure can work.

The Little Desert dispute coincided with and reinforced an international shift in ecological consciousness. Utilitarian conservation was meeting with growing opposition in many countries: technical and scientific solutions to problems were no longer regarded as sufficient to save the environment. But the Little Desert issue allowed utilitarian conservation a last 'fling', led by older-style conservationists. It is not accurate to describe the opponents of the Little Desert as 'eco-activists', as William Lines has done.[55] They came from a different conservation tradition and had a different world-view. Their style of operation was lobbying, negotiating, chatting with friends in high places. There was no direct action, no radical or 'Earth First!' element that advocated opposing the government or the establishment, either by non-violent or violent means.[56]

The importance of the older leaders lay in the fact that it was their contemporaries, and in some cases friends, who held the reins of power within the government. Claude Austin (who later became a foundation member of the Land Conservation Council) was chairman of the Western Victorian Conservation Committee. He campaigned tirelessly for the Lower Glenelg and Little Desert National Parks. He had also campaigned for the Liberal Party on behalf of Malcolm Fraser, his local federal member, who went on to become Prime Minister from 1975 to 1983. Austin played golf with the Premier, Sir Henry Bolte. He was also president of the Melbourne Club, which is at the heart of the Melbourne establishment's 'old boys' network'. Even Sir William McDonald recalled Austin as a friend, although he disagreed with him passionately about conservation.[57]

The Little Desert dispute marked both a convergence and a divide in the conservation movement. It was indeed a watershed. But a certain type of ecological consciousness was suggested by the widespread use of the watershed metaphor itself, which was based on a technical utilitarian conservationist term from the language of scientists. The choice of metaphor has dated. Latter-day greens label conservation crises differently—as battles fought and won or lost.[58]

They belong more clearly in the tradition of 'social movements'. They see the political system itself as suspect and 'attack' it accordingly. By contrast, the Little Desert dispute was dominated by those who fundamentally believed in the system. They were deeply convinced of the importance of science and of the scientific management of nature, and sought modifications of the system to facilitate scientific endeavour.

The political system was ultimately responsive to the pressure they brought to bear. Politicians such as Bill Borthwick saw science as a desirable and uncontroversial way of resolving disputes. With the toppling of Sir William McDonald, the chief advocate of the Little Desert scheme, the critics became organisational consultants. They negotiated and sought further to remodel the system along scientific lines. The centrepiece of this renegotiation was the Land Conservation Council, with its extensive public consultation and community representation, which managed to generate considerable support for its recommendations. The LCC's conflict-resolution process relied heavily on the supposedly objective and undoubtedly socially acceptable evidence of scientists and technical experts. Even the Aboriginal leader David Anderson was reported to have grudgingly condoned the advisory role of scientists with respect to the Little Desert, calling for political and economic interests to be put aside 'so that the public world interest can be dealt with by the most competent of the incompetent, the scientists'.[59] It seems that Anderson saw science as making the kind of case for the protection of the environment that would be most compatible with Aboriginal understandings of the land.

The LCC survived for twenty-seven years, mostly in the post-'green' age. The Little Desert dispute had made decision-making about land development both a scientific and a public concern. The LCC processes ensured that biological evidence became a factor in every major land-management decision as a matter of course, and that such information was publicly available. Yet, at a single stroke, the 1997 Environment Conservation Council Act took away both public representation and the necessity for scientific consultation.[60]

The rise of ecological consciousness was predicated both on 'consciousness'—including public awareness of decision-making procedures—and on a range of new ecological understandings of the world. The Little Desert dispute legitimised scientific ecological arguments as a dimension of the public interest in land-management matters. There are other dimensions, such as indigenous rights to land, which were not represented on the LCC, but its abolition spelt the end of an era of consensual decision-making that saved the State of Victoria much environmental anguish in the politically complex years of transition from conservation to environmentalism.

Since the 1970s the 'environmental revolution' has been evolving outside the scientific and bureaucratic powerhouses. The Land Conservation Council processes perhaps never fully addressed the concerns of radical environmentalists who felt that science alone was not enough. Not all agreed with Professor Turner's dictum that 'once you know the ecosystem scientifically you are compelled to conserve it'.[61] Radical ecology demands that 'knowing' must come from a different epistemology with a spiritual fount. 'Strong' or dark-green positions are difficult to accommodate within any mechanistic 'land-use' framework. But while the LCC existed, radical environmentalists at least had that space for discussion. Its abolition is likely to produce a backlash: fundamental shared values such as 'democracy' and 'fairness' are likely to re-emerge as common ground for utilitarian conservationists and radical environmentalists, and may also find support among those with concerns beyond the environmental agenda, including public service officials who have also lost their vehicle for providing government with advice 'in the public interest'.[62] By opting to go it alone and removing the negotiating table set up in the aftermath of the Little Desert dispute, the government risks a return to confrontational environmental politics. The history of the Little Desert dispute demonstrates the interdependence of political actions and the 'ecology of political networks'. A failure to understand the mutual dependence of government, bureaucracy and the community may have far-reaching environmental and political consequences.

Notes

Introduction: The Little Desert

1 Transcript of author's interview with Valerie Honey, 20 November 1990, p. 2.
2 Ibid., p. 3.
3 Ibid., p. 3.
4 Ibid., pp. 1, 3.
5 J. G. Mosley, 'The desert that spawned conservation reforms', *Australian*, 18 June 1971. Mosley was Deputy Director of the Australian Conservation Foundation at this time.
6 J. M. Powell, *An Historical Geography of Modern Australia*, p. 246.
7 Libby Robin, 'Ecology: a science of empire?', pp. 63–76.
8 George Sessions, 'Shallow and Deep Ecology', p. 422.
9 Roderick Frazier Nash, *The Rights of Nature: A History of Environmental Ethics*.
10 Ian D. Clark, *Aboriginal Languages and Clans: An Historical Atlas of Western and Central Victoria, 1800–1900*, pp. 336–353, refers to the group by its language, 'Wergaia'. The local Aboriginal people prefer 'Wotjabaluk'. See also Victoria: National Parks Service, *Little Desert Management Plan*, pp. 14–15.
11 Jan Critchett, *A Study of Aboriginal Contact and Post-Contact History and Places*, pp. 67–9; David Horton (ed.), *Encyclopaedia of Aboriginal Australia*, vol. 1., pp. 318–19; Aldo Massola, *Aboriginal Mission Stations in Victoria*, pp. 31–62.
12 D. J. Mulvaney, *Encounters in Place*, p. 159.
13 Ian D. Clark, *Scars in the Landscape: a register of massacre sites in western Victoria 1803–1859*.
14 Author's interview with Jack Kennedy, 19 September 1997.
15 Author's interviews with Peter Kennedy and 'Cape' Kennedy, 18 September 1997.
16 Jack Kennedy interview.
17 Alan E. J. Andrews (ed.) *Stapylton: With Major Mitchell's Australia Felix Expedition, 1836*, pp. 142–3.
18 Geoffrey Dutton, *Edward John Eyre: The Hero as Murderer*, pp. 41–2.
19 Les Blake, *Tattyara: A History of Kaniva District*, pp. 1–21; Les Blake, *Land of the Lowan: 100 years in Nhill and West Wimmera*, pp. 4–30.
20 Andrews, *Stapylton* [23 July 1836], p. 143.
21 Alexander Tolmer, *Reminiscences of an adventurous and chequered career*, Volume II, pp. 124, 126.

[22] Tom Griffiths (ed.) with Alan Platt, *The Life and Adventures of Edward Snell*, p. 276.

[23] Blake, *Land of the Lowan*, p. 2, records that the names 'Little Desert' and 'Big Desert' appeared in the *Narracoorte Herald* in 1884.

[24] Edwin Sherbon Hills, 'The Physiography of North-Western Victoria', pp. 297–323, especially p. 298. At the time that Hills named the ridges, County Lowan extended from Edenhope to Lake Hindmarsh, enclosing the whole of the Little Desert.

[25] Andrews, *Stapylton* [23 July 1836], p. 143.

[26] Charles Fenner, 'The Physiography of the Glenelg River', pp. 99–120.

[27] Hills, 'The Physiography of North-Western Victoria', pp. 302–3.

[28] R. L. Crocker, 'Post-Miocene climatic and geologic history and its significance in relation to the genesis of the major soil types of South Australia'.

[29] The name 'lunette' is a direct reference to Mitchell's 1836 description of the 'moonscape' that he saw from Mt Arapiles. The best summary of the scientific story is in G. Blackburn, R. D. Bond and A. R. P. Clarke, *Soil Development in Relation to Stranded Beach Ridges of County Lowan, Victoria*.

[30] Timothy Flannery, *The Future Eaters*, pp. 92–101.

[31] St Eloy D'Alton, 'The Botany of the "Little Desert", Wimmera, Victoria', pp. 64–78; Wimmera Regional Committee, *Need for Reservations in Desert Settlement*. The Little Desert Management Plan of 1996 records 631 native vascular plant species for the area.

[32] In 1962 CSIRO Wildlife scientist H. J. Frith produced a popular book on mallee-fowl to stir public interest in the plight of the bird: *The mallee-fowl: the bird that builds an incubator*. 'Brush' fencing was another industry that placed pressure on mallee-fowl habitat.

[33] The 'Disputed Zone' was about two miles wide and was the result of an error in the survey of the border, which was supposed to have been on the 141st meridian.

1 The Dispute

[1] Transcript of author's interview with Sir William McDonald, 12 November 1990, p. 8.

[2] Professor Ray Specht, a heathland ecologist who worked with the Waite team in the 1940s, said that the choice of site was determined by the presence or absence of grass trees (*Xanthorrhea spp.*). They referred to this as the 'Yacca line' (*pers. com.*, May 1991).

[3] FNCV Council, 28 August 1951 discussed a cutting from the *Sydney Morning Herald* sent to them by A. H. Chisholm, editor-in-chief of the *Australian Encyclopedia* and a keen ornithologist.

[4] FNCV Council, 31 July 1951, p. 3 'General Business: Reserves in Little Desert'. The Kaniva farmer and botanist Alex Hicks, who joined the FNCV at this time, was possibly responsible for the survey.

[5] FNCV Council, 30 October 1951, p. 594.

[6] Victoria, State Development Committee, *Report on National Parks*, No. 14–11522/51, 1951.

[7] Lands Department parish files for Booroopki and Morea parishes (both over-

lapping with the Lemon Springs Pastoral Run) show a number of new alienations made in the 1950s, especially 1956 and 1957.

8   Little Desert Settlement Committee (LDSC), *Report upon the Proposal to open the Little Desert to Settlement*, pp. 5–9.

9   McDonald transcript, p. 8.

10   [Victoria: Department of Lands], 'Departmental Report of Public Meeting at Kaniva on 28 June 1967, addressed by the Honourable Sir William McDonald, M.P., Minister of Lands', in LDSC, *Report*, Appendix B, pp. 14–15.

11   Newton S. Tiver (pastoral consultant) in transcript of evidence given before the Little Desert Settlement Committee (LDSC transcript, hereafter), pp. 60–70; R. J. Newman, 'Pasture Improvement in the Little Desert', pp. 1–9.

12   Alan Judge Holt, Secretary of Lands, Exhibit H, p. 15; see also Kaniva Council submission on 'Little Desert Development', 5 pp. (typescript). Holt's full submission to the LDSC and the Kaniva Council's written submission did not appear in the final transcripts, but copies were held in the private archive of Valerie Honey, who attended the whole inquiry.

13   LDSC, *Report*, Appendices E and F, pp. 20–3.

14   Tony Dingle, *The Victorians: Settling*, p. 58.

15   David Goodman, 'Gold Fields/Golden Fields', especially pp. 36–8.

16   Tom Griffiths, 'In Search of Classical Soil', pp. 21–38.

17   See Marilyn Lake, *The Limits of Hope*.

18   S. Wekey, Secretary to the Victorian Philosophical Institute, 1853, quoted in Goodman, 'Gold Fields/Golden Fields', p. 24 (emphasis in original).

19   Peter Cabena, Heather McRae and Elizabeth Bladin, *The Lands Manual*, pp. 2–4; See also Ray Wright, *The Bureaucrats' Domain*, esp. chapters 3–5.

20   [Department of Lands], 'Departmental Report of Public Meeting at Kaniva', p. 14.

21   LDSC transcript included statements by pastoral and agricultural consultants Newton S. Tiver, Christopher K. Shearer and William A. Beattie; economics academics from the University of Melbourne John S. Holden, Egon Donath and Alan G. Lloyd; and officers of the Department of Agriculture Rex J. Newman and Desmond R. Meadley.

22   Speakers included Alan Lloyd and John Holden, as well as Hugh Wynter, a farm management consultant from Nhill, Jack Vallance from Pier Millan, Victoria's largest wheat producer, and Emeritus Professor Sir Samuel Wadham, formerly Professor of Agriculture at the University of Melbourne. (Transcripts of ABC *Country Hour* programmes held in the personal archives of Peter Attiwill and Valerie Honey.)

23   Derek Ballantine, *Sun*, 12 August 1971. See also Michael Hayes, *Age*, 8 September 1969: 'The Little Desert is hardly a potential tourist attraction, despite the hopes of wild life protectionists and local businessmen. In six hours of scrub bashing we saw nothing in the desert apart from a few sparrows.'

24   Transcript of author's interview with W. G. D. Middleton, 9 February 1990, p. 32.

25   National Parks Act (Amendment), no. 87928, 16 December 1969.

26   Author's interview with L. H. Smith, 28 October 1991.

27   For example, Peter Attiwill, LDSC transcript, pp. 71–7.

28   Alfred Runte, *National Parks: The American Experience*, esp. pp. 48–64, where the notion of 'worthless lands' is discussed.

29 It was not 'pristine wilderness'. It was crossed with tracks, and pastoralists had grazed cattle throughout the Little Desert for over a hundred years.

30 Roderick Nash, *Wilderness and the American Mind.*

31 Richard Mabey, 'Richard Jefferies', pp. 133–49; Frederick Jackson Turner, 'The Significance of the Frontier'; Tom Griffiths, ' "The Natural History of Melbourne" ', pp. 339–65; Libby Robin, 'Visions of Nature', pp. 153–61.

32 SOBAC membership is listed in SOBAC, *Save Our Bushland and Bushlands Magna Carta.*

33 Wimmera Regional Committee, *Need for Reservations in Desert Settlement*; [Land Utilization Advisory Council], 'Report on land use in the Little Desert', (March 1968), reproduced in LDSC, *Report*, Appendix C, pp. 16–18. The Wimmera Regional Committee was established in 1947 under the auspices of the Central Planning Authority, with the Minister of Decentralization and State Development as its Chair.

34 SOBAC, *Save Our Bushland*; WVCC, *Kentbruck Heathland*, claimed the attendance at the 29 August 1969 meeting was 1100 and the 26 October 1969 meeting was 1500.

35 SOBAC, *Save Our Bushland*, pp. 25–31.

36 Transcript of author's interview with W. A. Borthwick, 8 June 1990, p. 12.

37 *Victoria's Resources*, vol. 2, no. 3, 1960, p. 5.

38 Graham Pizzey, personal communication, 21 March 1991.

39 The *Age* conducted a particularly personal campaign directed at the Minister, and finished up settling out of court an expensive legal dispute about a front-page article (4 October 1969), and an editorial (8 October 1969, p. 7) that implied the new developments in the Little Desert were being pursued because of their likely benefit to the Minister's brother-in-law. See also J. M. Powell, 'Action Analysis of Resource Conflicts', pp. 161–78.

40 The Botanic Gardens were under the control of the Minister of Lands, so McDonald was also at the centre of this dispute.

41 Borthwick transcript, pp. 12, 30.

42 Cartoon by Tanner, *Age*, 9 December 1969: 'I never knew the Little Desert was in Dandenong'; *Victorian Parliamentary Debates*, 9 December 1969, p. 2563.

43 Borthwick transcript, p. 13. It was not strictly true to say that Bolte had never campaigned on national parks. In 1955 the secretary of the VNPA, Ros Garnet, minuted that he had heard the Premier, Mr Bolte, mention his government's intention to act 'to preserve national parks', and that Miss Wigan had also heard the broadcast, but that 'it was not reported in any metropolitan daily newspaper' (VNPA Council Minutes, 20 June 1955).

44 The election promise was cited by Borthwick in his introduction to the second reading of the Land Conservation Bill, *Victorian Parliamentary Debates*, 15 September 1970, p. 147.

45 Liberal first-preference votes throughout the State fell from 37.5 per cent to 36.7 per cent. (Electoral information supplied by Dr Paul Thornton–Smith, Projects Branch, State Electoral Office, Victoria, 7 August 1990.)

46 For example, C. S. Elliott, 'A New Era?' (editorial), *Victoria's Resources*, vol. 12, no. 1, March–May 1970, p. 1.

47 Lake, *The Limits of Hope.*

48 Author's survey of letters to the editor in *Age*, *Herald*, *Sun* and several local papers between April and October 1969. Of 164 letters related to the Little Desert

or Lower Glenelg settlement schemes, 153 were against and 11 in favour of development. Letters stopped abruptly on 10 October 1969 because of litigation initiated by Sir William McDonald against the *Age*. Of the 153 letters opposed to the development, 33 per cent gave as their prime concern some combination of conservation, tourism or science, 20 per cent gave economics as the reason and 47 per cent expressed concern about the 'public interest' in land management matters, including 8 per cent congratulating the media on their role in publicising the dispute.

49 ABC Science Unit, 'The Little Desert: a Conservation Victory in Western Victoria'; exhibition, 'The Little Desert: A Conservation Victory', School of Botany, University of Melbourne, early 1970.

50 See *Victoria's Resources*, vol. 11, no. 2, 1969, p. 7; vol. 11, no. 4, 1969–1970, p. 31; and G. T. Thompson, 'Conservation Council of Victoria', *Victoria's Resources*, vol. 12, no. 1, 1970, pp. 27–9. The CCV is now known as Environment Victoria.

51 Cited by J. G. Mosley in 'The desert that spawned conservation reforms', *Australian*, 18 June 1971.

52 Jim Falk, *Global Fission*, p. 149.

53 The Ministry for Conservation Act (No. 8364 of 1972) came into operation on 23 January 1973. The Lands Ministry's land administration functions were transferred to a new Department of Conservation, Forests and Lands (CFL), and its survey and land sales functions to the Department of Property and Services. In 1990 the Victorian Government created a new 'superministry', Conservation and Environment, which subsumed CFL. In October 1992, following a change in government, this was reorganised as the Department of Conservation and Natural Resources, then restructured again as Natural Resources and Environment in April 1996.

54 Victoria. National Parks Service, *Little Desert National Park management plan* traces the history of park reservations.

2 Crosbie Morrison's National Parks Campaign

1 P. C. Morrison, Wild Life Broadcast, Script No 149, 'Stocktaking', 4 April 1946, Philip Crosbie Morrison Archive, Australian Science Archives Project (Series 3/010), State Library of Victoria, p. 1.

2 The 'National Trust' in Britain is an abbreviation for 'National Trust for Places of Historic Interest or Natural Beauty'. For a brief history, see Sir Dudley Stamp, *Nature Conservation in Britain*, pp. 32–5.

3 *Victorian Naturalist*, vol. 26, no. 2, June 1909, p. 14. Land reservations were sought at Mallacoota and Wingan Inlets, the islands surrounding Wilsons Promontory, and in the Mallee. (The Mallee reservation eventually became Wyperfeld National Park.)

4 Morrison, Editorial, *Wild Life*, January 1941, p. 4.

5 Peter Read, *Returning to Nothing*, makes the point that non-Aboriginal Australians generally have resisted the transcendentalism that Thoreau made famous in the United States, and have opted for a more pragmatic 'quasi-mystical' approach to nature—they *liken* their experience of wilderness to something mystical without actually being transformed by it (p. 141).

6 Tom Griffiths, *Hunters and Collectors*, pp. 121–49.

7 Graham Pizzey, *Crosbie Morrison*, pp. 114–17.

8 Robin, 'Visions of Nature', pp. 153–61; Stuart Brash, Anne-Marie Condé and Libby Robin with Gavan McCarthy and Tim Sherratt, *A Guide to the Records of Philip Crosbie Morrison*; Pizzey, *Crosbie Morrison*.

9 See *Parkwatch*, no. 115, December 1978, p. 3, where the then President of the VNPA, Geoff Durham, identified Sunday evening radio with Crosbie Morrison as something that 'sparked my interest in nature'.

10 Griffiths, *Hunters and Collectors*, p. 126.

11 Morrison, 'Stocktaking', p. 6.

12 Ibid., p. 4.

13 Sandra M. Bardwell, National Parks in Victoria, 1866–1956, p. 385, notes that in 1907 Wilsons Promontory was referred to as 'The National Park' (like Sydney's National Park—later Royal National Park).

14 J. B. Gregory (and A. H. S. Lucas), 'To Wilson's Promontory Overland' (4 parts).

15 Ibid., part 4, p. 154.

16 For an extended discussion of the significance and symbolism of islands see Richard H. Grove, *Green Imperialism*.

17 Later the Royal Australasian Ornithologists' Union, and from 1997 Birds Australia.

18 *Victorian Naturalist*, vol. 26, no. 1, May 1909, p. 12.

19 Ibid., vol. 4, no. 5, September 1887, p. 66.

20 Ibid., vol. 7, no. 1, May 1890, pp. 16–17; T. S. Hall, 'Wilsons Promontory as a National Park', *Victorian Naturalist*, vol. 21, no. 9, January 1905, p. 129.

21 *Victorian Naturalist*, vol. 4, no. 12, April 1888, pp. 197–8 (deputation); vol. 15, no. 5, September 1898, p. 60 (reference to *Government Gazette*, 8 July 1898, proclaiming national park).

22 Hall, 'Wilsons Promontory as a National Park', p. 130; see also Libby Robin, 'Thomas Sergeant Hall', pp. 485–92. Hall was FNCV president from 1901–03.

23 A. D. Hardy, 'Excursion to Wilsons Promontory', *Victorian Naturalist*, vol. 22, 1906, p. 191.

24 *Victorian Naturalist*, vol. 25, 1909, p. 153 and vol. 26, 1909, pp. 28–9.

25 Ibid., vol. 63, no. 1, pp. 1–2. Pizzey, *Crosbie Morrison*, pp. 228–50, describes what he calls 'the great National Park campaign 1946–1956'. The campaign for National Parks legislation is also well described by Bardwell, National Parks in Victoria, pp. 501–615.

26 Jane Lennon, 'Timeless Wilderness?', pp. 419–40.

27 The State Rivers and Water Supply Commission had been established in 1905, the Forests Commission in 1918 and the Soil Conservation Board in 1940.

28 For example, Australasian Association for the Advancement of Science, 'Committees of Investigation', *Report of the AAAS*, 1, 1888, Sydney, p. xxxiv and throughout the 1890s and later. See also Linden Gillbank, 'The Life Sciences', pp. 99–129.

29 *The Gould League* (brochure), 1976, p. 1.

30 VNPA Minutes of Provisional Council, first meeting, 17 September 1952, following conference 28 August 1952.

31 The Director of Fisheries and Game, Alfred Dunbavin Butcher, was, however, open to a broader definition of the department's role. In February 1949 when he addressed the FNCV, he stated that the main aims of the department were conser-

vation and management. Butcher was keen that the FNCV support the work of the Department of Fisheries and Game, as was his predecessor, Mr Fred Lewis, who joined the FNCV and was an active member after his retirement from the public service (FNCV Minutes, 12 April 1948, p. 378).

32 *Victorian Naturalist*, vol. 52, no. 1, 1935, p. 11.

33 Forests Commission, *Annual Report*, 1936–7, p. 4.

34 Libby Robin, *Building a Forest Conscience*, pp. 3–15.

35 C. E. Isaac, *Forest Policy*, p. 3.

36 Victoria: *Report of the Royal Commission to inquire into Forest Grazing* (L. E. B. Stretton). Judge Stretton had undertaken parliamentary Royal Commissions on the 1939 fires, and on fires at Yallourn in 1944.

37 *Report on Forest Grazing*, p. 5.

38 *Report on Bush Fires of 1939*, p. 5.

39 *Report on Forest Grazing*, p. 6.

40 Robin, *Building a Forest Conscience*, p. 106. The *Extracts* (SFC Leaflet 2/47) did not include the chapter containing the above quote, which was 'considered to be of such interest as to warrant its inclusion in a special publication' (p. 2). The special publication was C. E. Isaac (comp.), *An Inseparable Trinity*.

41 C. E. Isaac, 'An Inseparable Trinity', Broadcast no. 46, transcripts of 1955 radio broadcasts held in NRCL archives. Isaac's broadcasts were relayed over nine stations throughout metropolitan and country Victoria.

42 The strength of soil conservation by comparison with nature conservation was commented on several decades later by SOBAC in *Outline for a Bushlands Magna Carta*.

43 *Report on Forest Grazing*, p. 25. The National Parks mentioned by name in this context were Wilsons Promontory ('a ghost of its former self') and Mount Buffalo. The 'other harmful activities' clearly included military manoeuvres.

44 Ibid., pp. 25–6.

45 Soil Conservation and Land Utilization Act, no. 5226, 1947; Soil Conservation and Land Utilization Act, no. 5441, 1949, jointly enacted 15 February 1950.

46 Max Nicholson, *The Environmental Revolution*, p. 202.

47 *Argus*, 12 June 1948; *Age*, 15 and 18 June 1948; *Sun*, 15 June 1948.

48 The idea of sending a deputation came from C. E. Isaac (FNCV Council Minutes, 28 September 1948, p. 411). Isaac organised a luncheon for Crosbie Morrison to talk with the Premier, Mr Tom Hollway, who agreed to receive a small deputation on the subject of a 'properly constituted' National Parks Authority (FNCV Council Minutes, 26 July 1949, p. 467).

49 Resolution of the conference, 6 December 1948, FNCV Minutes, 13 December 1948, p. 427. See also FNCV, *National Parks and National Reserves in Victoria*, pp. 20–1, where details of the authority are spelt out.

50 SDC, *Report on National Parks*.

51 FNCV Council, 27 November 1951, p. 598.

52 Ros Garnet, a key founder of this organisation, was unaware of the earlier organisation of the same name until much later, when he was browsing through early copies of the *Victorian Naturalist* and came across the reference by accident (Transcript of author's interview with Ros Garnet, 20 April 1989, p. 32). The official launching of the VNPA was the cause of another public meeting on 23 July 1953. The role of Crosbie Morrison in the establishment of the VNPA is described by Pizzey, *Crosbie Morrison*, pp. 243–4.

53   Sources are 'Plan of the Campaign' (1944) (NRCL Archives, reproduced in Robin, *Building a Forest Conscience*, pp. 10–11) and VNPA *Newsletter*, no. 1, 1 July 1953.

54   These were the Forests Commission, Education Department, Department of Lands and Survey, State Rivers and Water Supply Commission, Soil Conservation Board and Melbourne and Metropolitan Board of Works.

55   The Save the Forests Campaign was supported by 37 organisations, the VNPA by 15. Only three overlapped: the FNCV, the Bird Observers' Club and the Gould League of Bird Lovers.

56   Obituary, Eric George Stewart (1902–82), *Parkwatch*, no. 131, Summer 1982, pp. 14–15.

57   See Robin, *Building a Forest Conscience*, pp. 90–2; Ian McCann, a member of the Wimmera FNC who was also an APPU member, represented the APPU at the deputation to the Premier on 17 November 1955 (VNPA Council Minutes 23 November 1955).

58   Goode claimed to have been unaware of the FNCV/VNPA campaign for national parks until he mooted the APPU conference (Transcript of author's interview with Dewar Goode, 20 November 1989, p. 9).

59   'They talk today on Park Bill', *Argus*, 18 September 1956 (Morrison archive, Scrapbook 2, p. 145, ASAP Series 9). Morrison's embarrassment would have been compounded by the fact that his position as editor of *Wild Life* had finished in 1954, following the death of Keith Murdoch (see Pizzey, *Crosbie Morrison*, pp. 200–3), and his situation at the *Argus* was by no means secure.

60   Conclusion to the first *Annual Report* of the National Parks Authority, 1957, p. 11. Nash, *Wilderness and the American Mind*.

61   Theodore Roosevelt (1858–1919), President of the USA from 1901 to 1909. His three-volume saga, *The Winning of the West*, extolled 'frontier virtues' and promoted a sort of 'virile nationalism'.

62   Smith interview, 28 October 1991.

3 The Local and the Global

1   The term 'limits to growth' became more famous in 1972 with the publication of a book of that title, the report of the Club of Rome's Project on the 'Predicament of Mankind' by D. H. and D. L. Meadows, but the 1969 Australian campaign was based on similar concerns.

2   Tim Bonyhady, *Places Worth Keeping: Conservationists, Politics and the Law*, pp. 1–20.

3   *Sydney Morning Herald*, 25 August 1997, pp. 1, 4; the Fitzroy case is like Pedder and the Franklin, in that the state government is supporting (indeed, indirectly initiating) the development proposal.

4   See Paul Erhlich, *The Population Bomb*.

5   Author's interview with J. S. Turner, 28 August 1990; Tape 2, side 1.

6   'The Proposed Glenelg National Forest and Sanctuary', *Victorian Naturalist*, vol. 64, no. 4, August 1947, pp. 62–91 (quote p. 62).

7   *Victorian Naturalist*, vol. 64, no. 3, July 1947, p. 40; see also 65th Annual Report of FNCV, *Victorian Naturalist*, vol. 62, no. 3, July 1945, p. 40.

8   FNCV Council, 28 June 1949, p. 463. The Minister for Forests had also indicated that it would be 'inadvisable to declare it a National Park' because of the fire risks associated with land managed by more than one body.

9   FNCV Minutes, 9 July 1951. Representatives from the Town and Country Planning Board had also been present for this visit.

10 Fred Davies, 'A Tribute to Noel F. Learmonth', *Victorian Naturalist*, vol. 88, February 1971, pp. 30–40.

11 Mr D. C. Smith of Grassdale proposed this, and it was endorsed by the FNCV, and passed to the Forests Commission (FNCV Council, 27 April 1948, p. 383). The decision that national parks should not be named after individuals was reported to FNCV Council, 26 March 1968.

12 Fred Davies, 'An Aussie looks at his environment', esp. pp. 16–24.

13 Ibid., p. 22.

14 Ibid., p. 23.

15 Transcript of author's interview with Fred Davies, 20 March 1989, p. 4; supported by correspondence between Learmonth and Ros Garnet on the subject, 14 April 1955, 24 April 1955, 11 May 1955, 17 May 1955, 27 June 1955, 13 August 1955, 28 August 1955 (Learmonth to Garnet), and reply from Garnet to Learmonth (1 May 1955, indicating VNPA's support) (VNPA Archives, 'Mt Richmond' file).

16 Davies transcript, pp. 2–3.

17 Letter from Fred Davies to Libby Robin, 18 October 1989, p. 5.

18 Western Victorian Conservation Committee, *The Case for a Lower Glenelg National Park*, p. 8.

19 FNCV Council Minutes, 30 January 1962, p. 1667.

20 Austin had been involved with Learmonth's initiative on the Mt Richmond reservation as early as 1955, according to a report in the *Hamilton Spectator*, 21 April 1955. He also had a much better knowledge of the Little Desert and Wyperfeld areas than Learmonth, so could represent 'western Victoria' more fully.

21 Logging in closed catchments, national parks and reserves became a general concern of natural history societies in the 1960s (FNCV Minutes, 11 July 1960, p. 1483). 'Closed catchments' had been a long-standing policy of the MMBW, unpopular with the Forests Commission. (See chapter 6.)

22 Frank R. Gibbons and R. G. Downes, *A Study of the Land in South-Western Victoria*.

23 On the Land Utilization Advisory Council, see chapter 6 below.

24 WVCC, *The Case for a Lower Glenelg National Park*.

25 FNCV Meeting, 11 November 1968, Item 4.

26 FNCV Council, 31 July 1951, p. 3.

27 FNCV Minutes, 10 December 1945, p. 266 and 11 November 1946, p. 308. Also FNCV Council Minutes, 26 March 1946, p. 278. Garnet was supporting the initiative of Mr Eric Muir and Jeparit Council in this proposal. The reservation of a new 'national park' was announced during the Back to Dimboola celebrations in October 1946, which were attended by a number of FNCV members. The local council undertook to fence and maintain the area, which was only thirteen hectares.

28 Melville also visited Mt Buller with Jim Willis and Norman Wakefield (FNCV Council Minutes, 24 February 1953). Ros Garnet's personal friendship with

Melville (which possibly arose through the Little Desert visit) resulted in continuing correspondence, and the circulation and discussion of British Nature Conservancy documents at a VNPA Annual Meeting, 26 September 1956. John Turner also had correspondence with Melville about the preservation of St Kilda Road trees. (Melville to Turner, 21 January 1954, J. S. Turner Collection, Box 20 (Civic Advisory Panel).)

29 Alec Hicks, interview with Libby Robin and Les Smith, 23 April 1989.

30 P. L. Williams mentioned this in the ABC Science Unit Broadcast, 'The Little Desert'.

31 Transcript of author's interview with Keith Hateley, 24 April 1989.

32 *Nhill Free Press*, 21 February 1955, reported on a public meeting held 20 February 1955.

33 The matter was also referred to the Native Plants Preservation Society. (VNPA Council Minutes, 17 March 1955).

34 Garnet to Learmonth, 1 May 1955 (VNPA Archives, 'Mt Richmond' file). Hateley transcript, pp. 4–6, also mentioned a strategy of asking for a small amount of land with the intention of expanding later. Hateley chose the Lowan sanctuary area because applications had been lodged to clear that land. The land was not strictly in the Little Desert, but it was more at risk from development than the Little Desert itself.

35 VNPA Council Minutes, 10 August 1955. Exhibition held 23 September 1955 to 2 October 1955.

36 Ros Garnet opened the Kiata Nature Shows on 24 September 1955 and 28 September 1957 as Secretary of the VNPA and President of the FNCV respectively. He reported the event to his sponsoring society in each case.

37 This was confirmed independently by both the then Secretary of Lands, A. J. Holt, and the Director of National Parks, L. H. Smith (author's interviews 18 November 1991 and 28 October 1991 respectively).

38 Honey transcript, pp. 1–2.

39 Author's second interview with Gwynnyth Taylor, 16 April 1990.

40 Honey transcript, p. 19. On R. G. Downes, see chapter 6 below.

41 'Sign here please and 3,500 did', *Age*, 25 July 1969; Honey claims that she had 4000 signatures by the time she actually presented the petition.

42 Honey transcript, p. 13.

43 Ibid., p. 5.

44 (Mrs) V. Honey, 'Urgent Need for Immediate, Thorough Investigation into Future Requirements for National Parks and Reserves: The Relevance of this to the Little Desert', typescript (9 pp.) accompanying petition to Acting Premier, Sir Arthur Rylah. Copy from the private archive of Mrs V. Honey, p. 2.

45 Honey, 'Urgent Need', p. 3.

46 Honey transcript, p. 25.

47 Honey, 'Urgent Need', p. 9.

48 Samuel P. Hays, *Beauty, Health and Permanence*.

4 The Ecologists

1 LDSC, *Report*, includes relevant extracts from the Minutes of the Proceedings of the Legislative Council, p. 2.

2   LDSC transcript, 23 December 1969, records the invitation issued to McDonald on 22 October and his reply on 15 December, declining to appear. Holt recalled that Galbally had apologised for placing him in an invidious position (Holt interview).

3   Geoff Edwards, personal file, 'Conservation and Applied Ecology'; also letter to Libby Robin 31 August 1991. Another of Ealey's students, Jenny Forse, addressed the FNCV soon after Gibbons' lecture about alienation in the Little Desert, which instigated the FNCV's press campaign about the area. (FNCV Minutes, 14 April 1969, General Business).

4   Author's interview with E. H. M. Ealey, 19 December 1995.

5   Libby Robin, 'Nature and Nation', pp. 55–66.

6   Transcript of author's first interview with J. S. Turner, (section 1, revised), 28 August 1990, p. 5.

7   Ibid., p. 5.

8   Transcript of second author's interview with Turner, 28 January 1991, p. 1.

9   Ibid., p. 3. 'Fire ecology' is possibly a term used with the hindsight of the 1990s. From the 1940s, however, Turner had staff (including David Ashton and Peter Attiwill) and postgraduate students undertaking ecological studies of *Eucalyptus regnans* (mountain ash) affected by the 1939 fires.

10   Professor Samuel Wadham had recommended Turner to Clark. When Turner arrived fresh from Cambridge, he frequently relied on Wadham's judgement in university and wider concerns (Turner, second transcript, p. 2; also letter from Turner to Wadham (early 1938), quoted in full in Roderick Alan Fawns, The Maintenance and Transformation of School Science, pp. 114–15).

11   Linden Gillbank, *The Biological Heritage of Victoria's Alps*, especially pp. 26–38. See also Gillbank, 'Into the Land of the Mountain Cattlemen', pp. 133–54.

12   A. S. Watt, 'On the Causes of Failure of Natural Regeneration in British Oakwoods', and 'On the ecology of British Beechwoods with special reference to their Regeneration'. Watt's later work on the ecology of Breckland was published by the *Journal of Ecology* in 1937, 1938 and 1940.

13   Gillbank, *The Biological Heritage of Victoria's Alps*, p. 63.

14   David Ashton, personal communication, 12 March 1993, remembered 1000 sites being examined in 1949 and 1950, but fewer in later years after D. W. Goodall had established statistically representative permanent points on numerous regular transect lines.

15   Gillbank, *The Biological Heritage of Victoria's Alps*, p. 30. R. L. Specht, 'Australia', pp. 404–5, also commented on the importance of fieldwork undertaken jointly by staff, postgraduates and undergraduate students at the University of Adelaide in the 1920s, and in interdisciplinary scientific societies like the Tate Society (University of Adelaide) and the McCoy Society (University of Melbourne) in the 1930s.

16   For example, it is probable that the ecological research station built by the Botany School in 1961 at Wilsons Promontory National Park was approved by the National Parks Authority because of the credibility the School had established with government work.

17   P. M. Attiwill, personal archive. Attiwill and Calder both returned to the Little Desert later in the year to add to the student work, and to recheck details for the report to the Galbally Committee (Calder, LDSC transcript, p. 193).

18   The lineage between the the 'metre plot' or quadrat and 'exclosures' has been

explained in an American context by the historian Ronald C. Tobey in *Saving the Prairies*, pp. 204–7.

19 'Ped' (F. G. Elford), 'Ecology in General Science', *Wild Life*, vol. 7, November 1945, p. 351.

20 Fawns, The Maintenance and Transformation of School Science, p. 2.

21 Ibid., p. 136.

22 Ibid., p. 5.

23 Turner's preface to the 1954 edition of James and Rowney's *New General Science*, which superseded Daniel and Turner's *General Science for Australian Schools*. Quoted by Fawns, The Maintenance and Transformation of School Science, p. 20.

24 Fawns, The Maintenance and Transformation of School Science, p. 32. According to Fawns, the 'science as essential humanity' idea was shared by Wadham and also James (later Sir James) Darling, headmaster of Geelong Grammar School, where Turner was on the Council. The turn of phrase was probably Darling's.

25 Ibid., p. 364.

26 [J. S. Turner] 'An Experiment in Teaching Biology' (file note on Australian Academy of Science file 3014). Details of print-runs in the early 1970s (e.g. 1971: text, 17 000; manual part 1, 29 000; manual part 2, 22 000; and teacher's guide, 1000) are on Australian Academy of Science file 1069, 'School Biology Project'.

27 Morgan setting out aims for the project in 1965, quoted by Fawns, The Maintenance and Transformation of School Science, p. 368.

28 The Academy in 1997 was also preparing a programme for lower secondary science.

29 Julian Huxley, 'Introduction' to Francis Ratcliffe, *Flying Fox and Drifting Sand*, p. ix.

30 Francis Ratcliffe to Sir David Rivett, 9 October 1936, CSIRO Archives, Series 3, PH/RAT/1 Part II, Canberra.

31 Ratcliffe, *Flying Fox and Drifting Sand*, p. 331.

32 Ibid., pp. 330–1.

33 Ibid., p. 317.

34 Francis N. Ratcliffe, *Conservation and Australia*, p. 1.

35 Edna Walling, *The Australian Roadside*, pp. 16–18.

36 Landscape Preservation Council, *Safeguarding the Victorian Landscape*.

37 *Safeguarding the Victorian Landscape*.

38 J. S. Turner, 'The threat to native Australian plants', in the six-part series, 'Going, Going, Gone', ABC Radio, 1962. His choice of examples is reminiscent of a description he made of himself in a letter to Sam Wadham in 1938, just before departing for Australia: 'As for my own views, I am what low brows call high brow, and what high-brows call middle-brow, if that conveys anything' (cited in full in Fawns, The Maintenance and Transformation of School Science, pp. 114–15). Beethoven, Shakespeare and greenhoods are all 'accessible' forms of high culture.

39 Stella Carr did later work on the plots, coming to Australia from Belfast in 1966 and from Canberra in 1979 with the assistance of the Soil Conservation Authority (Gillbank, *The Biological Heritage of Victoria's Alps*, p. 35).

40 Stella G. M. Carr and J. S. Turner, 'The Ecology of the Bogong High Plains', pp. 12–63.

41 *Report on Forest Grazing*, especially pp. 17–18. Stretton used an unpublished 'Interim Report, Ecological Work on the Bogong High Plains' by Turner and Fawcett in the preparation of his report (p. 20). In New South Wales, the report of A. B. Costin served as evidence of the need to reduce further the soil-erosion pressure from cattle. Some cattle-grazing leases have been renewed in Victoria and cattle continue to graze limited sections of the Australian alps in the 1990s.

42 Author's interview with R. L. Specht, 29 May 1991.

43 Malcolm Calder was also encouraged to support the VNPA by Turner, and was president for five years in the 1970s. Turner himself was vice-president 1969–1973.

44 Morrison, *National Parks Authority Director's Inaugural Report*.

45 For example, Turner had refused to take on a more active role in the Australian Conservation Foundation (established in 1965), despite constant requests from Francis Ratcliffe: 'I bitterly regret that you opted out of serving on the Executive Committee because you were already too busy in things of that kind' (Ratcliffe to Turner, 21 March 1967, Turner Collection, Box 8 (ACF)).

46 Turner to W. H. Algar, 10 October 1969, Turner Collection, Box 20 (Conservation).

47 Turner, first transcript, Section 2, pp. 3–4.

48 Ibid., Section 2, p. 4.

49 David Ashton, personal communication, 24 March 1993.

50 LDSC transcript, p. 71 (Attiwill) and p. 188 (Calder).

51 Peter Attiwill, personal communication, 18 September 1991.

52 Attiwill, LDSC transcript, p. 75.

53 Calder, LDSC transcript, p. 190.

54 Ibid., p. 190A.

55 Ibid., p. 190B.

56 Ibid., p. 192.

57 Dorothy Nelkin, 'Scientists and Professional Responsibility', pp. 75–95.

58 Turner to W. J. (Bill) Kilpatrick of Hawthorn, 17 June 1971, who, in a letter of 15 June 1971, was seeking an expert witness concerning the need for conservation in the rapidly developing Berwick Shire. (Turner Collection Box 20 (Conservation)).

59 Libby Robin, 'Radical Ecology and Conservation Science'.

5 A Wimmera Perspective

1 Les Blake, *The Land of the Lowan*, p. 2, notes the early use of the term Little Desert in the *Narracoorte Herald*, 1884. The writers of the 1870s referred to the area as 'mallee bush'.

2 Bardwell, National Parks in Victoria 1866–1956, pp. 375–80, 459–62, 480–480A. Wyperfeld National Park was enlarged again in 1992, to 3568 square kilometres. In the 1960s it was approximately 565 square kilometres.

3 S. R. Morton. 'Land of Uncertainty: The Australian Arid Zone', pp. 122–44. Another mallee area at Hattah Lakes National Park, north of Wyperfeld, was first reserved in 1960.

4 Libby Robin, 'Nature conservation as a national concern', pp. 1–24; FNCV

Council Minutes, 28 July 1959, p. 1407, mention the Little Desert among a number of suggestions for reservation in a VNPA proposal, which it endorsed.

5 FNCV Minutes, 9 August 1965; J. Ros Garnet, The vegetation of Wyperfeld National Park (North-West Victoria).

6 FNCV Council Minutes, 23 May 1967.

7 Middleton interview transcript.

8 Transcript of speech by W. G. D. Middleton, given at the handing over of Broughtons Waterhole, 24 June 1989, p. 12.

9 Middleton joined the FNCV on 13 February 1956.

10 Middleton interview transcript, p. 25.

11 Regional Conventions were held throughout Victoria by the NRCL in the period from 1953 to 1970; see Robin, Building a Forest Conscience, pp. 141–3. The AMP's proposal was made in September 1963, but there was earlier local knowledge of the likelihood of the scheme.

12 Mr E. Hanks, a Melbourne member of the FNCV, also attended the conference (FNCV Council Minutes, 28 July 1964, p. 2, 25 August 1964, p. 3 and 29 September 1964, p. 2).

13 Wimmera Regional Committee, Need for Reservations in Desert Settlement. The 'government expense' Middleton referred to was the roneoing of the maps showing where reservations were needed, done by himself and an employee of the Country Roads Board at the weekend (Middleton interview transcript). The recommendations were adopted without amendment by the National Parks Authority (Goode papers, Box 1/2 National Parks Authority (File: Tracks and Conservation), State Library of Victoria).

14 P. M. Attiwill in LDSC transcript, p. 73; the first published list of (about 200) plant species for the Little Desert was St Eloy D'Alton, 'The Botany of the "Little Desert", Wimmera, Victoria' (1913). In 1996 the tally was 631 species, according to The Little Desert Management Plan.

15 Cynthia Hicks (Bill's wife), personal communication, 29 April 1989. Bill Hicks was a Kaniva Shire Councillor for sixteen years.

16 A. Hicks to P. Attiwill, 9 December 1969 (Attiwill, Little Desert correspondence, personal archives).

17 Kaniva Times, 23 September 1969, p. 1.

18 Jean Holmes, The Government of Victoria, p. 6.

19 Newsday, 7 October 1969.

20 Nhill Free Press, 15 September 1969, news item and open letter to residents of Nhill district from Brian Pola, La Trobe University (a student activist).

21 Holmes, The Government of Victoria, p. 10.

22 Potts to Geoff Edwards, 16 July 1972 (Geoff Edwards personal archive).

23 Peter J. Schmitt, Back to Nature, p. xvii.

24 David R. Anderson, LDSC transcript, p. 165.

25 Nhill Free Press, 15 September 1969, editorial.

26 Minutes of Inaugural Meeting of Kaniva Promotion Committee, 29 September 1969 (Alec Hicks' personal archive).

27 Minutes of Kaniva Promotion Committee, Meeting 7, 25 January 1971; Wimmera Mail Times, 1 February 1971; Kaniva Times, 2 February 1971. This energetic small group also arranged for the compilation of a set of 116 slides to show bus tour guests at the motel. P. L. Williams had set up a 'Billyho Bushwalk'

on his property, and charged for a small pamphlet of the walk. Some of the proceeds from pamphlet sales were donated to assist the work of the Kaniva Promotion Committee (Minutes of Annual Meeting of KPC, 25 October 1971).

28 *Kaniva Times*, 23 May 1972.

29 Catalogue and Notes on Little Desert Art Exhibition (Alec Hicks' archive). *Kaniva Times*, 15 and 23 May 1972. More than 1000 people were reported to have visited the exhibition.

30 Hateley transcript; *Age*, 15 May 1972.

31 Douglas offered the painting entitled 'Such Savage and Scarlet as no Green Hills Dare' (after A. D. Hope's poem, 'Australia') at more than 30 per cent discount because it was to be bought by public subscription. The Council put in $100, and 'an anonymous person' guaranteed the purchase. Public response was described as 'disappointing' several months later (*Kaniva Times*, 18 July 1972).

32 Author's interview with R. C. (Wimpy) Reichelt, 30 October 1991.

33 Reichelt has a licence to breed the mallee-fowl (lowan) in captivity.

34 *Age*, 4 December 1971.

35 Reg Johnson, *One Man's Dream: Whimpey and the Little Desert Lodge*. Reichelt and his wife, Maureen, eventually bought out Johnson's share of the business.

36 The survey was undertaken by three biologists who spent three months living in the Little Desert. Dr Truda Howard, a botanist, was the leader of the group, which included Geoff Edwards and Ken Norris, a reptile specialist. The group became very friendly with the locals. Every Sunday their camp at Broughtons Waterhole was visited by the Hicks/Williams/Coutts triumvirate, who would bring lunch, conversation and research suggestions.

37 Potts to Edwards, 8 January 1974 (Geoff Edwards personal archive).

38 KPC Minutes 1971–74.

39 Trust for Nature—Victoria, is a non-profit, non-government statutory body responsible to Parliament. It was established by the *Victorian Conservation Trust Act 1972* (amended 1978) to enable covenants with landowners and to assist in the management of the conservation value of private land (Trust for Nature, *Annual Report 1994–5*, p. 4). The Trust also buys land, covenants it, and then sells it on through 'rolling funds', something it has found to be commercially successful. 'Covenants' do not seem to result in a fall in land values, contrary to predictions that they would.

40 A Blackburn and District Tree Preservation Society *Newsletter* is published irregularly, and usually appears about a month before the annual visit, which is held either in late September or early November to coincide with public holidays. 'Pilgrimage' is their term for their annual visit.

41 Not all the Urimbirra people came from Melbourne. One of the original directors of the co-operative was Don Merrett, the local entrepreneur behind West Wimmera Tours, mentioned above.

42 Author's interview with Clive Brownsea, 30 October 1990.

43 Les Smith, personal communication, 16 November 1995.

44 Author's interview with Auntie Joyce Kennedy, 18 September 1997.

45 At the time of writing (February 1998) the native title claim is undergoing an arbitration process before being heard by the High Court.

46 The Goolum Goolum Aboriginal Co-operative was established in late 1981 or early 1982 by Philip Pepper. See Clark, *Aboriginal Languages and Clans,* p. 350.

David Anderson and Philip Pepper were related, Anderson's grandmother being Nellie Stewart (née Pepper). Anderson died in the mid-1980s, according to relatives.

47 Peter Kennedy interview.
48 *Little Desert Management Plan*, p. 32.
49 Peter Kennedy interview.

6 The Bureaucrats

1 Hugh Stretton, 'ABC: Just the beginning'; K. S. Inglis, *This is the ABC*.
2 Powell, *An Historical Geography of Modern Australia*. Powell's other works include 'Action Analysis of Resource Conflicts', pp. 161–79; *Environmental Management in Australia, 1788–1914*; *Watering the Garden State*; and 'Enterprise and dependency', pp. 102–21. See also Bardwell, National Parks in Victoria, 1866–1956; R. Wright, *The Bureaucrats' Domain*; David Mercer, '"A Question of Balance"'.
3 Until the mid-1960s there was a ban on married women's employment in the Victorian public service; even after the ban was lifted, it took a long time for women to move into positions of seniority.
4 Middleton interview transcript; also speech transcript.
5 Max Weber, *Economy and Society*, pp. 1417–18.
6 Transcript of author's interview with A. G. Lloyd, 31 October 1991. Also David Wishart, personal communication, 2 September 1992.
7 McDonald transcript, p. 8.
8 Lloyd transcript, pp. 5–6.
9 McDonald transcript, p. 5.
10 *Age*, 30 August 1969, 27 October 1969, 17 November 1969, 24 December 1969; *Herald*, 30 July 1969, 23 December 1969; *Sun*, 30 August 1969, 17 November 1969, 24 December 1969.
11 R. J. Newman, 'Pasture Improvement in the "Little Desert"', *Journal of the Department of Agriculture, Victoria*, vol. 57, part 1, 1959, pp. 1–9; quote is on p. 8.
12 Honey, 'Urgent Need', p. 7. The relevant *Journal of the Department of Agriculture, Victoria*, was filed with this document.
13 Incident reported in both the *Age* and the *Sun*, 17 November 1969. Lloyd (transcript) named his source as David Wishart, then Director of Agriculture, but said that others were also concerned. Wishart said 'I'm not saying I was the source, but I'd have been quite happy to have been and may well have been.' (Transcript of author's interview with Wishart, 30 September 1992, p. 13).
14 Terence J. Johnson, *Professions and Power*, pp. 9, 12.
15 Samuel P. Hays, *Conservation and the Gospel of Efficiency*, 1959.
16 Nicholson, *The Environmental Revolution*.
17 In his book *The Fight for Conservation*, Pinchot claimed to have originated the term 'conservation', but see Susan R. Schrepfer, *The Fight to Save the Redwoods*, p. 11 for a dissenting view. The Conservation League and President Roosevelt's National Conservation Commission (1909) certainly ensured the popularity of the term.

18 *Gum Tree*, vol. 1, no. 1, March 1917.
19 Ibid., vol. 3, no. 11, September 1919, p. 1.
20 Powell, 'Enterprise and dependency', pp. 102–21.
21 G. T. Thompson, *A Brief History of Soil Conservation in Victoria 1834–1961*.
22 Victorian Institute of Surveyors, *Soil Erosion in Victoria*. On the history of the New South Wales Soil Conservation Service, see Roland Breckwoldt, *The Dirt Doctors*.
23 Alan Holt, Secretary of Lands from 1965, remembered Clark from his early days as a public servant, and claimed that Clark got his nickname from his determination and tenacity, particularly in pursuing the issues of soil erosion and the professional status of surveyors (Holt interview).
24 Patrick O'Shaughnessy, *Melbourne and Metropolitan Board of Works Catchment Management Policies*; Tom Griffiths, *Fire, Water, Timber and Gold*, p. 65; Tony Dingle and Carolyn Rasmussen, *Vital Connections*.
25 Figures drawn from K. O. Campbell, 'Land Policy', p. 172.
26 Australia: Rural Reconstruction Commission, Reports 1–10, 1944–46, especially Third Report, 'Land Utilization and Farm Settlement', issued 30 June 1944.
27 Lake, *The Limits of Hope*.
28 Rural Reconstruction Commission, Third Report, Section 449, p. 96.
29 Ibid., Section 396, p. 71; See also R. G. Downes, *The Land Utilization Advisory Council*.
30 Victoria: *Report of the Royal Commission to inquire into Forest Grazing*, p. 29.
31 *Soil Conservation and Land Utilization Act*, no. 5226, 1947; *Soil Conservation and Land Utilization Act*, no. 5441, 1949.
32 Land Utilization Advisory Council, Minutes, Meeting 1, 26 April 1950, p. 1.
33 David Wishart, a veterinary scientist, was appointed Director of Agriculture in 1967, and this was one of the differences in style he introduced. His predecessors were mostly agricultural scientists and horticulturalists (author's interview and discussion, 2 September and 30 September 1992).
34 Holt interview. The Director of National Parks was Leonard H. Smith.
35 Thompson, *Brief History of Soil Conservation*, pp. ix–x.
36 LUAC Minutes, 1950–70; Meeting 50, Reefton (22 November 1962); Meeting 56, Werribee (21 February 1964); Meeting 67, Wilsons Promontory (22 April 1966).
37 This process of centralisation is analysed in the context of the Little Desert dispute by Powell in *An Historical Geography of Modern Australia*, p. 235, and in his 'Action Analysis of Resource Conflicts', esp. pp. 162–4.
38 LUAC Minutes, Meeting 66, 11 March 1966, p. 3, item 8.
39 LUAC Minutes, Meeting 21, 21 June 1956, p. 1, item 3.
40 LUAC Minutes, Meeting 22, 4 October 1956, item 5.
41 Report signed 1 August 1957, following meetings 13 June 1957 (reconvened 21 June 1957), 12 July 1957, 25 July 1957.
42 LUAC Minutes, Meeting 25, 12 July 1957, item 3.
43 LUAC Minutes, Meeting 27, 20 November 1957, item 7.
44 LUAC Minutes, Meeting 29, 26 June 1958, item 3, records a dissenting view from W. T. Long, Assistant Secretary for Lands.
45 LUAC Minutes, Meeting 31, 16 December 1958, item 4; Meeting 32, 11 February 1959, item 3.

[46] Soil Conservation and Land Utilization Act, Section 14(c), p. 7.
[47] R. G. Downes memorandum, 28 May 1959, reported in LUAC Minutes, Meeting 33, 3 June 1959, item 10.
[48] LUAC Minutes, Meeting 34, 16 July 1959, item 3(b).
[49] LUAC Minutes, Meeting 37, 6 May 1960, item 3.
[50] Transcript of author's interview with Frank Gibbons, 30 September 1991.
[51] WRC, *Need for Reservations in Desert Settlement*, pp. 47–8.
[52] Downes was later awarded a Doctor of Agricultural Science by the University of Melbourne, on the basis of a thesis comprising selected scientific papers (SCA, *23rd Annual Report*, to 30 June 1972, p. 9).
[53] LUAC Minutes, Meeting 61, 12 March 1965, item 6, pp. 4–5 (decision deferred); Meeting 62, 28 May 1965, item 2 (decision to co-opt).
[54] LUAC Minutes, Meeting 71, 21 December 1966; Premier's Directive, 19 April 1966, see below.
[55] Downes had hosted a meeting on the subject of 'National Parks and Reserves, Victoria: A Master Plan' early in 1964, which was attended by Professor J. S. Turner and Dr R. L. Specht from the Botany School, University of Melbourne, and Dr L. H. Smith, Director, National Parks Authority. (Letter from J. S. Turner to L. H. Smith, 9 March 1964, J. S. Turner Archive, Box 8.)
[56] R. G. Downes, 'Conservation and the Community', in D. S. White and C. S. Elliot (eds), *Man, The Earth and Tomorrow*, p. 96.
[57] The clash between John Muir and Gifford Pinchot is well described in Nash, *Wilderness and the American Mind*, pp. 129–40.
[58] For example, Gibbons and Downes, *A Study of the Land in South–Western-Victoria*.
[59] LUAC Minutes, Meeting 67, 22 April 1966, item 1.
[60] LUAC Minutes, Meeting 74, 5 July 1967; quotes from p. 1, p. 3 and p. 3 respectively.
[61] Gibbons transcript; the authorised version was approved at the 78th meeting of the LUAC on 14 March 1968. The original Study Group report dated 10 November 1967 and amended 28 November 1967 (from the personal archive of Frank Gibbons) was discussed in detail at the LUAC's 77th Meeting (25 January 1968), but the minutes were brief on the subject. It was concluded that the council should inspect the area on 23 February 1968 (by implication, before the report was finalised).
[62] LUAC Minutes, Meeting 78, 14 March 1968, pp. 2–5.
[63] LUAC Minutes, Meeting 87, 26 November 1969, p. 2.
[64] LUAC Minutes, Meeting 92, 17 December 1970. No formal meetings were held between 17 December 1970 and 15 February 1971, when the Land Conservation Act (1970) introduced the Land Conservation Council.
[65] Ray Wright unravels some of the complexities of the term 'public interest' in *The Bureaucrats' Domain*, pp. 10–14. He concludes that there was never a fixed definition of the term. Rather it was controlled by the pragmatic situation of the day, the fashions and the personal views of the actors. Nonetheless, the term dates back to the seventeenth century, and was always regarded by politicians and bureaucrats as self-evident.
[66] LUAC Minutes, Meeting 51, 21 February 1963, item 12.
[67] Downes, *The Land Utilization Advisory Council*.
[68] The term 'Wisconsin idea' was coined in the United States by Robert M. la

Follette Sr about 1912 to describe the participation of Wisconsin academics in the policy-making processes of the State. See Christine L. Thomas, 'One Hundred & Twenty Years of Citizen Involvement with the Wisconsin Natural Resource Board', esp. p. 63; also Thomas R. Huffman, 'Defining the Origins of Environmentalism in Wisconsin', p. 51.
69   LUAC Minutes, Meeting 85, 25 June 1969, p. 3.

7   Public Participation and New Bureaucracies

1   Professor Gustav A. Swanson (Head of the Department of Fishery and Wild Life Biology at Colorado State University), ABC Broadcast, 2FC, 7.15 p.m., 15 December 1968, Script, p. 4.
2   Presidential address to the FNCV, 1969, by Mr Allen, Item 7, AGM March 1969.
3   CCV News, *Victoria's Resources*, vol. 12, no. 3, 1970.
4   'League' was a popular name for conservation groups founded in the first half of the twentieth century, some examples being the Gould League (1909), Australian Forest League (1912), League of Junior Tree Lovers (1922), League of Youth (1933) and Natural Resources Conservation League (1951). By 1969, however, it had a decidedly old-fashioned ring. Other possibilities mooted were: Conservation Co-ordination Committee of Victoria, and Nature Conservation Council of Victoria (FNCV Council Agenda, 29 April 1969, Correspondence).
5   The VNPA also started off as a collaboration of societies, but later introduced individual membership, probably as its bushwalking element grew.
6   Robin, *Building a Forest Conscience*, pp. 39, 91, 95–6, 110, 126, 132. Lewis Godfrey, in an interview with the author on 23 November 1989, explained that the NRCL met all his travelling expenses and provided a small honorarium for his work at the CCV. School Forestry was a branch or section of the Education Department from 1924 until 1988.
7   'CCV News', later changed to 'Point of View' (contributed by the CCV) was published in *Victoria's Resources* throughout the 1970s. It stopped abruptly in 1980, with the publication of the issue 'Minerals for People' (vol. 22, no. 4).
8   *Age*, 21 November 1969.
9   C. S. Elliott, 'Editorial', *Victoria's Resources*, vol. 12, no. 1, March–May 1970, p. 1. The FNCV also opposed the Land Resources Council 'in line with the CCV' (FNCV Council Minutes, 27 January 1970, p. 3), and both the Western Victorian Conservation Committee and VNPA provided commentaries on the proposed legislation (FNCV Council Agenda, 24 February 1970).
10   Letter from Gwen Piper to David Lee, Secretary of the FNCV, 17 September 1970, p. 2 (courtesy Mrs Dora Lee).
11   The NRCL had been the recipient of a government grant administered through the Forests Commission since the mid-1940s, when it was known as the Save the Forests Campaign. When the CCV was established, the Forests Commission channelled this money via the CCV. Thus the NRCL quickly lost its status as senior partner in the CCV–NRCL co-operative partnership, as it lost its direct access to government funding.
12   Sir Samuel Wadham, 'Some historical background of land settlement with reference to the Little Desert proposals', describes the agricultural development ethic behind the failed soldier and migrant settlement schemes of the 1920s and 1930s.

¹³ The 'values planning' style is associated with the R. J. Hamer years (1972–81), and contrasted with the directive 'program planning' mode of the corporatist ALP government of John Cain (1982–88). See N. P. Low and J. M. Power, *Policy systems in an Australian metropolitan region: political and economic determinants of change in Victoria*, p. 159 and David Mercer, 'Victoria's Land Conservation Council and the Alpine Region', pp. 107–30.

¹⁴ The fortunes of the EPA are critically analysed in P. Russ and L. Tanner, *The Politics of Pollution.*

¹⁵ W. A. Borthwick, Second Reading Speech on Land Conservation Bill, *Victorian Parliamentary Debates*, 299, September 1970, p. 150.

¹⁶ Borthwick transcript, p. 1.

¹⁷ Borthwick, Second Reading Speech, p. 147.

¹⁸ Borthwick transcript, p. 1.

¹⁹ Dr Mick Lumb, Director of Land Use Planning (1978–87) and Principal Research Officer for the LCC (1974–78) made this point in relation to the Mallee region. (personal communication, 24 May 1993). 'Resource allocation' was his term.

²⁰ *Age*, 21 November 1969.

²¹ LUAC Minutes, Meeting 89, 29 April 1970, Item 2, p. 2.

²² J. S. Turner, author's first interview, Tape 3, Side 1, 28 August 1990.

²³ Dimmick told Henry Bland: 'It is important that the Chairman of the Council be seen as completely independent and not biased towards "conservation". Unless members of the Council and the public see the Chairman as having no commitments to any particular group the Council will not operate effectively'. (LCC to Henry Bland, (undated; c. 1974), LCC archives, p. 2).

²⁴ Land Conservation Act, 1970, No. 8008, Section 3.1 (k). Under McDonald's proposed legislation the number of 'outsiders' (non-government employees) was increased to six, but all were appointed by the Governor in Council. Those who did not trust McDonald or Bolte perceived this as a serious problem.

²⁵ Land Conservation Council, *18th Annual Report*, 1987/88, p. 4.

²⁶ Mercer, 'Victoria's Land Conservation Council', pp. 108–9.

²⁷ Turner (first interview) commented that he did not have time to be 'constantly attending meetings'.

²⁸ Mercer, 'Victoria's Land Conservation Council', p. 108.

²⁹ Gerard McPhee, 'Land Conservation Council: Conservation or Exploitation', pp. 16–20.

³⁰ The example was qualified with a late disclaimer, 'I stress that these are avenues open to the FCV, and I do not offer them as a description of FCV activities, Heaven forbid!' (McPhee, 'Land Conservation Council', p. 20).

³¹ CCV Archives, State Library of Victoria. Director's correspondence file, 1980.

³² In 1983 the Forests Commission was absorbed into the Department of Conservation, Forests and Lands, so the linking of FCV and LCC interests was no longer directly relevant.

³³ Freedom of Information legislation affected all Victorian government agencies, offering interested members of the public access to documents previously withheld. The numbers of FoI requests made to the LCC were, according to *Annual Reports*: 16 in 1984/85; 36 in 1985/86; 31 in 1986/87; 13 in 1987/88; 11 in 1988/89; 1 in 1989/90. No numbers were given thereafter.

³⁴ I asked nearly all informants how they valued the LCC, and most indicated a high

level of satisfaction with its processes, recommendations and publications. Two or three gave neutral or 'I don't really know' responses, but none of the 1969 activists were *dissatisfied* with its design and role.

35 J. B. Dargavel and I. S. Ferguson, 'Forest Use Conflicts in Victoria', pp. 215–24.

36 Dargavel and Ferguson, 'Forest Use Conflicts in Victoria', p. 219.

37 John H. Taylor, 'Planning the Future Use of Public Land in Victoria', *Australian Forestry*, no. 37, 1975, p. 211.

38 David Scott, 'The Quality of Environmental Decision Making', p. 6. Scott cited the use of economic consultants in the case of the Central Highlands region, the report on which was published in April 1993.

39 [H. A. Bland], *Second Report of the Board of Inquiry into the Victorian Public Service*, p. 7.

40 Ibid., p. 8.

41 Ibid., p. 9.

42 Ibid., p. 12.

43 *Age*, 4 December 1974. The *Age* had associated itself strongly with the feeling against the Little Desert Settlement Scheme in 1969, and did not waste this new opportunity to ally itself with Little Desert development critics.

44 LCC response to Bland, p. 2.

45 Ibid., p. 4 and p. 3 respectively.

46 LCC *Annual Report* 1977/78 indicated that the descriptive report covering the alpine area (published July 1977) had resulted in 1538 submissions and the second-stage 'proposed recommendations' (published April 1978) had attracted a further 5362 submissions. Dick Johnson's book, *The Alps at the Crossroads*, was published by the VNPA in December 1974. It was reprinted twice in 1975, and again in 1979.

47 LCC response to Bland, p. 4.

48 The Ministry for Conservation Act was passed in December 1972 and implemented in January 1973.

49 *Ministry of Conservation* (pamphlet reprinted from the 1977 *Victorian Year Book*) p. 5.

50 Letter from A. L. Godfrey, Secretary, CCV, to R. J. Hamer, Premier, 16 December 1974 (copy on LCC file, 'Bland Report'). This letter was probably the result of a verbal report on the Bland Report given to the CCV by Professor Turner, since Godfrey's longhand minutes of Turner's report were also on the LCC file.

51 Quoted *Age* editorial, 19 December 1974.

52 National Parks Act 1975. See also D. S. Saunders, *The Role of the National Parks Service*, NPS pamphlet, July 1978.

53 'Borthwick: We need the LCC', *Age*, 18 December 1974.

54 Restructuring abolished the long-standing Soil Conservation Authority, the Forests Commission of Victoria, the separate Lands Department and the Vermin and Noxious Weeds Destruction Board. The Department of Conservation, Forests and Lands was the first of the 'superministries' in the area (a Labor government initiative in 1983). This was superseded by the Department of Conservation and Environment (another Labor initiative in 1990), the Department of Conservation and Natural Resources in 1992, a Liberal/National (conservative) coalition initiative and under the same government, the Department of Natural Resources and Environment in 1995. In December 1996, the National Parks Service became

part of 'Parks Victoria', administered by Melbourne Water. The former distinction between 'metropolitan' and 'country' has disappeared with this arrangement.
55 Bland, *Second Report*, p. 43.
56 Ibid., p. 16.
57 'Aircraft to drop "bombs" on fire', *Age*, 6 January 1976; 'Desert burn-off worries farmers', *Herald* 26 February 1976 (Lowan Shire sought more controlled burning); Army manoeuvres by eleven heavy-track vehicles without permits, resolved when the army agreed to pay to rectify damage (*Age*, 29 August 1980, 30 August 1980; *Herald*, 29 August 1980; *Sun*, 29 August 1980, 3 September 1980); the Little Desert Farm plan was rejected by the Town Planning Appeals Tribunal, and the Kaniva Shire Council, but not before there had been suggestions that the State would have to buy the 60 farmlets in question (for about $2 million) in order to protect the national park potential of the area. (*Age*, 30 April 1974, 7 January 1976, 6 July 1976).
58 Scott, 'The Quality of Environmental Decision Making', p. 7.
59 This point was drawn to my attention by Mick Lumb (personal communication, 24 May 1993).
60 The Mountain District Cattlemen's Association of Victoria was established in response to moves in New South Wales banning cattle from the high country. Its publication *Voice of the Mountains* first appeared in November 1972. The second issue carried a short history of the Association (*Voice of the Mountains*, no. 2, December 1973, p. 3).
61 Scott, 'The Quality of Environmental Decision Making', p. 15.
62 Ibid., p. 2. Efforts were made in at least two States (Queensland and Tasmania) to establish similar bodies in the late 1980s and early 1990s, but they did not succeed (Edwards interview).
63 Sheldon Krimsky, 'Beyond Technocracy: New Routes for Citizen Involvement in Social Risk Assessment', p. 58.
64 Krimsky, 'Beyond Technocracy', p. 43.
65 Scott, 'The Quality of Environmental Decision Making', p. 2.
66 David Scott, 'What is Lost with the LCC', unpublished typescript (3 pp.), May 1997. VNPA Archives.
67 *Environment Conservation Council Act*, 41/1997, assented to 11 June 1997, s.5 (1).
68 Ibid., s.5 (3).
69 Ibid., s.22 (2a).
70 Ibid., s.19 (1–3).
71 Letter from Environment Victoria, quoted by Cheryl Garbutt in Second Reading Debate for Environment Conservation Council Bill, *Victorian Parliamentary Debates*, 20 May 1997.

8 Conservation and Environmentalism

1 Francis N. Ratcliffe, *Conservation and Australia*, p. 5.
2 *Sydney Morning Herald*, 18 June 1973. This quote was promptly picked up by the Australian Conservation Foundation and published in their next *Newsletter* (July 1973), p. 4.

[3] The term 'environmentalism' gained currency following the publication in 1976 of Tim O'Riordan's book of that title.

[4] Ratcliffe, *Conservation and Australia*, p. 5.

[5] The 'subversive' dimension of ecology was first directly mentioned in 1964 by Paul B. Sears in 'Ecology—a subversive subject'.

[6] Judith Wright, *Conservation as an Emerging Concept*.

[7] Neil Evernden, *The Natural Alien*, pp. 3–4.

[8] The 'shades of green' terminology was more common in Australia in the early than the late 1990s. For example, in the *Age*, 1 May 1990, p. 17, Geoffrey Blainey was reported as using the light/dark green distinction in an address concerned with the interference by green activists with what Blainey considered to be good economic management of the country. In a politically different context, Rosaleen Love in 'Should Australia have a green party?' reported British environmentalist Jonathon Porritt using the distinction at an Ecopolitics conference in Sydney in April 1991.

[9] The term 'watershed' occurs in many of the author's interview transcripts, and also occurred in informal discussion about the Little Desert dispute. On ABC radio (interview by Doug Aiton, 3LO, 22 August 1991) the former State Premier, Sir Rupert (Dick) Hamer, referring to a rising culture which valued the environment and concern for quality of life, mentioned 1970 as 'a watershed' year.

[10] A. D. Butcher, interview with the journalist Jennifer Byrne, as reported in the *Age*, 23 February 1978, p. 4.

[11] Andrew Jamison, Ron Eyerman and Jacqueline Cramer with Jeppe Laessoe, *The Making of the New Environmental Consciousness*, pp. 9–11.

[12] 'Baby boomers' is a common term for the demographically large generation born immediately after World War II. The group is generally seen to begin with those born in 1946, but its 'ending dates' vary between 1955 and 1970, depending on the source. Since 'conservation generations' are relatively short (for example, there is a real difference between the conservationists of the 1970s and the 1980s), an end date of 1955 is assumed in the following discussion.

[13] See Libby Robin, 'Nature conservation as a national concern', pp. 1–24.

[14] Mark Davis in *Gangland* has commented on the success of baby-boomers as keepers of the 'public culture'. He uses the term 'boomer whinge' to refer to the combined views of the era of the demographic bulge and its immediate predecessor, in arguing for the powerlessness of Generation X-ers to have a space in 'public culture'. My argument is that the noise of the demographic bulge masks not only 'younger' but also 'older' views.

[15] Transcript of author's interview with Geoff Edwards, 30 May 1991; also letter to author, 31 August 1991. Edwards commented that the year after the Little Desert dispute the Monash University Biological Students' Society split and a group formed a more radical 'Environment Society'. At the time of the dispute, however, it was very much a scientific society.

[16] See for example Richard Mabey, *The Common Ground*; Nash, *Wilderness and the American Mind*; Hays, *Beauty, Health and Permanence*; Carolyn Merchant, *The Death of Nature*.

[17] Nitmiluk Visitor Centre, Katherine, Northern Territory, August 1997 (personal observation).

[18] D. R. Anderson, LDSC transcript, 4 February 1970, p. 168. The spelling of the

Aboriginal groups' names has changed since 1970 (AIAS preferred spelling in brackets).

[19] *Little Desert Management Plan*, pp. 14–16.

[20] Graeme Davison, 'Sydney and the bush: An urban context for the Australian legend'. See also Wayne Hudson and Geoffrey Bolton (eds), *Creating Australia*.

[21] Quoted in Davison, 'Sydney and the bush', p. 253.

[22] Russel Ward, *The Australian Legend*.

[23] Raymond Williams, *The Country and the City*, p. 12.

[24] Peter Attiwill, personal communication, May 1989.

[25] The Royal Australian Air Force used the Nhill airport during the war as a Air Navigation and Armament School, and a section of the Little Desert was cleared for bombing target practice (Ivan Anderson, former RAAF Fitter Armourer, personal communication, 18 September 1997). See also *Little Desert Management Plan*, p. 16.

[26] They include: Robyn Eckersley, *Environmentalism and Political Theory: Toward an Ecocentric Approach*; Warwick Fox, *Towards a Transpersonal Identity*, P. R. Hay, 'The Politics of Tasmania's World Heritage Area and Freya Mathews, *The Ecological Self*.

[27] William Ramson, 'Wasteland to Wilderness: Changing Perceptions of the Environment', pp. 5–19 (especially pp. 17–18); Richard J. Roddewig, *Green Bans: the Birth of Australian Environmental Politics*, pp. 3–14.

[28] Roddewig, *Green Bans*, p. 33. The Victorian BLF leadership resented the publicity Jack Mundey of New South Wales had achieved simply by changing 'black' to 'green'. See also Patricia Grimshaw and Katie Holmes, 'A Search for Identity: Carlton's History, Carlton's Residents', pp. 154–67.

[29] Australia, *Australian Heritage Commission Act 1975*, s. 4, pp. 3–4.

[30] Falk, *Global fission*, pp. 247–55; William J. Lines, *Taming the Great South Land*, pp. 228–30.

[31] 'UNSEAT SIR WILLIAM IS THEIR CLAIM', headline in *Portland Observer*, 8 August 1969. The article said the Western Victorian Conservation Committee and its prominent Liberal-supporting President, Claude Austin, were preparing to encourage conservative voters to back the Country Party rather than the Liberal Party in Sir William's seat of Dundas.

[32] Gregory Bateson, *Steps to an Ecology of Mind*. The anthropological linguists C. F. Voegelin and F. M. Voegelin used the term 'ecology of language' to describe the language system of immigrant bilingual communities in 1964, according to M. W. J. Garner, Ecology of language: Swedish and Russian in Melbourne, p. 1. See also Charles Rosenberg, 'Towards an Ecology of Knowledge'.

[33] Transcript of author's first interview with Gwynnyth Taylor, 25 February 1990, p. 9.

[34] Garnet transcript.

[35] R. and V. Routley, *The Fight for the Forests*.

[36] Ibid., p. 11. Brian Wynne, 'Knowledges in Context', p. 116.

[37] R. and V. Routley, *The Fight for the Forests*, p. 10.

[38] Ibid., acknowledgments. The disclaimer is in darker type, slightly crooked, at the bottom of the page. It was clearly added later.

[39] Richard Routley and Val Plumwood, 'The "Fight for the Forests" Affair', p. 72. When this critique was published, the former Acting Head of the Department of

Forestry, Australian National University (Dr L. T. Carron) declined to comment (postscript by Brian Martin, p. 73).

[40] *Focus on the Forester*, Proceedings of the eighth annual conference of the Institute of Foresters of Australia, Adelaide 1977.

[41] L. M. Duffy, 'Impacts and Influences', p. 1. The mining industries are also proud of their 'record in conservation'. See George Seddon, 'The Australian Rural Landscape: Its Qualities and Conservation', p. 16.

[42] Transcript of author's interview with Peter Attiwill, 21 October 1991, p. 1.

[43] Robin, 'Nature conservation as a national concern'.

[44] Attiwill transcript, p. 1.

[45] Letter to the Editor from University of Melbourne Agricultural Science Students, *Age*, 24 June 1969.

[46] Middleton transcript, p. 16.

[47] Examples include: Friends of the Earth (Victoria), 'Killing Corporations', *Nuke News*, July 1990; Greenpeace Australia, 'Shame File' (naming 'Australia's top five polluters'), *Greenpeace Australia News*, vol. 4, no. 2), Winter 1993, p. 14.

[48] Gibbons transcript, p. 31.

[49] Ibid., p. 28. Gibbons did not use the term 'monkey-wrenching', but he made it clear that he would not have approved 'ecotage', or the sabotage of property for ecological ends.

[50] Ibid., p. 29.

[51] Lynn White Jr, 'The Historical Roots of our Ecologic Crisis', pp. 1203–7.

[52] Nash, *Wilderness and the American Mind*, p. 44.

[53] David Meagher, *Macmillan Dictionary of the Australian Environment*, p. 180.

[54] The Save Lake Pedder Committee was founded in 1967. The period from 1972 onwards marked the peak of opposition.

[55] Lines, *Taming the Great South Land*, p. 225.

[56] The earliest Australian example of 'ecotage' (or sabotage for environmental ends) was by two Western Australians, Michael Haabjoern and John Chester, who attacked the Western Australian Chip and Pulp Company's woodchip loader in Bunbury, Western Australia, in July 1976. See Bonyhady, *Places Worth Keeping*, p. 40.

[57] McDonald, personal communication, 12 November 1990.

[58] Ian Watson, *Fighting over the Forests*, for example, 'Sally Johnston', pp. 83–4; J. G. Mosley and J. Messer (eds), *Fighting for Wilderness*, Part One: Battles Lost and Won; Part Two: Winning Future Battles.

[59] NRCL News, *Victoria's Resources*, vol. 12, no. 2, June–August 1970, p. 33.

[60] Victoria, *Environment Conservation Council Act* 41/1997. See also Libby Robin, 'Lessons of history forgotten as green watchdog silenced', *Age*, 20 May 1997, p. A11.

[61] Turner first transcript, section 2, pp. 3–4.

[62] See for example Moira Rayner, *Rooting Democracy*.

Bibliography

Interviews and discussions

Ivan Anderson, David Ashton, Peter Attiwill, Cliff Beauglehole, Budg. Bleakley, Bill Borthwick, Clive Brownsea, Malcolm and Jane Calder, Fred Davies, Keith Dempster, Neil Douglas, Sophie Ducker, Tim Ealey, Lance Edgar, Geoff Edwards, Charles Elsey, Judith Frankenberg, Richard Frankland, Carole Fraser, Angus Frith, Ros Garnet, Sarah Gebert, Frank and Pat Gibbons, Lewis Godfrey, Dewar Goode, Bill Grauer, Keith Hateley, Alex Hicks, Cynthia Hicks, Alan Holt, Valerie Honey, 'Cape' Kennedy, Jack Kennedy, Joyce Kennedy, Peter Kennedy, Dora Lee, Alan Lloyd, Mick Lumb, Ray Madden, Sir William McDonald, Jane Marshall, 'Matt' Matthews, Bill Middleton, Lucy Crosbie Morrison, Graham Pizzey, Wimpy and Maureen Reichelt, David Scott, Edna Smith (née Isaac), Len Smith, Les and Helen Smith, Ray Specht, Gwynnyth Taylor, John Turner, Norman Wettenhall, Perce Williams, Jim Willis and David Wishart.

Newspapers

Age
Argus
Australian
Countryman
Hamilton Spectator
Herald (Melbourne)
Kaniva Times
Newsday
Nhill Free Press
Portland Observer
Sun
Sydney Morning Herald
Wimmera Mail Times

Other sources

ABC Science Unit Broadcast. 'The Little Desert—a Conservation Victory in Western Victoria', 19 September 1971. (Narrator: Ronald Falk; Writer and Producer: John Challis. Tape and transcript held in the private archive of Valerie Honey.)

Andrews, Alan E. J. (ed.). *Stapylton: With Major Mitchell's Australia Felix Expedition, 1836* [largely from the Journal of Granville William Chetwynd Stapylton]. Blubber Head Press, Hobart, 1986.

Ashton, D. H. and Ducker, Sophie C. 'John Stewart Turner 1908–1991', *Historical Records of Australian Science*, vol. 9, no. 3, 1993, pp. 278–90.

Attiwill, Peter. Private archive on 'The Little Desert', kindly lent to the author.

Australasian Association for the Advancement of Science. 'Committees of Investigation', *Report of the AAAS, 1*, Sydney, 1888.

Australia: Rural Reconstruction Commission. *Third Report: Land Utilization and Farm Settlement*. The Commission, Canberra, 30 June 1944.

Australian Academy of Science. Archives, Basser Library, Canberra.

Australian Conservation Foundation. *Australian Habitat*, 1973– .

—— *Landscape Conservation: Rural Landscape Conservation with particular reference to the rural–urban fringe*. ACF, Melbourne, 1975.

—— *Newsletters*, 1967– .

—— *Occasional Publications*, 1968– .

—— *The Pedder Papers: Anatomy of a Decision*. ACF, Parkville, December 1972.

—— *Special Publications* 1968– .

Australian Forest League. *The Gum Tree*. Published irregularly, 1917–56.

Bardwell, Sandra M., National Parks in Victoria, 1866–1956, PhD thesis, Monash University, 1974.

Barr, Neil and Cary, John. *Greening a Brown Land: The Australian Search for Sustainable Land Use*. Macmillan, Melbourne, 1992.

Bateson, Gregory. *Steps to an Ecology of Mind*. Ballantine, New York, 1972.

Bayly, Ian A. E. 'The Destruction of Lake Pedder: Getting to know the HEC', *Overland*, no. 61, August 1975.

Blackburn, G., Bond, R. D. and Clarke, A. R. P. *Soil Development in Relation to Stranded Beach Ridges of County Lowan, Victoria*. CSIRO (Soil Publication No. 24), Melbourne, 1967.

Blackburn and District Tree Preservation Society. *Newsletter*, 1973– .

Blake, Les. *Tattyara: A History of Kaniva District*. Shire of Kaniva, Kaniva, 1981.

—— *Land of the Lowan: 100 years in Nhill and West Wimmera*. Nhill and District Historical Society, Nhill, 1976.

Bolton, Geoffrey. *Spoils and Spoilers: Australians Make their Environment, 1788–1980*, Allen & Unwin, Sydney, 1981.

Bonyhady, Tim. *Places Worth Keeping: Conservationists, Politics and Law.* Allen & Unwin, Sydney, 1993.

Brash, Stuart, Condé, Anne-Marie and Robin, Libby with McCarthy, Gavan and Sherratt, Tim. *A Guide to the Records of Philip Crosbie Morrison.* Australian Science Archives Project, Melbourne, 1993.

Breckwoldt, Roland. *The Dirt Doctors: A Jubilee History of the Soil Conservation Service of NSW.* SCSNSW, Sydney, 1988.

Burgmann, Verity. *Power and Protest: Movements for Change in Australian Society.* Allen & Unwin, Sydney, 1993.

Cabena, Peter, McRae, Heather and Bladin, Elizabeth. *The Lands Manual.* Royal Historical Society of Victoria, Melbourne, 1989.

Campbell, K. O. 'Land Policy' in Williams, D. B. (ed). *Agriculture in the Australian Economy.* Sydney University Press, Sydney, 1967, pp. 171–84.

Carr, Stella G. M. and Turner, J. S. 'The Ecology of the Bogong High Plains' (Parts I and II) *Journal of Australian Botany*, vol. 7, no. 1, 1959, pp. 12–63.

Carson, Rachel. *Silent Spring.* Hamish Hamilton, London, 1963 [American first edition 1962].

Clark, Ian D. *Aboriginal Languages and Clans: An Historical Atlas of Western and Central Victoria, 1800–1900.* Monash Publications in Geography No. 37, Clayton, 1990.

—— *Scars in the Landscape: a register of massacre sites in western Victoria, 1803–1859.* AIATSIS, Canberra, 1995.

Clifford, H. Trevor (ed.). *Cambridge–Castlemaine: A Tribute to John Stewart Turner on the Occasion of his 80th Birthday.* Department of Botany, University of Queensland, St Lucia, 1988.

Commonwealth Scientific and Industrial Research Organisation (CSIRO) Archives. Fyshwick, Canberra.

Conservation Council of Victoria Collection. Australian Manuscripts Section, State Library of Victoria, Melbourne.

Costin, A. B. *A Study of the Ecosystems of the Monaro Region of New South Wales with special reference to soil erosion.* New South Wales Soil Conservation Service, Sydney, 1954.

Costin, A. B. and Frith, H. J. (eds). *Conservation.* Penguin, Harmondsworth, 1971.

Critchett, Jan. *A Study of Aboriginal Contact and Post-Contact History and Places.* Report prepared for the Land Conservation Council, Deakin University, Warrnambool, 1995.

Crocker, R. L. *Post-Miocene climatic and geologic history and its significance in relation to the genesis of the major soil types of South Australia.* CSIR *(Australian Bulletin*, no. 193), Melbourne, 1946.

D'Alton, St Eloy. 'The Botany of the "Little Desert", Wimmera, Victoria', *Victorian Naturalist*, vol. 30, August 1913, pp. 64–78.

Dargavel, John. *Fashioning Australia's Forests*. Oxford University Press, Melbourne, 1995.

Dargavel, J. B. and Ferguson, I. S. 'Forest Use Conflicts in Victoria', *Australian Forestry*, no. 37, 1975, pp. 215–24.

Davidson, B. R. *Australia—Wet or Dry?: The Physical and Economic Limits to the Expansion of Irrigation*. Melbourne University Press, Carlton, 1969.

—— *The Northern Myth: A Study of the Physical and Economic Limits to Agricultural and Pastoral Development in Tropical Australia*. Melbourne University Press, Carlton, 1965.

Davies, Fred. 'An Aussie Looks at his Environment', Unpublished typescript (96 pp), (n.d., approx 1988).

Davis, Mark. *Gangland*. Allen & Unwin, Sydney, 1997.

Davison, Graeme. 'Sydney and the bush: An urban context for the Australian legend' in Russell, Penny and White, Richard (eds). *Pastiche 1: Reflections on nineteenth-century Australia*. Allen & Unwin, St Leonards, 1994, pp. 241–59. (First published in *Historical Studies*, vol. 18, no. 71, 1978.)

Dingle, Tony. *The Victorians: Settling*. Fairfax, Syme & Weldon Associates, McMahons Point, 1984.

Dingle, Tony and Rasmussen, Carolyn. *Vital Connections: Melbourne and its Board of Works, 1891–1991*. Penguin, Ringwood, 1991.

Downes, R. G. 'Conservation and the Community', in White, D. S. and Elliot, C. S. (eds). *Man, The Earth and Tomorrow*. Cassells, North Melbourne, 1969, pp. 96–100.

—— *The Land Utilization Advisory Council: Its Functions and Responsibilities*, pamphlet reprinted from *Fur, Feathers and Fins*, Newsletter of the Department of Fisheries and Wildlife, Victoria, November 1966 [second reprint June 1968].

Dutton, Geoffrey. *Edward John Eyre: The Hero as Murderer*, Penguin, Ringwood, 1977.

Eckersley, Robyn. *Environmentalism and Political Theory: Toward an Ecocentric Approach*. UCL Press, London, 1992.

The Ecologist (journal of radical ecology, published by Ecosystems Ltd and founded by British radical ecologist Edward Goldsmith), July 1970– .

Edwards, Geoff. Private archive on 'The Little Desert', kindly lent to the author.

Erhlich, Paul. *The Population Bomb*, Sierra Club–Ballantyne Books, New York, 1968.

Evernden, Neil. *The Natural Alien*. University of Toronto Press, Toronto, 1985.

Falk, Jim. *Global Fission: The Battle Over Nuclear Power*. Oxford University Press, Melbourne, 1982.

Fawns, Roderick Alan, The Maintenance and Transformation of School Science, PhD thesis, Monash University, Clayton, 1987.

Fenner, Charles. 'The Physiography of the Glenelg River', *Proceedings of the Royal Society of Victoria*, vol. 30, 1918, pp. 99–120.

Fenner, Frank (ed.). *A National System of Ecological Reserves in Australia*. Australian Academy of Science, Canberra, 1975.

—— *The First Forty Years*, Australian Academy of Science, Canberra, 1995.

Field Naturalists' Club of Victoria. 'The Proposed Glenelg National Forest and Sanctuary', *Victorian Naturalist*, vol. 64, no. 4, August 1947, pp. 62–91.

—— *Victorian Naturalist* [monthly (later bimonthly)], Melbourne, particularly 1945–75.

—— Minutes of Council, National Herbarium Library, South Yarra.

Field Naturalists' Club of Victoria, National Parks and National Monuments Sub-Committee. *National Parks and National Reserves in Victoria*. Field Naturalists' Club of Victoria, Melbourne, 1948 [Copy from the Royal Australian Ornithologists' Union Archives, Box 22A, Australian Manuscripts Section, State Library of Victoria].

Flannery, Timothy. *The Future Eaters*, Reed Books, Sydney, 1994.

Focus on the Forester, see Institute of Foresters of Australia.

Fox, Warwick. *Towards a Transpersonal Identity: Developing New Foundations for Environmentalism*. Shambala, Boston, 1990.

Frankel, O. H. 'Conservation in Perpetuity: Ecological and Biosphere Reserves', in Frank Fenner (ed.). *A National System of Ecological Reserves in Australia*, Australian Academy of Science, Canberra, 1975, pp. 7–10.

Frankel, Sir Otto. 'The biological structure of the landscape', in George Seddon and Mari Davis (eds), *Man and Landscape in Australia: Towards an Ecological Vision*, Australian UNESCO Committee for Man and the Biosphere, Publication no. 2, Australian Government Publishing Service, Canberra, 1976, pp. 49–62.

Frankenberg, Judith (edited by Turner, J. S.). *Nature Conservation in Victoria*. Victorian National Parks Association, Melbourne, 1971.

Frawley, Kevin. 'The History of Conservation and the National Park Concept in Australia: A State of Knowledge Review', in Frawley, Kevin J. and Semple, Noel M. (eds). *Australia's Ever Changing Forests: proceedings of the First National Conference on Australian Forest History*. Department of Geography and Oceanography, Australian Defence Force Academy, Campbell, ACT, 1988, pp. 395–417.

—— and Semple, Noel M. (eds). *Australia's Ever Changing Forests: pro-*

ceedings of the First National Conference on Australian Forest History. Department of Geography and Oceanography, Australian Defence Force Academy, Campbell, ACT, 1988.

Friends of the Earth (Victoria). 'Killing Corporations', *Nuke News*, July 1990.

Frith, H. J. *The mallee-fowl: the bird that builds an incubator.* Angus & Robertson, Sydney, 1962.

Garner, M. W. J., Ecology of language: Swedish and Russian in Melbourne. PhD thesis, University of Melbourne, 1986.

Garnet, J. Ros. *The vegetation of Wyperfeld National Park (North-West Victoria): a survey of its vegetation and plant communities, together with a check-list of the vascular flora as at December 1964.* Field Naturalists' Club of Victoria in conjunction with the Committee of Management of Wyperfeld National Park, Melbourne, 1965.

Gibbons, Frank R. and Downes, R. G. *A Study of the Land in South-Western Victoria.* Soil Conservation Authority, Melbourne, 1964.

Gillbank, Linden. *The Biological Heritage of Victoria's Alps: An Historical Exploration.* mimeo report (72 pp.) prepared for the Historic Places Section, Department of Conservation & Environment, Melbourne, 1991.

—— 'Into the Land of the Mountain Cattlemen: Maisie Fawcett's ecological investigations on the Bogong High Plains', in Farley Kelly (ed.), *On the Edge of Discovery: Australian Women in Science*, Text Publishing, East Melbourne, 1993, pp. 133–54.

—— 'The Life Sciences: Collections to Conservation', in Roy MacLeod (ed.), *The Commonwealth of Science: ANZAAS and the Scientific Enterprise in Australasia 1888–1988*, Oxford University Press, Melbourne, 1988, pp. 99–129.

Goldsmith, Edward. 'Gaia: Some implications for theoretical ecology', *The Ecologist*, vol. 18, no. 2, 1988, pp. 64–74.

Goode [Dewar] Collection. Australian Manuscripts Section, State Library of Victoria, Melbourne.

Goodman, David. 'Gold Fields/ Golden Fields: The Language of Agrarianism and the Victorian Gold Rush', *Australian Historical Studies*, 23 (90), 1988, pp. 19–41.

—— *Gold Seeking : Victoria and California in the 1850s.* Allen & Unwin, St Leonards, 1994.

Greenpeace Australia. *Greenpeace Australia News.* Adelaide, 1990–1997.

Gregory, J. B. 'To Wilson's Promontory Overland', *Victorian Naturalist*, vol. 2, no. 4, August 1885, pp. 43–8; Parts 2, 3 and 4 followed, co-authored by A. H. S. Lucas, in vol. 2, no. 5, September 1885, pp. 54–9; vol. 2, no. 7, November 1885, pp. 87–90; vol. 2, no. 12, April 1886, pp. 150–4.

Griffiths, Tom. *Fire, Water, Timber and Gold: A History of the Melbourne East Study Area*. Report to the Land Conservation Council, Department of Conservation, Forests & Lands, Melbourne, 1989.

—— *Hunters and Collectors: The Antiquarian Imagination in Australia*, Cambridge University Press, Melbourne, 1996.

—— 'In Search of Classical Soil: A Bicentennial Reflection', *Victorian Historical Journal*, vol. 59, nos 3 and 4, November 1988, pp. 21–38.

—— *Secrets of the Forest*. Allen & Unwin, Sydney, 1992.

—— ' "The Natural History of Melbourne": The Culture of Nature Writing in Victoria 1880–1945', *Australian Historical Studies*, Vol. 23 (93), Oct. 1989, pp. 339–65.

—— and Robin, Libby (eds). *Ecology and Empire: Environmental History of Settler Societies*. Keele University Press, Edinburgh, 1997.

—— (ed.) with assistance from Alan Platt, *The Life and Adventures of Edward Snell*. Angus & Robertson with the State Library of Victoria, Sydney, 1988.

Grimshaw, Patricia and Holmes, Katie. 'A Search for Identity: Carlton's History, Carlton's Residents', in Graeme Davison and Andrew May (eds), *Melbourne Centre Stage: The Corporation of Melbourne 1842–1992*, [*Victorian Historical Journal*, vol. 63, nos 2 and 3], RHSV and the City of Melbourne, Melbourne, October 1992, pp. 154–67.

Grove, Richard. *Green Imperialism: Colonial Expansion, Tropical Island Edens and the Origins of Environmentalism, 1600–1860*. Cambridge University Press, Cambridge, 1995.

Hall, T. S. 'Wilsons Promontory as a National Park', *Victorian Naturalist*, vol. 21, no. 9), January 1905, pp. 128–131.

Harris, Colin R., The National Parks and Reserves of South Australia, MA thesis, University of Adelaide, 1974.

Hay, P. R. 'The Politics of Tasmania's World Heritage Area: Contesting the Democratic Subject', *Environmental Politics*, vol. 3, no. 1, Spring 1994, pp. 1–21.

Hays, Samuel P. *Beauty, Health and Permanence: Environmental Politics in the United States 1955–1985*. Cambridge University Press, Cambridge, 1987.

—— *Conservation and the Gospel of Efficiency*. Harvard University Press, Cambridge Mass., 1959.

Hicks, Alec. Private archive on 'Conservation', kindly lent to the author.

Hills, Edwin Sherbon. 'The Physiography of North-Western Victoria', *Proceedings of the Royal Society of Victoria*, vol. 51, Part II, 1939, pp. 297–323.

Holmes, Jean. *The Government of Victoria*. University of Queensland Press, St Lucia, 1976

Home, R. W. (ed.). *Australian Science in the Making*. Cambridge University Press (in Association with the Australian Academy of Science), Cambridge, 1988.

Home, R. W. and Kohlstedt, Sally Gregory (eds). *International Science and National Scientific Identity*. Kluwer, Dordrecht, 1991.

Honey, Valerie. Private archive on 'The Little Desert', kindly lent to the author.

Honey, (Mrs) V. 'Urgent Need for Immediate, Thorough Investigation into Future Requirements for National Parks and Reserves: The Relevance of this to the Little Desert', typescript (9 pp.) accompanying petition to Acting Premier, Sir Arthur Rylah. Copy in Honey archive.

Horton, David (ed). *Encyclopaedia of Aboriginal Australia*. (2 vols) Aboriginal Studies Press, Canberra, 1994.

Hudson, Wayne and Bolton, Geoffrey (eds.). *Creating Australia: Changing Australian History*. Allen & Unwin, St Leonards, 1997.

Huffman, Thomas R. 'Defining the Origins of Environmentalism in Wisconsin: A Study in Politics and Culture', *Environmental History Review*, vol. 16, no. 3, Fall 1992, pp. 47–69.

Inglis, Ken. *This is the ABC*. Melbourne University Press, Carlton, 1983.

Institute of Foresters of Australia. *Focus on the Forester*. Proceedings of the eighth annual conference, IFA, Adelaide, 1977.

Isaac, C. E. *Forest Policy* [speech to Victorian Parliament 1 December 1943, published as pamphlet]. Victorian Government Printer, Melbourne, 1943.

—— *An Inseparable Trinity: The Story of the 'Save the Forests' Campaign*, SFC, Springvale, 1950.

Jamison, Andrew, Eyerman, Ron and Cramer, Jacqueline with Laessoe, Jeppe. *The Making of the New Environmental Consciousness: A Comparative Study of the Environmental Movements in Sweden, Denmark and the Netherlands*. Edinburgh University Press, Edinburgh, 1990.

Johnson, Dick. *The Alps at the Crossroads: the quest for an alpine national park in Victoria*. Victorian National Parks Association, Melbourne, 1974.

Johnson, Reg. *One Man's Dream: Whimpey and the Little Desert Lodge*. R. C. Reichelt & H. R. Johnson, Nhill, 1983.

Johnson, Terence J. *Professions and Power*. Macmillan, London, 1972.

Kamenka, Eugene and Krygier, Martin (eds). *Bureaucracy: The Career of a Concept*. Edward Arnold (Australia), Port Melbourne, 1979.

Kelly, Farley (ed.). *On the Edge of Discovery: Australian Women in Science*, Text Publishing, East Melbourne, 1993.

Krimsky, Sheldon. 'Beyond Technocracy: New Routes for Citizen Involvement in Social Risk Assessment', in James C. Petersen (ed.). *Citizen Participation in Science Policy*. University of Massachusetts Press, Amherst, 1984, pp. 43–61.

Lake, Marilyn. *The Limits of Hope: Soldier Settlement In Victoria 1915–1918*. Oxford University Press, Melbourne, 1987.

Land Conservation Council. Archives, Melbourne.

—— *Annual Reports.* 1971–1997

—— *Statewide Assessment of Public Land Use.* LCC, Melbourne, July 1988.

Land Utilization Advisory Council. Minutes of Meetings (1950–1971). Department of Natural Resources & Environment Archives, East Melbourne.

[Land Utilization Advisory Council]. 'Report on land use in the Little Desert' (March 1968), reproduced in Little Desert Settlement Committee. *Report upon the Proposal to open the Little Desert to Settlement.* Legislative Council, Melbourne, 17 March 1970, Appendix C, pp. 16–18.

Landscape Preservation Council (National Trust of Victoria). *Safeguarding the Victorian Landscape.* [undated publicity pamphlet], early 1960s, Melbourne, in Box 15, J. S. Turner Collection, University of Melbourne Archives, Carlton.

Lennon, Jane. 'Timeless Wilderness? The Use of Historical Source Material in Understanding Environmental Change in Gippsland, Victoria', in Frawley, Kevin J. and Semple, Noel M. (eds). *Australia's Ever Changing Forests: proceedings of the First National Conference on Australian Forest History.* Department of Geography and Oceanography, Australian Defence Force Academy, Campbell, ACT, 1988, pp. 419–40.

Lines, William J. *Taming the Great South Land: a History of the Conquest of Nature in Australia.* Allen & Unwin, Sydney, 1991.

'The Little Desert: A Conservation Victory', photographic exhibition held in School of Botany, University of Melbourne, early 1970 [Captions and photographs in private archive of Peter Attiwill].

Little Desert Settlement Committee. *Report upon the Proposal to open the Little Desert to Settlement.* Legislative Council, Melbourne, 17 March 1970.

—— Transcript of Evidence, 30 October–23 December 1969, unpublished manuscript held in the Library of the Parliament of Victoria. 256 pp.

Love, Rosaleen. 'Should Australia have a green party?' *Australian Society*, May 1991, pp. 6–7.

Low, N. P. and Power, J. M. *Policy systems in an Australian metropolitan region: political and economic determinants of change in Victoria.* Pergamon Press, Oxford, 1984.

Mabey, Richard. *The Common Ground: a Place for Nature in Britain's Future?* Hutchinson (in association with the Nature Conservancy Council), London, 1980.

—— 'Richard Jefferies', in Mabey, Richard (ed). *In a Green Shade: Essays on Landscape 1970–1983*, Hutchinson, London, 1983, pp. 133–49.

McClosky, Michael. 'Wilderness Movement at the Crossroads 1945–1970', *Pacific History Review*, 41, 1972, pp. 346–61.

[McDonald, Sir William, Minister of Lands]. *The Victorian Drought 1967/68*. [Melbourne, Lands Department], undated (63 pp.).

McIntosh, Robert P. *The Background of Ecology: Concept and Theory*. Cambridge University Press, Cambridge, 1985.

McKenry, Keith. 'The Little Desert: A history and critical analysis of the abortive scheme to open the area for settlement', unpublished report, Monash University, 1972 [Personal archive of Geoff Edwards].

MacLeod, Roy (ed.). *The Commonwealth of Science: ANZAAS and the Scientific Enterprise in Australasia 1888–1988*, Oxford University Press, Melbourne, 1988.

McPhee, Gerard. 'Land Conservation Council: Conservation or Exploitation', in Westbrook, Phillipa and Farhall, John (eds). *What State is the Garden In?* CCV & Native Forests Action Council, Melbourne, 1980, pp. 16–20.

Marshall, A. J. (ed.). *The Great Extermination: A guide to Anglo-Australian cupidity, wickedness and waste*. Heinemann, London and Melbourne, 1966.

Martin, Brian, Baker, C. M. Ann, Manwell, Clyde and Pugh, Cedric (eds). *Intellectual Suppression: Australian Case Histories, Analysis and Responses*. Angus & Robertson, North Ryde, 1986.

Massola, Aldo. *Aboriginal Mission Stations in Victoria: Yelta, Ebenezer, Ramahyuck, Lake Condah*. Hawthorn Press, Melbourne, 1970.

Mathews, Freya. *The Ecological Self*. Routledge, London, 1991.

Meadows, D. H. and Meadows, D. L. *The Limits to Growth: a Report for the Club of Rome's Project on the Predicament of Mankind*. Potomac Associates, London, 1972.

Meagher, David. *Macmillan Dictionary of the Australian Environment*, Macmillan, South Melbourne, 1991.

Meinig, D. W. (ed.). *The Interpretation of Ordinary Landscapes: Geographical Essays*. Oxford University Press, New York, 1979.

Mercer, David. *'A Question of Balance': Natural Resources Conflict Issues in Australia*. Federation Press, Sydney, 1991.

—— 'Victoria's Land Conservation Council and the Alpine Region', *Australian Geographical Studies*, vol. 17, no. 2, October 1979, pp. 107–30.

Merchant, Carolyn. *The Death of Nature: Women, Ecology and the Scientific Revolution*. Harper & Row, San Francisco, 1980.

Michael, Mike and Grove-White, Robin. 'Talking about Talking about Nature: Nurturing Ecological Consciousness', *Environmental Ethics*, vol. 15, no. 1, 1993, pp. 33–47.

[Morrison, P. Crosbie]. *Inaugural Report of Director of the National Parks Authority*. Reproduced in *VNPA News Letter*, August 1957.

Morrison, P. Crosbie (ed.). *Wild Life* [monthly magazine]. 1938–54.

Morrison [Philip Crosbie] Collection. Australian Manuscripts Section, State Library of Victoria, Melbourne.

Morton, S. R. 'Land of Uncertainty: The Australian Arid Zone', in Recher, Harry F., Lunney, Daniel and Dunn, Irina (eds.), _A natural legacy: ecology in Australia_. 2nd ed. Pergamon Press, Sydney, 1986, pp. 122–44.

Mosley, J. G., Aspects of the Geography of Recreation in Tasmania, PhD thesis, Australian National University, 1963.

—— 'Toward a History of Conservation in Australia', in Amos Rapoport (ed.), _Australia as Human Setting_, Angus & Robertson, Sydney, 1972, pp. 136–54.

—— 'Trends in the Planning of Australia's National Parks and Reserves', _Australian Journal of Science_, vol. 30, no. 8, 1968, pp. 281–4.

Mosley, J. G. and Messer, J. (eds). _Fighting for Wilderness_. Fontana/ACF, Sydney, 1984.

Mountain District Cattlemen's Association. _Voice of the Mountains_, 1972– .

Mulvaney, D. J. _Encounters in Place_, Queensland University Press, St Lucia, 1989.

—— (ed). _The Humanities and the Australian Environment_. Australian Academy of the Humanities, Canberra, 1991.

Nash, Roderick. _The Rights of Nature: A History of Environmental Ethics_. Primavera Press, Leichhardt, 1990 (first edition Wisconsin, 1989).

—— _Wilderness and the American Mind_. Yale University Press, New Haven and London, third revised edition, 1982 (first edition 1967).

Natural Resources Conservation League, _Victoria's Resources_. (Quarterly journal), Springvale, 1959–80; renamed _Trees and Victoria's Resources_. (1980–84) and _Trees and Natural Resources_. (1985–).

Nelkin, Dorothy. 'Scientists and Professional Responsibility: The Experience of American Ecologists', _Social Studies of Science_, no. 7, 1977, pp. 75–95.

Newman, R. J. 'Pasture Improvement in the Little Desert', _Journal of the Department of Agriculture, Victoria_, vol. 57, part 1, January 1959, pp. 1–9.

Nicholson, Max. _The Environmental Revolution_. Hodder & Stoughton, London, 1970.

—— _The New Environmental Age_. Cambridge University Press, Cambridge, 1987.

O'Riordan, T. _Environmentalism_. Pion Limited, London, 1981 (first edition 1976).

Osborn, T. G. B. 'On the Ecology of the Vegetation of Arid Australia, No. 1. Introduction and General Description of the Koonamore Reserve for the study of Salt-bush Flora', _Transactions of the Royal Society of South Australia_, no. 49, 1925, pp. 290–7.

Osborn, T. G. B., Wood, J. G. and Paltridge, T. B. 'On the Growth and

Re-action to Grazing of the Perennial Salt-bush, *Atriplex vesicarium*', *Proceedings of the Linnean Society of New South Wales*, no. 57, 1932, pp. 377–402.

O'Shaughnessy, Patrick. *Melbourne and Metropolitan Board of Works Catchment Management Policies: A History and Analysis of their Development.* CRES Working Paper 1986/28, Australian National University, Canberra, 1986.

Pinchot, Gifford. *The Fight for Conservation.* University of Washington Press, Seattle, 1967 (first edition 1910).

Piper, Gwen. *My One Fourteen Millionth Share.* Temnor Publications, West Ryde, 1980.

Pizzey, Graham. *Crosbie Morrison: Voice of Nature.* The Law Printer, Melbourne, 1992.

Powell, J. M. 'Action Analysis of Resource Conflicts: The Little Desert Dispute, Victoria 1963–72', in J. M. Powell (ed.). *The Making of Rural Australia.* Melbourne, Sorrett, 1974, pp. 161–79.

—— 'Enterprise and dependency: water management in Australia', in Tom Griffiths and Libby Robin (eds). *Ecology and Empire: Environmental History of Settler Societies.* Keele University Press, Edinburgh, 1997, pp. 102–21.

—— *Environmental Management in Australia, 1788–1914. Guardians Improvers and Profit: An Introductory Survey.* Oxford University Press, Melbourne, 1976.

—— *An Historical Geography of Modern Australia: The Restive Fringe.* Cambridge University Press, Cambridge, 1988.

—— *Watering the Garden State: Land, Water and Community in Victoria 1834–1988.* Allen & Unwin, Sydney, 1989.

Pybus, Cassandra and Flanagan, Richard (eds). *The Rest of the World is Watching: Tasmania and the Greens.* Sun Books, Sydney, 1990.

Ramson, William. 'Wasteland to Wilderness: Changing Perceptions of the Environment', in D. J. Mulvaney (ed). *The Humanities and the Australian Environment.* Australian Academy of the Humanities, Canberra, 1991, pp. 5–19.

Ratcliffe, Francis N. *Conservation and Australia.* ACF, Canberra, 1968 (pamphlet 7 pp.) [Reprinted from *Australian Quarterly*, March 1968, vol. 40, no. 1.]

—— *Flying Fox and Drifting Sand.* Angus & Robertson, Sydney, 1947.

Rayner, Moira. *Rooting Democracy.* Allen & Unwin, Sydney, 1997.

Read, Peter. *Returning to Nothing: the meaning of lost places.* Cambridge University Press, Cambridge, 1996.

Robin, Libby. *Building a Forest Conscience: An Historical Portrait of the Natural Resources Conservation League of Victoria.* NRCL, Springvale, 1991.

—— 'Ecology: a science of empire?', in Tom Griffiths and Libby Robin (eds). *Ecology and Empire: Environmental History of Settler Societies*. Keele University Press, Edinburgh, 1997, pp. 63–76.

—— 'Nature and Nation: *The Great Extermination* and Australian political nature writing', in Nick Drayson (ed.), *The Literature of Australian Natural History*. ADFA, Canberra, 1996, pp. 55–66.

—— 'Nature Conservation as a national concern: the role of the Australian Academy of Science', *Historical Records of Australian Science*, vol. 10, no. 1, 1994, pp. 1–24.

—— 'Radical Ecology and Conservation Science: An Australian Perspective', *Environment and History*, 1998 (forthcoming).

—— 'Thomas Sergeant Hall (1858–1915): Scholar and Enthusiast', *Historical Records of Australian Science*, vol. 6, no. 4 (July 1987), pp. 485–92.

—— 'Visions of Nature: *Wild Life*, 1938–1954', *Victorian Naturalist*, no. 105 (September/October 1985), pp. 153–61.

Roddewig, Richard J. *Green Bans: the Birth of Australian Environmental Politics*. Hale & Iremonger, Sydney, 1978.

Roosevelt, Theodore. *The Winning of the West*. 3 vols, G. P. Putnam's, New York, 1889–1894.

Rosenberg, Charles. 'Towards an Ecology of Knowledge: On Discipline, Context and History', in Oleson, Alexandra and Voss, John (eds). *The Organization of Knowledge in America, 1860–1920*. Johns Hopkins University Press, Baltimore, 1979.

Rosenbloom, Henry. 'The Greening of Australia: Hugh Stretton's Environmentalism', *Meanjin*, 1/1977, pp. 110–16.

Routley, R. and V. *The Fight for the Forests*. RSSS, Australian National University, Canberra, 1973.

Routley, Richard and Plumwood, Val. 'The "Fight for the Forests" Affair', in Martin, Brian, Baker, C. M. Ann, Manwell, Clyde and Pugh, Cedric (eds). *Intellectual Suppression: Australian Case Histories, Analysis and Responses*. Angus & Robertson, North Ryde, 1986, pp. 70–3.

Runte, Alfred. *National Parks: The American Experience*, University of Nebraska Press, Lincoln and London, 1979.

——'The National Park Idea: Origins and Paradox of the American Experience', *Journal of Forest History*, vol. 21, no. 2, April 1977, pp. 65–75.

Russ, Peter and Tanner, Lindsay. *The Politics of Pollution*. Widescope, Camberwell, 1978.

Russell, Jim. 'Plantation Forestry and the Australian Landscape,' in J. Dargavel and N. Semple (eds). *Prospects for Australian Forest Plantations*. CRES, Australian National University, Canberra, 1990.

Samuels, M. S. 'The biography of landscape: cause and culpability, in D. W. Meinig (ed.), *The Interpretation of Ordinary Landscapes: Geographical Essays*. Oxford University Press, New York, 1979, pp. 51–88.

Saunders, D. S. *The Role of the National Parks Service*. (National Parks Service pamphlet), Government Printer, Melbourne, July 1978.

Save Our Bushlands Action Committee. *Outline for a Bushlands Magna Carta*. Brochure presented to a public meeting at the Palais Theatre, St Kilda, on Sunday, 26 October 1969, SOBAC, Melbourne, 1969.

—— *Save Our Bushland: A Record of the Proceedings of the Public Meeting held in the Lower Melbourne Town Hall and Scots Church Hall on Friday 29/8/1969*. SOBAC, Melbourne, 1969.

Schedvin, C. B. *Shaping Science and Industry: A History of Australia's Council for Scientific and Industrial Research, 1926–1949*. Allen & Unwin, Sydney, 1987.

Schmitt, Peter J. *Back to Nature: the Arcadian Myth in Urban America*. Oxford University Press, New York, 1969.

Schrepfer, Susan R. *The Fight to Save the Redwoods*. University of Wisconsin Press, Madison, 1983.

Scott, David, 'The Quality of Environmental Decision Making: The Principles and Practice of the Victorian Land Conservation Council', unpublished typescript, based on a paper prepared for Ecopolitics IV Conference, University of Adelaide, September 1989, revised 1993, 17 pp. LCC Archives.

—— 'What is Lost with the LCC'. Unpublished typescript (3 pp.), May 1997. VNPA Archives.

Sears, Paul B. 'Ecology—a subversive subject', *Bioscience*, no. 14, 1964, pp. 11–13.

Seddon, George. 'The Australian Rural Landscape: Its Qualities and Conservation', in Australian Conservation Foundation, *Landscape Conservation*, ACF, Melbourne, 1975, pp. 11–17.

—— 'The Rhetoric and Ethics of the Environmental Protest Movement', *Meanjin*, 4/1972, pp. 427–38.

Seddon, George and Davis, Mari (eds). *Man and Landscape in Australia: Towards an Ecological Vision*. Australian UNESCO Committee for Man and the Biosphere, Publication no. 2, Australian Government Publishing Service, Canberra, 1976.

Sessions, George. 'Shallow and Deep Ecology: A review of the philosophical literature', in Robert C. Schultz and J. Donald Hughes (eds). *Ecological Consciousness*. University Press of America, Washington DC, 1981.

Shepard, Paul and McKinley, Daniel (eds). *The Subversive Science: Essays toward an Ecology of Man*. Houghton Mifflin, Boston, 1969.

Shortland, Michael (ed.). *Science and Nature: essays in the history of the environmental sciences*. British Society for the History of Science, Monographs Series, no. 8, Oxford, 1993.

Specht, R. L. 'Australia', in Edward J. Kormondy and J. Frank McCormick (eds), *Handbook of Contemporary Developments in World Ecology*, Greenwood Press, Westport, Connecticut, 1981, pp. 387–415.

Stamp, Sir Dudley. *Nature Conservation in Britain*. The New Naturalist/ Collins, London, 1969.

Stretton, Hugh. 'ABC: Just the beginning. Why Australia needs more books like Inglis's history', *Age Monthly Review*, vol. 3, no. 9, January 1984, pp. 14–15.

Swanson, Gustav A. Transcript of Radio Broadcast, ABC 2FC, 7.15 p.m., 15 December 1968.

Taylor, John H. 'Planning the Future Use of Public Land in Victoria', *Australian Forestry*, no. 37, 1975, pp. 208–14.

Thomas, Christine L. 'One Hundred & Twenty Years of Citizen Involvement with the Wisconsin Natural Resource Board', *Environmental History Review*, vol. 15, no. 1, Spring 1991, pp. 61–81.

Thompson, G. T. *A Brief History of Soil Conservation in Victoria 1834–1961*. Soil Conservation Authority, Melbourne, 1979.

Tobey, Ronald C. *Saving the Prairies: The Life Cycle of the Founding School of American Plant Ecology, 1895–1955*. University of California Press, Berkeley, 1981.

Tolmer, Alexander. *Reminiscences of an adventurous and chequered career at home and in the antipodes*, Libraries Board of South Australia, Adelaide, 1972 (facsimile).

Turner, Frederick Jackson. 'The Significance of the Frontier', in E. E. Edwards (ed.), *Early Writings of Frederick Jackson Turner*, University of Wisconsin Press, Madison, 1938.

Turner, J. S. (ed.). *A Report on the Condition of the High Mountain Catchments of New South Wales and Victoria*. Australian Academy of Science, report no. 1, Canberra, May 1957.

—— 'The threat to native Australian plants', in the six-part series, 'Going, Going, Gone', ABC Radio, 1962 in Box 15, J. S. Turner Collection, University of Melbourne Archives, Carlton.

Turner [John Stewart] Collection. University of Melbourne Archives, Carlton.

Victoria (Acts of Parliament). *Environment Conservation Council Act* (no. 41/97), June 1997; *Land Conservation Act* (no. 8008), 24 November 1970; *Ministry for Conservation Act* (no. 8364 of 1972), 23 January 1973; *National Parks Act (Amendment)* (no. 87928), 16 December 1969.

Victoria: Department of Conservation, Forests and Lands (Portland Region and National Parks and Wildlife Division). *Lower Glenelg National Park: Proposed Management Plan*, December 1988.

[Victoria: Department of Lands] 'Departmental Report of Public Meeting at Kaniva on 28 June 1967, addressed by the Honourable Sir William McDonald, M.P., Minister of Lands', reproduced in Little Desert Settlement Committee, *Report upon the Proposal to open the Little Desert to Settlement*. Legislative Council, Melbourne, 17 March 1970, Appendix B, pp. 14–15.

Victoria: Forests Commission. *Annual Reports*.

Victoria: National Parks Service. *Little Desert Management Plan.* Department of Natural Resources and Environment, East Melbourne, 1996.

Victoria. *Report of the Royal Commission to inquire into the Causes and Measures Taken to Prevent the Bush Fires of January 1939* [L. E. B. Stretton], Government Printer, Melbourne, 1939.

Victoria. *Report of the Royal Commission to inquire into Forest Grazing* [L. E. B. Stretton], Government Printer, Melbourne, 1946.

Victoria. *Second Report of the Board of Inquiry into the Victorian Public Service* [H. A. Bland], Government Printer, Melbourne, 1974.

Victoria. State Development Committee. *Report on National Parks.* Government Printer, Melbourne, 1951 [Forests Commission Archives].

Victorian Institute of Surveyors. *Soil Erosion in Victoria.* Government Printer, Melbourne, 1940.

Victorian National Parks Association. Archives, 10 Tasma Terrace, East Melbourne.

—— *Parkwatch* (quarterly journal). (Called *Parkwatch* March 1978– 'Newsletter no. 112'. *Newsletters* have also continued to be issued).

—— *VNPA Newsletter* 1952– .

Victorian Naturalist, see Field Naturalists' Club of Victoria.

Victoria's Resources, see Natural Resources Conservation League of Victoria.

Wadham, Sir Samuel. 'Some historical background of land settlement with reference to the Little Desert proposals', *Victoria's Resources,* March– May 1970, pp. 2–5.

Walling, Edna. *The Australian Roadside* (1952). Republished posthumously as *Country Roads: The Australian Roadside.* Pioneer Design Studio, Lilydale, 1985.

Ward, Russel. *The Australian Legend.* Oxford University Press, Melbourne, 1958.

Watson, Ian. *Fighting over the Forests.* Allen & Unwin, Sydney, 1990.

Watt, A. S. 'On the Causes of Failure of Natural Regeneration in British Oakwoods', *Journal of Ecology,* no. 7, 1919, pp. 173–203.

—— 'On the ecology of British Beechwoods with special reference to their Regeneration', *Journal of Ecology,* no. 11, 1923, pp. 1–48.

Webb, Leonard J., Whitelock, Derek and le Gay Brereton, John (eds). *The Last of Lands.* Jacaranda, Milton, 1970.

Weber, Max. *Economy and Society.* Guenther Roth and Claus Wittich (eds), University of California Press, Berkeley, 1978 (first edition 1968) (based on Weber's *Wirtschaft und Gesellschaft,* 4th edition, 1956).

Westbrook, Phillipa and Farhall, John (eds). *What State is the Garden In?* CCV and Native Forests Action Council, Melbourne, 1980.

Western Victorian Conservation Committee. *Boundaries of Kentbruck Heathland,* WVCC, Portland, April 1969.

—— *The Case for a Lower Glenelg National Park,* WVCC, Portland, June 1968.

—— *Kentbruck Heathland*, WVCC, Portland, December 1969.

—— Private archive on 'Conservation', kindly lent to the author by Fred Davies (compiler).

White, D. C. and Elliott, C. S. *Man, The Earth and Tomorrow.* NRCL, Springvale, 1969.

White, Lynn, Jr. 'The Historical Roots of our Ecologic Crisis', *Science*, no. 155, 10 March 1967, pp. 1203–7.

Wild Life Preservation Society of Australia. *Australian Wild Life* (intermittent journal). Society began in 1909, and was active in the 1950s.

Williams, D. B. (ed.). *Agriculture in the Australian Economy.* Sydney University Press, Sydney, 1967.

Williams, Michael. *The Making of the South Australian Landscape.* Academic Press, London and New York, 1974.

Williams, Raymond. *The Country and the City.* Penguin, London, 1985 (first published 1973).

Wimmera Regional Committee. *Need for Reservations in Desert Settlement.* WRC, Horsham, 1964.

Wright, Judith. *Conservation as an Emerging Concept.* Australian Conservation Foundation (Occasional Publication No. 2), Melbourne, 1970.

Wright, R. *The Bureaucrats' Domain: Space and the Public Interest in Victoria 1836–84.* Oxford University Press, Melbourne, 1989.

Wynne, Brian. 'Knowledges in Context', *Science, Technology and Human Values*, no. 6, 1991, pp. 113–16.

Index

Aboriginal land rights, 83, 88, 138, 141, 154

Aboriginal Protection Law Act, 6

Aborigines, *see* Jawoyn people; Wotja-baluk people

Academy of Arts, 30

Adelaide, South Australia, 8, 80, 148

Age, 1–2, 18, 52, 81, 84–5, 126, 148

agricultural science, 56, 60–1, 63

Agriculture, Victorian Department of, 15, 20, 58, 91, 94–5, 100–2, 106

Alpine National Park, 127, 131

Alps: Australian, 68; Victorian, 58–62, 67, 123, 129

Anderson, David, 83–4, 88, 141, 153

Antwerp, Victoria, 6

Ararat, Victoria, 43

Argus, 27, 31, 38, 65

arid zone, 76–7

Ashton, Dr David Hungerford, 60, 70–1

Attiwill, Dr Peter Muecke, 56, 60–2, 72–5, 79, 148–9

Austin, Claude N., 47, 52, 79, 122, 152

Australasian Association for the Advancement of Science, 32

Australasian Ornithologists' Union, *see* Royal Australasian Ornithologists' Union

Australian Academy of Science, 52, 64, 68, 77, 139

Australian and New Zealand Association for the Advancement of Science, 63

Australian Association for Scientific Workers, 63

Australian Broadcasting Commission (ABC), 15

Australian Conservation Foundation (ACF), 52, 66, 144, 148

Australian Forestry Council, 103

Australian Heritage Commission, 144

Australian Institute of Agricultural Science, 81

Australian Institute of Foresters, 147–8

Australian Labor Party (ALP), 19, 81, 138, 149

Australian Mutual Provident (AMP) Society, 11–13, 78, 110

Australian National University, School of Forestry, 147

Australian Primary Producers Union (APPU), 38

Bangham, South Australia, 14

Bardwell, Dr Sandra, 90

Barrett, Charles, 65

Barrett, Sir James, 25, 58, 76

Barwick, Sir Garfield, 134

Beauglehole, Alexander Clifford (Cliff), 46

Big Desert, Victoria, 12, 88

Bill's Gully, Victoria, 87

biodiversity politics, 3, 72, 136, 140–3, 153

biology, in schools, 63–4

Bird Observers' Club, 52–3

Birds Australia, *see* Royal Australasian Ornithologists' Union

Blackburn, Gerard, 9

Blackburn and District Tree Preser-
  vation Society, 87
Bland, Sir Henry, 126–9
Bolte, Sir Henry, 13, 16, 18–23, 79, 81,
  101, 103, 106, 117, 121, 137–8, 152
Bordertown, South Australia, 12
Borthwick, William Archibald (Bill),
  MLA, 21, 23–4, 119–20, 122–3, 128,
  153
Boy Scouts Association, 37
Breckland, England, 59
Broughtons Waterhole, Victoria, 10, 86
Brownsea, Clive, 87
Builders Labourers Federation (BLF),
  144
bureaucratic systems, 4, 23–4, 32, 55,
  60, 62, 70, 78, 90–133, 143–5, 154
Burke, A., 44
bushfires, 1939, 35, 58
Butcher, Dr Alfred Dunbavin, 52, 112,
  139

Calder, Dr (Donald) Malcolm, 56, 60–2,
  72–5, 85
Cambridge, England, 59
Cambridge University, 57
Carr, Dr Denis, 68
Carr, Stella G. M., *see* Fawcett, (Stella
  Grace) Maisie
Carson, Rachel, 42, 46, 65, 136, 139
Central Planning Committee, 104, 107
Ceylon Forest Service, 97
Chisholm, A. H., 27
Clark, Charles Tate, 58, 98
Clements, Professor Frederic E., 59
'closed catchment' policy, 98
Colac Field Naturalists' Club, 77
Commission for Conservation, the En-
  vironment and Land-Use Planning,
  129
Commoner, Barry, 139
Commonwealth Scientific and Industrial
  Research Organisation (CSIRO), (be-
  fore 1949, Council for Scientific and
  Industrial Research), 32, 59, 65, 116
conservation, utilitarian, 32–6, 92–3,
  96–8, 108, 120, 135–6, 138, 145,
  149–50, 152, 154
Conservation, Victorian Department of,

13, 19, 24, 101–3, 106, 109, 119,
  127–8
Conservation and Environment, Vic-
  torian Department of (DCE), 128
Conservation and Natural Resources,
  Victorian Department of (DCNR), 129
Conservation, Forests and Lands, Vic-
  torian Department of (CFL), 149
Conservation Council of Victoria
  (CCV), 23, 78, 85, 114–18, 122–4,
  128, 133, 144
Conservation League of America, 96,
  108
conservation science, 3, 32–3, 56, 62,
  66–73, 85, 104–9, 116, 119, 143, 153
Cornell University, 60–1
Costin, Alec Baillie, 46, 68
Council of Adult Education, Tourist
  Development Authority, 77
Country Party, 19, 81, 138
Country Women's Association (CWA),
  37
Countryman, 81
Coutts, Avelyn, 49–50, 52, 61–2, 77
The 'Crater', Victoria, 10
Cudmore, F. A., 44

D'Alton, St Eloy, 9
Dandenong, Victoria, 21, 82
Daniel, Frederick, 63
Dargavel, Dr John B., 125
Davidson, Bruce, 42, 46, 93
Davies, Fred, 11, 43, 45–6, 118
Davison, Professor Graeme, 141
Deniliquin, New South Wales, 45
Dimboola, Victoria, 6–7, 10, 12, 49–50,
  77, 82
Dimmick, Samuel Guy McLaren, 121,
  127–8
Douglas, Neil, 84
Downes, Dr (Ronald) Geoffrey, 52, 102,
  105, 107–8, 111–12, 120
Downes, Stephen, 52
Duffy, L. M., 148
Dundas, Victoria, 22, 104
Dunstan, Albert, MLA, 81

Ealey, Dr E. H. M. (Tim), 56–7, 71
Earth First!, 152

East, Sir Ronald, 111
Ebenezer Moravian mission station, 6
ecocentrism, 143, 145–6
ecological consciousness, definition, 4, 136, 146, 150–4
ecology, science of, 3, 55–8, 60, 62–4, 66–8, 70–5, 108–9, 119, 127, 148
economics: agricultural, 56, 65–6, 72–4, 81, 93–5, 104–5, 110, 138; land-use, 125
ecosystems, 130
ecotourism, 83, 86, 88–9
Edelman, Murray, 113, 124
Edenhope, Victoria, 5
Edwards, Geoff, 85
Ehrlich, Paul, 42, 46
Elford, F. G., 63
Elliott, C. Sibley, 116
Environment Conservation Council (ECC), 131–3; *see also* Land Conservation Council
Environment Conservation Council Act, 133, 153
Environment Protection Authority (EPA), 119–20
Environment Victoria, *see* Conservation Council of Victoria
environmental justice, 135–6, 139, 154
environmentalism, 5, 22, 41–2, 53–4, 92, 113–14, 123–5, 134–54
Erosion Investigation Committee, 98
Evernden, Neil, 55, 137
exclosure, 59
Eyre, Edward John, 7

Fawcett, (Stella Grace) Maisie, 58–9, 62, 67–8
Fawns, Dr Roderick, 63
Federation of Victorian Walking Clubs, 38, 124
Fenner, Charles, 9
Ferguson, I. S., 125
Field Naturalists Club of Victoria (FNCV), 9, 12, 18, 25–6, 29–30, 32–3, 36–7, 40–1, 43–4, 47–50, 52–3, 77, 79, 114, 116, 118; Australian Natural History Medallion, 77
Fisheries and Game, Victorian Department of, 33, 100

Fisheries and Wildlife, Victorian Department of, 52, 85, 91, 106–7, 112
Fitzroy River, Western Australia, 42
forestry, 47–8, 57, 60, 77–8, 90, 96–8, 100, 103, 105, 107, 115, 118, 125, 127, 146–9
Forests Commission of Victoria (FCV), 34–6, 40, 44, 47–8, 78, 90–1, 94, 97, 101, 103–6, 112, 118, 124, 127, 149
Frankenberg, Judith, 46, 69
Franklin River, Tasmania, 41, 150
Fraser, A. J., MLA, 103, 105–6
Fraser, Malcolm, MHR, 152
Fraser Island, Queensland, 42
Fraser Island Defence Organisation, 42
Freedom of Information requests, 124
Friends of the Earth, 149
Friends of the Little Desert National Park, 87
Frith, H. J., 46
frontier, 142–3

Galbally, J. W., MLC, 19, 55, 74
Galbally inquiry, 55–6, 62, 71–5, 79, 83, 85, 117, 141, 148
Galbraith, A.V., 34
Garnet, John Roslyn (Ros), 12, 33, 41, 43–5, 49–50, 52, 77, 146
'General Science', 63–4
Gibbons, Frank Ross, 56, 110, 149–50
Gillbank, Dr Linden, 60
Glenelg River, Lower, Victoria, 42–8, 118
Godfrey, A. Lewis, 115
Goodall, Dr David W., 62
Goode, Dewar Wilson, 38
Goolum Goolum Aboriginal Cooperative, 88, 141
Gould League of Bird Observers, 33
Grampians, Victoria, 104, 130
Grampians Fringe Dwellers' Association, 130
Graetz, Len, 76
green politics, 3, 22–3, 88, 135, 137, 139, 144–6, 149–53
Gregory, J. B., 29–30
Gum Tree, 97

Hall, Thomas Sergeant, 30

Hardy, Alfred D., 30–1, 33
Hamer, R. J. (Dick, later Sir Rupert), MLA, 21, 128
Hateley, Keith, 49–50, 62, 79, 84, 87
Herald, 18
Heytesbury scheme, 13, 93–4
Hicks, Alec, 49–50, 52, 61–2, 77, 79–80
Hicks, Cr Bill, 79
High Plains, *see* Alps, Victorian
Holsworth, Bill, 123
Holt, Alan Judge, 55
Honey, Valerie, 1–2, 51–3, 95
Horsham, Victoria, 7, 43, 78, 88
Housewives Association, 37

Imperial Forestry School, Oxford, 97
International Biological Program (IBP), 68
irrigation, 45, 97, 102
Isaac, Cyril E., MLC, 34–5

Jakarta, 121
James, D., 80
Jamison, Andrew, 139
Jawoyn people, 141
Johnson, President L. B., 54
Johnson, Reg, 85
Jones, Owen, 97
Jordon, K. W., 50
Judaeo-Christian traditions, 150

Kakadu National Park, 88
Kaniva, Victoria, 9, 12, 14, 43, 49, 61, 79–80, 84–5, 95, 129; Council, 84; Promotion Committee, 84
Kaniva Times, 80, 82, 85–6
Kelly's Bush, New South Wales, 144
Kennedy, 'Cape', 7, 89
Kennedy, Peter, 7, 88–9
Kennedy, Jack, 6–7
Kentbruck Heath, Victoria, 11, 16, 41, 48, 53–4, 110, 118, 122
Kiata, Victoria, 12, 49–50; Lowan Sanctuary, 9–10, 49–50
Kiewa River, Victoria, 58; Kiewa catchment, 58–9
Kinnear, Bobby, 6
Koonamoore Vegetation Reserve, South Australia, 59

Kosciuszko Tops, New South Wales, 68
Krimsky, Sheldon, 131

Lake Hindmarsh, Victoria, 7
Lake Hume, New South Wales, 58
Lake Pedder, Tasmania, 41, 148, 151–2
Lake Tyers, Victoria, 6
Land Conservation Act, 117, 126, 132
Land Conservation Council (LCC), 23–4, 75, 86, 118–33, 138, 152–4
Land (Plantation Areas) Act, 47–8, 103, 107, 110
Land Resources Council, 24, 116–7
Land Utilization Advisory Council (LUAC), 47–8, 52, 92–3, 100–12
Lands, Victorian Department of, 1–2, 11, 13–15, 19, 21, 23–4, 30, 36–7, 40, 44, 48, 50, 58, 79, 91, 98, 100–1, 104–7, 109–10, 113, 119–20, 126, 138
landscape conservation, 63, 67
Landscape Preservation Council, National Trust, 67, 74, 93
Landy, John, 123
Lawloit Ranges, Victoria, 50, 77
Lawrence, Alfred Oscar Platt, 78–9, 90, 112, 118
Lawson, Henry, 142
Learmonth, Noel, 43–7, 50
Lee, R. D., 44
Lemon Springs, 12
Lennon, Jane, 31
Liberal Party, 21, 79, 82, 138, 152
Lindros, Joan, 122–3
Lines, William, 152
Little Desert, description of, 5–10, 62, 72, 129
Little Desert Lodge, 85
Little Desert National Park, 16, 24, 49, 73–4, 77–9, 82–3, 86–9, 95, 110, 129, 143, 152
Little Desert Settlement Committee, *see* Galbally inquiry
Little Desert Settlement Scheme, 2, 11, 14–16, 19, 21–4, 53, 55–7, 61–2, 71–4, 78–83, 91–5, 109–10, 113, 117, 122, 126, 138, 141–2, 146, 150–3
Lloyd, Professor Alan Graham, 42, 94–5

lowan, *see* mallee fowl
Lowan, County (Shire), 9, 50
Lower Glenelg National Park, 118, 152
Lucas, A. H. S., 29–30
Lyons, Gerald, 52

McCann, Ian, 79
Macdonald, Donald, 27, 65
McDonald, Sir William, MLA, 1, 11, 13–22, 48, 50–2, 55, 73, 79–81, 83, 91–5, 104–6, 109-10, 113, 116–17, 119–20, 138, 141–2, 146, 152–3
McIlroy, W., 98
McLennan, Charles, 31
McLennan, Dr Ethel I., 58
McMichael, Jessie, 32
McPhee, Gerard, 124
Mallee, Victorian, 5, 76–7, 102
mallee fowl, 9–10, 50, 76, 85
Marshall, Professor A. J. (Jock), 46, 57, 65
Mattingley, Arthur Herbert Evelyn, 76
Mead, Elwood, 97
Melbourne, Victoria, 1, 18–19, 38, 45, 48, 51, 80–1, 87, 102, 114, 144, 151
Melbourne and Metropolitan Board of Works, 98
Melbourne Club, 152
Melbourne Olympic Games (1956), 38
Melville, Dr Ronald, 49
Mercer, David, 90, 123–4
Michigan State, USA, 119
Middleton, W. G. D. (Bill), 52, 77–9, 87, 90, 92, 118, 149
Midwest, American, 59
Mineral Deposits Limited, 134
Mines, Victorian Department of, 107
Minimay, Victoria, 12
Mirimbiak Nations Aboriginal Corporation, 88
Mitchell, Major Thomas, 7–8
Mitta Mitta River, Victoria, 58
Mole Creek, Victoria, 46, 48
Monash University: Biological Students' Society, 56, 85, 140; Department of Zoology, 56; Environmental Science Program, 57, 71
Moon, May, 67
Morgan, David, 64

Morrison, Philip Crosbie, 25–9, 31, 33, 36, 38–41, 45, 65, 69
Mosley, Geoff, 2
Moulds, Dr Frank, 48
Mount Alexander, Victoria, 8
Mount Arapiles (Mount Broughton), Victoria, 8
Mount Richmond, Victoria, 44–5, 50
Mount Richmond National Park, 46–7
Mountain District Cattlemen's Association, 130–1
Muir, John, 108
Municipal Association of Victoria, 123
Murray River, New South Wales, 7
Museum of Victoria, *see* National Museum of Victoria

Nash, Roderick, 5, 17
Natimuk, Victoria, 12, 51
National Environmental Policy Act (USA), 131
National Estate, 144
National Herbarium of Victoria, 37, 53
national identity, 134–5, 141–3
National Museum of Victoria, 33, 37–8
National Parks Act, 16, 38
National Parks Association of Victoria, 25, 30, 76
National Parks Authority, 17, 39, 44, 47, 50, 69, 102, 106–8
National Parks Service, 121, 128
National Trust, 25, 67, 93
Native Forests Action Council, 124
Native Title claim, 88
Natural Resources Conservation League (NRCL), 18, 67, 78, 115–16
Natural Resources and Environment, Victorian Department of (NRE), 129, 133
Neales, Dr Tom, 61
Nelkin, Dorothy, 74
Newman, Rex James, 52, 95
Nhill, Victoria, 12, 49, 77–8, 81–4, 87; Chamber of Commerce, 81–2; Progress Association, 49–50
Nhill Free Press, 84
Nicholson, Max, 46
Nitmiluk Gorge, Northern Territory, 141

Nixon, President Richard, 137

Omeo, Victoria, 58
ornithology, 47, 77, 79, 122
Osborn, Professor T. G. Bentley, 59

Paris, IBP meeting, 68
Pepper, Nathaniel, 6
Pepper, Phillip, 6
Pinchot, Gifford, 96, 108
Pine Hills (Mayrung), New South Wales, 44
Pine Plains, Victoria, 5
pine plantations, 47–8, 103, 107, 110, 118, 146
Piper, Gwen, 117–18
Pizzey, Graham, 19, 38, 52
Planning, Victorian Department of, 119
plant physiology, 57, 61
Portland, Victoria, 16, 43–5, 47–8
Portland Field Naturalists' Club, 44–5, 47
Potts, J. J., 80, 82, 85–6
Powell, Professor J. M., 3, 90
Pretty Valley (Victorian Alps), 59

quadrats, 61, 72

Ratcliffe, Dr Francis Noble, 46, 65–6, 134–6, 143
Reichelt, Maureen, 85
Reichelt, R. C. (Wimpy), 84–5
Returned Soldiers', Sailors' and Airmen's Imperial League of Australia, 37
Richardson River, Victoria, 5
Rocklands settlement scheme, 104–6, 109–10
Rocky Valley (Victorian Alps), 59
Roe, Dr Dick, 59
Roosevelt, President Theodore, 36, 39
Routley, Richard (later Richard Sylvan), 146
Routley, Val (later Val Plumwood), 146
Royal Australasian Ornithologists' Union (RAOU), 30
Royal Botanic Gardens, Melbourne, 19
Royal Commission: into the Fires of

1939, 35; into Forest Grazing, 34, 68, 100–1, 120–1
Royal Geographical Society of Australasia, 30
Royal Society of Victoria, 30
Rural Reconstruction Commission, 99, 103, 109

Saunders, Don, 121
Save Our Bushlands Action Committee (SOBAC), 5, 18, 23, 51, 54, 72–3, 87, 114–15, 140, 142, 146
Save the Dandenongs League, 67
Save the Forests Campaign, 34–8
Schmitt, Peter J., 83
Scott, David, 121, 125, 130–1
Sherbrooke Forest, Victoria, 40
Sierra Club, 108
Smith, Dr Leonard H., 40, 102
Smith, Leslie, 87
Snell, Edward, 8
Snowy River Hydro-Electric Scheme, 68
Soil Conservation Authority, Victoria (SCA), 52–3, 56–7, 67, 91, 93, 98, 101–2, 104–10, 115, 120, 150
Soil Conservation Board, Victoria (SCB), 36, 58–60, 98, 100–1, 108
Soil Conservation Service, New South Wales (SCS), 98, 100
soil erosion, 34–5, 58, 68, 93–4, 97–8, 102, 105, 118
soldier settlement schemes, 15, 22, 99–100
South Downs, England, 59
Specht, Professor Raymond L., 68–9
Spencer, Sir (Walter) Baldwin, 31
Stapylton, G. W. C., 7–9
State Development Committee, 12, 37, 44, 91, 103
State Electricity Commission of Victoria (SEC), 58–9
State Rivers and Water Supply Commission (SRWSC), 58, 97, 100–2, 111
Stawell, Victoria, 50
Stewart, Ena, 38
Stewart, Eric, 38
Stoneham, Clive, MLA, 12

Stretton, Hugh, 90
Stretton, Judge Leonard E. B., 34–6, 68, 100–1, 120–1
Sun, 18
Swanson, Gustav, 113–14
Sydney Morning Herald, 134

Tasmanian Hydro-Electric Commission (HEC), 41, 151
Taylor, Gwynnyth, 1–2, 48, 51, 146
Taylor, John, 125
technopessimism, 136–7, 144
Thompson, George T., 102, 115
'Three Blind Mice', *see* 'PL' Williams, Avelyn Coutts and Alec Hicks
Tolmer, Alexander, 8
Town and Country Planning Act, 126
Town and Country Planning Association, 25
Town and Country Planning Authority, 129
Town and Country Planning Board, 127
Trust for Nature —Victoria, 86–7
Turnbull, Keith H., 105
Turner, Professor John Stewart, 43, 56–64, 67–71, 73–5, 121, 123, 154

Uluru, Northern Territory, 88
United States Forest Service, 96
University of Melbourne, 31, 37, 52, 56–8, 63, 94, 121; Botany School, 56–62, 69, 73–4; Forestry School, Creswick, 57, 147
University of Queensland, 68
Urimbirra Cooperative, 87–8

Victorian Alps, *see* Alps, Victorian
Victorian Conservation Trust, *see* Trust for Nature—Victoria
Victorian Curriculum Board, 63
Victorian Institute of Surveyors, 98
Victorian Legislative Council Select Committee to inquire into the Little Desert Settlement Scheme, *see* Galbally inquiry
Victorian National Parks Association

(VNPA), 1–2, 16, 18, 25, 33, 37–8, 40, 43, 48, 50–2, 68, 79, 114–16
Victorian Public Service, Board of Inquiry into, 126
Victoria's Resources, 19, 115–17

Wadham, Sir Samuel, 52, 63
Wail, Victoria, 77
Waite Agricultural Research Institute, 12
Walling, Edna, 67
Ward, Russel, 142
Warrandyte State Park, 69
Watson, Ina, 44
Watt, Dr A. S., 59–60
Webb, Dr Leonard J., 46
Wemba Wemba (language group), 141
Wergaia (language group), 141
Wescott, Dr Geoffrey, 124
West Wimmera Tours, 84
Western Victorian Conservation Committee, 47–8, 152
Western Victorian Field Naturalists' Clubs Association, 47, 114
Wettenhall, Dr H. Norman B., 93
Wild Life, 26–7, 31, 40, 65
'wilderness', 140–3, 150–1
Wildlife Preservation Society of Australia, 137
Wilkins, Ormsby, 52
Williams, John, 86
Williams, Percival, 86
Williams, 'PL', 49–50, 52, 61–2, 77, 86
Willis, Dr James Hamlyn, 53
Wilsons Promontory National Park, 28–32, 37, 61, 102
Wimmera, Victorian, 4, 10, 13, 51, 76–9, 83–9
Wimmera Field Naturalists' Club, 77
Wimmera Regional Committee, 18, 52, 78–9, 104, 106–7, 110
Wimmera River, Victoria, 5–7, 9, 88
'Wisconsin idea', 111
Wotjabaluk people, 5–7, 83–4, 88, 141
Wright, Judith, 137, 144
Wright, Dr Raymond, 90
Wyperfeld National Park, 2, 12, 76–7